"*The modern conversation on biblical sexuality is dominated by either politically correct social justice warriors or over-the-top shock jocks. Clary's plain spoken approach is refreshing and helpful. There are no cheap shots but neither are there any pulled punches.*"

MICHAEL FOSTER, PASTOR, EAST RIVER CHURCH, BATAVIA, OHIO; AUTHOR, *IT'S GOOD TO BE A MAN*

"*Michael Clary has written a profound and important book. In it he addresses a subject that many powerful and influential people wish he hadn't addressed. I wish those people were just outside the church, but unfortunately, they're in it as well. He has had the temerity to speak clearly, and persuasively as an advocate for sexual sanity in an insane time. He's joined a small resistance movement by doing so. I'm pleased that he's quoted me—but he also quotes a number of my friends and acquaintances. That says something. There aren't many of us. A few years ago, it seemed like there were many men and women who could be counted on to endorse sanity. I'm sad to say that has not proven to be the case. But you hold in your hands an invitation to join our intrepid band as we make an appeal for moral and biblical sense in a world of sexual nonsense.*"

C. R. WILEY, AUTHOR OF *THE HOUSEHOLD AND THE WAR FOR THE COSMOS* AND *IN THE HOUSE OF TOM BOMBADIL*

"God the Father. Male and female he created them. Jesus as the bridegroom to his bride, the church. All throughout Scripture, we see God's creational design for the two sexes. Yet our culture has so suppressed the significance of manhood and womanhood that they are now not just interchangeable but exchangeable. Michael Clary offers a deep, biblical corrective to the gnostic thinking that has plagued the Western world for at least six decades now. The irrefutable truth he presents takes the American church to task for its complicity in suppressing God's good design and reminds us of our call to be distinct from the culture in the matters of sex and sexuality."

MEGAN BASHAM, REPORTER FOR THE DAILY WIRE

"God's design really is a beautiful design. Those given eyes to see it will come away from Michael Clary's strong book thinking just that. In these packed pages, you'll find many insights here, much pastoral wisdom, and a lot of courageous care for Christ's church. This is not a book that shames and scorches the reader; it's a book that tells the truth, but always points us to the upward call of God in Christ. We live out God's good design entirely, it turns out, by God's amazing grace."

DR. OWEN STRACHAN, PROVOST, GRACE BIBLE THEOLOGICAL SEMINARY; AUTHOR, THE WAR ON MEN

GOD'S
GOOD
DESIGN

A BIBLICAL, THEOLOGICAL, AND PRACTICAL GUIDE TO HUMAN SEXUALITY

D. MICHAEL CLARY

REFORMATION ZION PUBLISHING

Unless otherwise indicated, Scripture quotations are from the ESV® Bible (The Holy Bible, English Standard Version®), copyright © 2001 by Crossway, a publishing ministry of Good News Publishers. 2016 Text Edition. Used by permission. All rights reserved.

Scripture quotations marked (NIV) are taken from the Holy Bible, New International Version®, NIV®. Copyright © 1973, 1978, 1984, 2011 by Biblica, Inc.™ Used by permission of Zondervan. All rights reserved worldwide. www.zondervan.com The "NIV" and "New International Version" are trademarks registered in the United States Patent and Trademark Office by Biblica, Inc.™

Published 2023.
Printed in the United States of America
ISBN: 978-1-956521-09-2 Paperback
ISBN: 978-1-956521-10-8 eBook

To the household God has given me:

Laura, wife of my youth and fruitful vine,

To the arrows in our quiver, Reese, Isaiah, Owen, and Judah,

May the Lord shine his steadfast love on our house for a thousand generations!

Contents

Introduction

"There are a lot of ways to fall down, but only one way to stand up straight."[1]

G. K. CHESTERTON

"So if a person lives many years, let him rejoice in them all; but let him remember that the days of darkness will be many. All that comes is vanity."

ECCLESIASTES 11:8

My great grandfather, Gallie Robertson, built a house during the Great Depression for $450. He and his wife, Mary, lived there for the rest of their lives. It was a modest house, certainly not built to code. They built what they could afford, doing much of the work with their own hands. The ceilings, for example, were so low that I had to duck to avoid hitting my head on the light fixtures. They didn't have much, but they were thankful for what they had. He was 102 years old when he died.

---

1. Gilbert K. Chesterton, *Orthodoxy* (New York: John Lane Company, 1909), 186. This is a popularized paraphrase of Chesterton's original quote.

Gallie and Mary Robertson were married for 74 years. He was 22 when they got married. She was 14. That would be a scandal in today's world. Both were highly intelligent but barely educated. Momo (pronounced "maw maw") received a sixth grade education. A sponge for knowledge, she read everything she could get her hands on, memorizing much of it. Popo (pronounced "paw paw") was not so fortunate, receiving only a third grade education. But who has time for school when there's so much work to be done? Soon after their wedding day, Mary got pregnant. Her labor was extraordinarily difficult, and she was fortunate to survive. After giving birth to their baby daughter, Ethel, they never had another child.

Popo Gallie was a hard-working man, who could tell jokes as naturally as swinging a hammer. He built a small church on his property, which is also where he served as a preacher. At Christmas time, he would take fruit baskets to the shut-ins, most of whom were much younger than he was. He also built a small wood shop behind his house, next to the small garden Momo Mary kept. Their poverty taught them to be resourceful. She grew vegetables and canned them for the winter every year. My mother and sisters all learned canning from her. Having lived through many hard times, being prepared came second nature to her. Rumor had it she always kept $2000 in her bra. That was her emergency fund.

Realizing that our time remaining with Popo Gallie and Momo Mary was short, the family threw them an anniversary party almost every year. My own daughter was born shortly before their final party in the summer of 2005. The highlight of the party was watching Momo Mary, seated in her wheelchair, holding my infant daughter for the first time. She lived long enough to meet my infant son also, who was born the following year. She died a few months later. Popo Gallie lived for several more years, reaching 102, long enough to meet my third and fourth children, both boys.

Psalm 127:3 says, "Behold, children are a heritage from the LORD, the fruit of the womb a reward." One of my favorite memories of Popo Gallie is listening to him try to keep track of all his grandchildren, great grandchildren, and great-great grandchildren. There were so many people that he'd get the names mixed up. Even though they lived their whole lives in poverty, they were rich in other ways. Their wealth came from embodying the ancient wisdom of Scripture. They were rich because they'd built a productive household together, according to God's good design.

In a relatively short period of time, the traditional, sexual norms and beliefs embodied by my great grandparents have been cast aside in favor of novel sexual ethics that would have been unthinkable when they were my age. The changes have happened at an incredible pace, with little regard given to how these changes will play out in the future.

However, this book is not about nostalgia. I'm not writing with a starry-eyed desire to live in the past because people in those days got everything right. Rather, this book is an attempt to recover and apply the doctrine of sexuality for our modern context. Some of the concepts in this book may seem strange or even frightening to many readers. This is understandable, as the way Scripture presents sexuality is so radically different from the way it is presented in pop culture.

In this book, we will demonstrate the truth, goodness, and beauty of God's design for sexuality. We will show how God's story of his covenant love for his people, ultimately revealed in the gospel, was a profound mystery, written into the created order from the beginning of time. In other words, God's design for sexuality, with all its limits and possibilities, should be freeing, not frightening.

The Purpose of This Book

The topic of sexuality can be controversial, painful, or even scary for people, because it's so personal. This isn't some abstract doctrine that can be studied in a library, detached from the realities of everyday life. It touches on the deepest longings of the human soul. I will argue later in this book that human beings are embodied souls, a unity of the physical and spiritual realms. We don't experience life as generic humans with a few masculine and feminine tweaks to make things interesting. Everything about us is lived and experienced within the reality of our sexual nature, such as our need for connection, the desire for transcendent meaning, and the hope of finding someone who will truly love us.

The issue of sexuality can also be connected to painful experiences. For example, those who have been sexually abused have been violated in the most intimate way. Someone who grows up without a father experiences life like driving a car with a flat tire. He may get where he's going, but it's a rough ride. Many single men and women live with the daily feeling of being unwanted and unloved, fearing that they may die alone. So they bury themselves in their careers or other hobbies to replace the ache of a missing family. Some Christians are sexually attracted to others of the same sex, knowing it is a sinful desire.

Although we will explore all these topics which may strike fear or anger in people's hearts, my purpose is not to self-righteously launch verbal grenades at the evils of the world. My purpose in this book is to demonstrate the goodness of sexuality and the wisdom of God in how he's designed it so we will delight in it rather than fear it. My purpose is not to "reimagine sexuality," but to reexplain to a modern audience what our great grandparents knew instinctively. We've had too many books reimaging things for the modern

4

world and too little reexplaining things that should be obvious. In other words, this book is not an argument for something new. It's an argument for something very, very old.

I'll state my goal directly: my desire is to persuade readers to consider again the beauty of God's good design for sexuality and to delight in it. My aim is for men and women to reject the androgyny of the modern world and joyfully embrace their vocations as men and women. You might bristle at some of these ideas. I get that. No one likes having their ideas challenged. But I ask you to keep an open mind. I'm not claiming to have all the right answers. I've changed my positions on a few things as I've written this book. In fact, over the years I've realized how wrong I've been on many issues of sexuality. I unreflectively assumed my opinions were biblical, only to realize that I had been more influenced by feminist thinking than Scripture.

I suspect many readers of this book are similar to me. You are a Christian. You believe the Bible. You love Jesus and want to honor him with your life. You believe God created us male and female, and that means something for how we live our lives. But once you get into the particulars, it gets murky. Why does the Bible tell wives to submit to their husbands? Why doesn't God accept homosexuality? Why does the Bible teach that only qualified men can be elders in the church? After all, there are lots of godly women who are better preachers than many male preachers, right? That seems like an arbitrary rule. So what does masculine and feminine actually mean anyway? In other words, it's easier to believe the concepts as long as we don't apply them. I was troubled by these things because it didn't seem fair. I didn't realize it at the time, but on paper, I believed what has been called "complementarian" theology. But I was more of a feminist at heart. I believed the specific doctrines because I saw them in Scripture, but I didn't see the beauty in them. My heart had been shaped by the values of the world. From my experience as a pastor, I see this all the time. There is a disconnect between what the head believes and what the heart delights in. I wrote this book for people like me, to help them connect these dots. I wrote this book because I wanted to help Christians rejoice at the profound mystery of sexuality and delight in the beauty of sexuality, while addressing their fears and misgivings in a respectful way. As a pastor, I wanted a book that I could freely recommend to others without worrying about its tone.

Like me, many Christians have been affected by the world's value system as they encounter its messaging every day. The world's values permeate nearly every movie and every TV show, TV commercials, and online ads, and they are championed by cultural elites. Even though the Bible teaches us how to think about sexuality, the world often shapes our desires and feelings in ways that we don't perceive. The stories celebrated within our culture contain an alternate vision of truth, goodness, and beauty, and we can't help but be deeply affected by those things. Modern Christians have been so thoroughly catechized by the world's values that we scarcely notice. Some of our most foundational beliefs about sexuality come from a blend of Disney movies, romantic comedies, novels, and diversity posters. This is the power of story. Stories can make us feel good about bad things and feel bad about good things.

In this book, you will be presented with a vision of sexuality that is good, true, and beautiful. It is the vision of Scripture, not the vision of culture. And yet, because we have been so thoroughly shaped by the subversive messaging of culture, you might agree with your mind that it is good but resist it in your heart because it may not *feel* good. This is because of how compelling stories are. A well-written screenplay, talented actors, a beautiful soundtrack, and a gripping plotline can combine to move our emotions so powerfully that they change our values and even form new desires. It's so predictable. In recent years, LGBTQ activists have deliberately worked to promote their values through various Hollywood media channels. Gay characters must always be presented sympathetically and heroically, often as victims of oppression. Entertainment is propaganda. The goal is not merely entertainment but persuasion. And it has worked. After decades of this sort of messaging, it's broken through. We have been trained for so long in an alternate vision of sexuality that it's hard to imagine it was ever any different. Plato once said that a country cultivates what it honors. In our society, we honor sexual immorality and dishonor God's design. When you honor immorality, you get more and more of it.

But here's the truth. God created human sexuality to reflect his own nature and uniquely bring glory to himself. Men and women of various personality types and gifts can glorify God with their individuality, but this freedom of expression is not without limit. Men and women will honor God in ways that are distinct from one another, and these distinctions are important. I will elaborate on these distinctions throughout this book.

How Did We Get Here?

I love these lines from Ernest Hemingway's famous poem, "The Sun Also Rises," where one man asks another how he went bankrupt: "How did you go bankrupt?" Bill asked. "Two ways," Mike said. "Gradually, then suddenly."[2] Our culture has significantly changed in its understanding of sexuality in recent years. The seeds of change were already in the ground many decades ago. But

---

2. Ernest Hemingway, *The Sun Also Rises* (Mineumsa, 2012).

then, major changes happened, seemingly overnight. But how did it happen so quickly? For a detailed account of what happened, see Carl Trueman's excellent work, *The Rise and Triumph of the Modern Self.*[3] For our purposes in this book, this brief sketch will suffice.

Gnosticism

The modern confusion around sexuality bears much resemblance to ancient Gnosticism, a heresy condemned by the early church. The Gnostics believed in a strict separation of body and spirit. The body (and all the rest of the material world) was thoroughly evil and corrupt, but the spirit (and the whole spiritual realm) was pure and good. For the gnostic, your "true self" was spiritual. In fact, the inner man was considered divine. Thus, the immaterial part of the person was the only thing that mattered. However, the true self was trapped in a fallen, evil, physical body. Being composed of corrupt matter, the physical body was morally tainted and vile. Thus, salvation occurred at the end of one's life when the individual finally escaped the material world, having his or her corrupt physical body stripped away, entering completely into the heavenly realm.[4]

Sound familiar? It should, because Gnosticism is making a comeback in our day. The modern claim that someone's gender can be different than their biological sex is a gnostic idea. It is not uncommon to hear a man say he feels like a "woman trapped in a man's body." For such a man, his subjective experience of "gender" is who he *really* is, regardless of his body parts and chromosomes. In this view, the Creator God is replaced by the individual who

---

3. Carl R. Trueman, *The Rise and Triumph of the Modern Self: Cultural Amnesia, Expressive Individualism, and the Road to Sexual Revolution* (Wheaton, IL: Crossway Books, 2020).

4. Walter A. Elwell and Philip Wesley Comfort, *Tyndale Bible Dictionary*, Tyndale *Reference Library* (Wheaton, IL: Tyndale House Publishers, 2001), 535.

re-creates himself according to his subjective feelings. Just as God created by speaking words (Gen 1:3), men and women can simply declare that they identify as another gender and everyone else is expected to go along. Only in a gnostic world could anyone make this claim, and clearly, we are living in such a world.

Unsurprisingly, Gnosticism was condemned by the early church, just as it should be rejected today. Anyone who claims to be a woman trapped in a man's body is essentially telling God that he needs to repent for making a mistake when he created him or her. Yet Jesus said God created us male and female from the beginning. Not only this, but Jesus affirmed the value of the physical body by inhabiting one himself. Jesus was born, died, and rose again in a physical human body. Jesus also ascended and now sits at the right hand of the Father in his resurrected human body. The body matters, and God's design for the human body is male and female.

Feminism

The modern feminist movement has largely embraced this gnostic view of sexuality. Feminism is a fruit plucked off the gnostic tree. This is evident in two key ways. First, modern feminists downplay the unique female function of childbearing. Modern feminism trains women to view their ability to bear children either as a curse or an optional accessory to their lives, not the blessing God created it to be. Modern feminism presses the idea that women need to be liberated from their fertility in order to progress in society and be equal to men. What God calls "blessed" in Scripture is considered "cursed" by the world. Even though distinctions can be made between first, second, and third-wave feminism, the goal of liberating women from the burden of fertility has always been an essential feature. It is no small irony that feminism produces a hatred and fear of anything that reflects the true womanly beauty of bearing new life.

Secondly, the unique goodness of the female body is denied under the banner of "equality," the outcome of which is not equality but sameness. Werner Neuer said, "the current feminist movement is more or less intent on totally destroying the traditional conception of what constitutes male and female."[5] When he wrote that in 1990, it would have seemed absurd that this would actually become a hot-button issue in our culture. It's not so absurd anymore. The drive for equality demands that women be treated the same as men in nearly every aspect of life, particularly in the workplace. One major casualty of flattening out the differences between men and women is childbearing. Feminism doesn't promote the unique goodness of women. It forces women to act more like men.

Androgyny

Feminism has joined forces with Gnosticism to bring forth androgyny, the true child of their union. Androgyny refers to the blending of both male and female characteristics in a single person. In modern parlance, androgynous people might call themselves "non-binary" or "queer," meaning neither male nor female. Though androgyny is gaining popularity in the modern world, it is nothing new. Gender bending goes all the way back to ancient Gnosticism, which regarded androgyny as the ideal form of human existence. In his book *Different By Design*, John MacArthur cites

---

5. Werner Neuer, *Man and Woman in Christian Perspective* (London, England: Hodder & Stoughton Religious, 1990), 16.

one feminist scholar who claims that a person can become more enlightened as he or she becomes more androgynous.[6] Androgyny is fast becoming the sexual ideal in the modern world.

Gnosticism is a philosophical framework that was smuggled in and mainstreamed under the respectable banner of feminism. When Gnosticism combines with feminism, androgyny is the inevitable result. Men become more like women. Women become more like men. Neither become more like Christ. Catholic writer J. Budziszewski said, "the underlying wish is that both sexes would be men, but that some of these men would look like women."[7]

Feminism is now the assumed paradigm in every part of Western society, so much so that any critique of feminism is considered as a critique of femininity itself. Even though feminism ultimately undermines the goodness of God's design for women, many Christians see feminism as a positive force for women in society and in the church. But this belief is false. Femininity is a gift of God, designed by God for his own glorious purpose. Christianity does not need feminism to regard women with their rightful value and respect. Feminism adds nothing to the glory of women. Rather, it obscures the unique glory of women by making them less feminine. At its core, feminism is misogynistic. It tries to advance women by making them more manly.

Contraception

The Scriptures teach, and most people throughout history have recognized, that three things naturally belong together: marriage, sex, and childbearing. The birth control pill changed that perception

---

6. John MacArthur, *Different by Design*, MacArthur Study Series (Wheaton, IL: Victor Books, 1996), 26–27.

7. J. Budziszewski, *On the Meaning of Sex* (Wilmington, NC: ISI Books, 2014), 42–43.

dramatically. For the first time, women could have sex without the risk of getting pregnant. Once the possibility of casual sex without pregnancy was widely adopted, marriage itself was gradually stripped of its practical obligations, reducing it to a legal contract of personal fulfillment. It is no surprise, then, that the decades that followed were marked by skyrocketing divorce rates, plummeting birth rates, and an out-of-control sexual revolution. Predictably, unplanned pregnancies often led to abortion, which became legal in 1973.[8] Abortion turns a mother's body into a graveyard. Someone once observed that if feminism were a religion, abortion would be its chief sacrament, because someone must die to purchase your freedom.

The trajectory of feminism was evident in the writings of prominent feminist Simone de Beauvoir back in 1949. Trueman writes, "De Beauvoir's rhetoric reinforces the idea that biology is ultimately regarded as a form of tyranny, a potentially alienating form of external authority. Rather than seeing reproduction as the fulfillment – or at least a fulfillment – of what it means to be a woman, de Beauvoir sees it instead as a potential obstacle to the identity of any individual woman. The body is something to be overcome; its authority is to be rejected; biology is to be transcended by the use of technology; who or what woman really is is not her chromosomes or her physiology; Rather, it is something that she becomes, either as an act of free choice or because society coerces her into conformity with its expectations… Everything, even the male-female binary, must be revised in the world of the psychologized self."[9] Not to be outdone, Betty Friedan famously compared the suburban home to a "comfortable concentration camp."[10]

---

8. Thankfully, the *Roe v. Wade* decision was overturned in 2022.

9. Trueman, *The Rise and Triumph of the Modern Self*, 259.

10. Kirsten Fermaglich, "'The Comfortable Concentration Camp': The Significance of Nazi Imagery in Betty Friedan's 'The Feminine Mystique' (1963)," *American Jewish History*, 91 (2003), no. 2: 205–32, http://www.jstor.org/stable/23887200.

The Obergefell Decision

A cultural atomic bomb exploded in 2015 when the Supreme Court issued its ruling in the *Obergefell* case that legalized homosexual marriage. This is where the "gradually" of our cultural change became a "suddenly," like a rocket ship propelling our society into the uncharted outer reaches of what was thought unimaginable just a few years prior. At the time of this ruling, many states had passed laws explicitly rejecting gay marriage. Even California passed Prop 8 in 2008, a ballot proposition that banned gay marriage in their state constitution.

This ruling was particularly significant. Even though God created marriage and gave it to humanity as a gift, the nine, unelected Justices of the Supreme Court took it upon themselves to redefine it. By creating a new category of marriage, "gay marriage,"[11] the court decided that two gay men could be just as married as a man and a woman. Foolish as this decision was, it fit the logic of our times. Marriage was no longer the covenant bond that produced, provided for, and protected children. Instead, it was reduced to little more than a legal sex contract. Absurd as it might seem, the *Obergefell* decision indicated that reality itself was something under the Supreme Court's jurisdiction. With marriage redefined in this way, what prevents us from redefining "male" and "female" as the only categories of personhood? That's exactly what happened. The next logical step, transgenderism, previously a fringe phenomenon, was given legal and cultural legitimacy practically overnight.

---

11. I put quotation marks around "gay marriage" because it doesn't exist. There is no such thing as gay marriage, no matter what the Supreme Court rules.

Transgenderism

The transgender revolution might seem like it came out of left field, but it, too, follows the same logical progression. Feminists have long desired the ideal where men and women are interchangeable. The birth control pill accelerated this idea by enabling women to have sex without getting pregnant, just like men. Marriage was no longer a necessary institution for the provision and protection of children, but it was reduced to a means of formalizing sentimental attachment. German theologian Werner Neuer observed, "in feminism the tendency is either to deny completely, or to count as insignificant, all sexual differences apart from the incontestably biological ones. The non-biological differences between men and women are socially conditioned and therefore seen as open to correction."[12] Having achieved many of its goals of securing equal treatment for men and women, modern gender ideologies eliminate the categories of male and female entirely. With the widespread acceptance of transgenderism, there is little left to restrain the endless creation of novel sexual identities. We have now been forced into a new, androgynous reality where "male" and "female" are merely two options along an ever-expanding gender continuum.

Amazingly, C. S. Lewis recognized the same flawed thinking of feminism back in 1948. In an essay opposing the ordination of women into the Anglican priesthood, he wrote, "The innovators are really implying that sex is something superficial, irrelevant to spiritual life. To say that men and women are equally eligible for certain professions is to say that for the purposes of that profession their sex is irrelevant. We are, within that context, treating both as neuters... This may be inevitable for our secular life. But in our Christian life we must return to reality. There we are not

---

12. Neuer, *Man and Woman*, 18.

homogenous units, but different and complementary organs of a mystical body… And the kind of equality which implies that the equals are interchangeable… is, among humans, a legal fiction. It may be a useful legal fiction. But in church we turn our back on fictions. One of the ends for which sex was created was to symbolize to us the hidden things of God. One of the functions of human marriage is to express the nature of the union between Christ and the Church. We have no authority to take the living and semitive figures which God has painted on the canvas of our nature and shift them about as if they were mere geometrical figures."[13]

Lewis may not have anticipated transgenderism as it exists today, but he did recognize the basic logic that led to it. Feminism is a form of sexual Gnosticism that practically eliminates the categories of male and female, instead fashioning us into generic "persons," or, as Lewis called them, "neuters." The modern calls to "reject the gender binary" in favor of a "gender spectrum" is the application of the basic logic that was embedded in feminism from the beginning. Ironically, feminism has produced a movement that promotes equality by eliminating "woman" as a meaningful category. Yet feminism can't exist if women don't exist.

This reminds me of a species of spider, the desert spider, known for its strange practice of matriphagy. Matriphagy is when a mother is consumed by its offspring. This is what has happened to feminism. Transgenderism, the offspring of feminism, is now consuming its own mother. This can particularly be seen in women's athletics, where biologically male athletes can dominate women's sports (not to mention take their collegiate scholarships) as "transgender women." The boundary lines between men's and women's sports, which once protected female athletes, has been eliminated.

---

13. C. S. Lewis, "Priestesses in the Church," in *God in the Dock: Essays on Theology and Ethics* (New York, NY: HarperCollins Publishers Inc, 2014, Kindle Edition), 323.

Transgenderism has given biological males new ways to oppress and dominate women. All a man must do is *say* he is a woman, and he will be granted easy access to spaces once designed to prevent such intrusions. It's only a matter of time before every major sports record held by female athletes will be broken by taller, faster, stronger men who identify as women. Isn't it a strange tribute when Glamour Magazine named Caitlyn Jenner, a biological male formerly known as Bruce Jenner, its "Woman of the Year"? Evidently, Glamour Magazine thought a biological male was better at being a woman than all the other women. Without a hint of irony, Jenner said, "maybe this is why God put me on earth."[14]

The Christian faith teaches that men and women, created in the image of God, have dignity and value as men and women. Diminishing the differences between men and women ultimately diminishes our unique glory. In an essay entitled *Why Man and Woman are Not Equal*, Glenn Stanton wrote, "Woman is the most powerful living force on the globe. She creates, shapes, and sustains human civilization. The first step in weakening her power is to convince her that she must overcome her femininity. This, ironically, is precisely what the most vocal strains of feminism have advocated. Yes, woman should have equality in the workplace, in politics, and in the public square. But to render her more like man in order to accomplish this, and to judge her womanliness a hindrance to her ascendancy, is to get things exactly backwards. It is to treat her as much less than she truly is."[15]

---

14. Thomas Page McBee, "Caitlyn Jenner, Trans Champion: 'Maybe This Is Why God Put Me on Earth,'" https://www.glamour.com/story/caitlyn-jenner (accessed July 22, 2022).

15. Glenn T. Stanton, "Why Man and Woman Are Not Equal," https://www.firstthings.com/blogs/firstthoughts/2016/08/why-man-and-woman-are-not-equal (Accessed July 22, 2022).

The Future

Unfortunately, the sexual revolution is like a runaway train that has no brakes. Gender ideologies have gone viral, infecting every level of society. Every lifestyle, kink, or fetish must now be celebrated as a legitimate identity. After all, isn't that what the plus sign of the LGBTQ+ is supposed to represent? Once the logic of the sexual revolution has been adopted by the world, there is no limit to where it can go. As God took note of the rebellion at the Tower of Babel, he said, "this is only the beginning of what they will do" (Gen 11:6). Our modern world has identified true happiness with sexual gratification, and the way to create a happy society is to allow for a maximum amount of erotic gratification.[16]

For example, I once forced myself to sit through a TED talk that claimed pedophilia is a legitimate sexual orientation. Currently, this is not a mainstream view, but we have already adopted the logic that would eventually normalize it. Advocates have labeled themselves "minor attracted persons," and they want nothing less than to normalize and mainstream pedophilia. On what basis could anyone oppose it? The only moral standard that everyone still agrees on is consent. But that won't last long. Children can be manipulated into giving consent. There is no longer a meaningful, transcendent standard to which everyone agrees for governing our sexuality. This being the case, on what basis could anyone oppose polygamy? Polyamory? Bestiality? I once saw another news article defending "zoophilia" as a sexual orientation. Why not? This is our world. It's only a matter of time until each of these practices gain mainstream approval, because after all, who are we to judge? Like boiling a frog in a kettle, these ideas slowly gain traction until they are normalized. LGBTQ+ activists are playing the long game.

---

16. Trueman, *The Rise and Triumph*, 240.

What would have been shocking 20 years ago is now openly celebrated during Pride Month. What we find shocking now may very well be celebrated 20 years from now. And so it goes.

Some Qualifications and Caveats

This book is not a diatribe against sexual immorality. I've devoted one chapter to that subject towards the end. More than anything, this book is a reminder of the goodness of God's design for sexuality—things our grandparents would have called "common sense." Since sexuality is a touchy and emotional subject, I want to get a few qualifications out of the way here at the outset.

First, let me get the log out of my own eye. I'm not writing as one who has it all together. I don't have the perfect marriage or perfect family. I've got a long way to go as a husband and father. My life and marriage are not the standard for everyone else's life and marriage. Christians of good conscience may make different yet God-honoring decisions based on their particular circumstances. I fall short of many of the ideals I believe in, and I need the grace of Jesus like everyone else.

Second, we need to keep the grace of God securely in view throughout this study. This subject matter is deeply theological and deeply personal. Some of the personal matters are painful too. For example, some Christians have sexual sin in their past that produced a child they love with someone they now despise. That's complicated, and this book cannot untangle that web. My parents' divorce when I was seven years old was a defining experience of my childhood. I took it really hard. And yet that situation has given me family members I can't imagine life without. If God can raise the dead, his grace can bring life out of any situation. This book is not about looking down on people in judgment. Rather, it's about putting forth a positive vision to aspire to, recognizing that we all fall short. In other words, remember that "he gives more grace" (James 4:6). Assume the grace of God on every page of this book.

Third, I'm writing primarily as a pastor, not some kind of academic or "expert" on sexuality. My interest is to help ordinary Christians keep their grip on sexuality in a world that's losing it. Readers who would like a more thorough and academic study of sexuality, I commend to you Stephen B. Clark's *Man and Woman in Christ: An Examination of the Roles of Men and Women in Light of Scripture and the Social Sciences*.[17]

Finally, this book is a study of God's design for sexuality. It would not be realistic to examine every text in Scripture about sexuality or to tease out every "what if" scenario that doesn't exactly fit our framework. Moses said, "Thou shalt not commit adultery," which lays down the basic principle, followed by lots of case laws for the various "what if" scenarios. I readily acknowledge that issues of sexuality can be extraordinarily complicated. Jesus taught us to understand sexuality "from the beginning," where God's design is clear (Matt 19:4, 8). If someone's situation isn't quite ideal, that doesn't necessarily mean they're living in sin. Sometimes it could mean a faithful Christian strives to honor Christ but is suffering the effects of a fallen world. So this book cannot address every question, nor can it replace the practical wisdom best provided by a pastor or trusted church leader.

---

17. Stephen B. Clark, *Man and Woman in Christ: An Examination of the Roles of Men and Women in Light of Scripture and the Social Sciences* (Bloomington, IN: Warhorn Media, 2021).

Conclusion

There are two truths at the heart of this book. First, obeying God with our sexuality is an essential part of Christian holiness. Second, sexuality is a persistent area of deception, temptation, and spiritual attack. We will return to these two themes in the conclusion. The premise of this book is that God has a design for human sexuality patterned after his own household and given for a good and glorious purpose.

This book might be frustrating for some readers not for what it says but for what it leaves unsaid. There is not enough paper and ink to write all that could be said about human sexuality. The mystery is that profound. I have chosen to write about issues I find pressing and interesting. This book is about answering the "why" questions. We might know what the Bible says about sexuality, but if we don't understand *why* those things are true, it will be difficult for people to relate to those commands and want to obey them.

CHAPTER 1

God's Cosmic Household

"Earthly marriage images the heavenly, and serves to prepare for this heavenly marriage; for the ultimate goal of history is that a humanity may emerge of which Christ is the Head and in which God is all in all."[1]

HERMAN BAVINCK

"So then you are no longer strangers and aliens, but you are fellow citizens with the saints and members of the household of God."

EPHESIANS 2:19

Introduction

The theory of evolution teaches that human beings came about as the result of time and chance. We are nothing more than a

---

1. Herman Bavinck, *The Christian Family*, ed. Stephen J. Grabill, trans. Nelson D. Kloosterman (Grand Rapids, MI: Christian's Library Press, 2012), 44.

collection of soulless atoms bound together, like Lego bricks. The mindless, impersonal universe, through random mutation and natural selection, made us male and female. There is no purpose or design. It's just what happened. There's no need for gratitude, and there's no one to thank. We are nothing more than matter plus energy plus chance plus time. Everything we consider meaningful is an illusion, and it will all disappear and be forgotten in the meaningless void after we're gone. It's depressing.

The Bible tells a different story. God is not random. He has a glorious purpose in all that he does. He created human beings for a particular reason. He also created male and female to express something eternal and beautiful. The story of God's purpose in creating human beings, as male and female, begins with God himself. God was building a household to dwell with his people who were created in his image.

The idea of a "household" did not begin when God created man and woman and joined them in marriage. It's older than that. God's heavenly, cosmic household is the original. Human households are the copy. God's cosmic household is comprised of two realms: the angelic, spiritual realm (Job 38:7; Ps 82:1), and the human, material realm (Ps 8:3-8). God is the eternal Father. There is no eternal mother. Motherhood is part of the created order. But we'll get to that later in this chapter.

The Person of God

God's Purpose in Creation

The Scriptures tell us that God is eternal. God is, always has been, and always will be. He is also triune—Father, Son, and Holy Spirit, and he has joyfully existed for all eternity in perfect fellowship and delight within the godhead. To put it another way, God is eternally happy. He needs nothing. Nor is he deficient in any way. Therefore, God did not create us to satisfy any need he has. He did not create us because he was lonely and needed companionship. He is God! And yet it was God's good pleasure to create a world and fill it with creatures that would reflect, behold, and display the wonders of his glory. This is our Father's world.

Unlike Eastern religions such as pantheism, God is not a part of his creation, nor is creation part of God's own being. God is distinct from his creation, yet he is still connected to his creation. The Apostle Paul spoke of Jesus Christ in this way: "for by him all things were created, in heaven and on earth, visible and invisible, whether thrones or dominions or rulers or authorities—all things were created through him and for him. And he is before all things, and in him all things hold together" (Col 1:16-17). The author of Hebrews says that Jesus Christ was the one through whom God created the world, and he "upholds the universe by the word of his power" (Heb 1:3). God delights in his creation. He is himself the glue that holds it all together.

In the early chapters of Genesis, creation is depicted as a dwelling place for God, like a cosmic household, or a temple. God authored light, land, water, stone, soil, trees, orcas, eagles, and every other object and creature in existence. But God's work reached its zenith when he made man and woman in his image. We are the crown of his creation, having received from him the highest honor.

Genesis 2 tells us that he created Adam and placed him in the Garden of Eden to work it and keep it. Eden was a special place where heaven and earth met like a temple sanctuary. Thus, the scene was set: the whole universe belongs to God, the earth is a special place where God's image-bearers live, Eden was God's garden-temple on the earth, and Adam served God in a dual role as king and priest. Further, God created Eve, Adam's wife, to help him accomplish the task of subduing the earth and filling it with people who bear God's image (Gen 1:28).

Though God began the work, he left it to man to finish it. Adam and Eve were commanded to continue forming and filling the earth, just as God did before them. As they multiplied and subdued the earth, they were expanding God's household on the earth through generations of multiplying human households. And it was very good.

God's Purpose for Sexuality

This background is important because it shows us how human sexuality is part of God's eternal purpose. Sex was not incidental to the world God made. God could have created people that reproduced all by themselves, like trees. But that's not what he made. Instead, God made a world where sex was a necessary act for the creation of more humans. By God's good design, sex produces the most valuable being in all creation: a person. And God protected this act by building a marriage covenant around it. Sex is like a priceless work in a museum—it's the design of a genius mind, a masterpiece of such mystery, wonder, and beauty that thieves will want to steal it and vandals will want to destroy it. God, however, wants to protect it. It is valuable because of its unique power to convey eternal truths of love, trust, vulnerability, giving, receiving, pleasure, fulfillment, and life. Like a Christmas gift waiting under the tree, God protects the gift of sexuality by wrapping it in a covenant, only to be opened at the right time, when it can be most fully expressed and enjoyed for God's glory and our good. And it's the gift that keeps giving because it contains the potential to create. The ability to create new life is, perhaps, where human beings are most like God, because the new life we create bears God's image.

The image of God is both a human identity and a human activity. Men and women "image" God in their beings as those made to do something uniquely God-like. Men and women also "image" God in their work to continue the work of creation that God began. As humans establish households of their own for the glory of God, God's own household is being expanded as well. And the establishment of each human household is accomplished through marriage, sex, and children.

Simply put, God designed sex to reveal something good, true, and beautiful about himself. The earth was God's garden-temple where he dwelt with his ever-growing human household. So ultimately, sex is about God because he created it and it is good. This is why Paul calls it a profound mystery (Eph 5:32). Viewing it as a mere physical act of pleasure distorts what it is and why it was crafted.

Further, since the image of God is expressed in male and female humans (Gen 1:27), the masculine and feminine qualities of each are not random or incidental. They are not social constructs to be changed as we see fit. Masculinity and femininity are both grounded in God's nature and his purpose for creation.

Cosmic Fatherhood and Motherhood

The Fatherhood of God is eternal. The word "father" implies relationship—a father is one who "begets." Since the early church, Christians have officially affirmed that Jesus Christ is eternally "begotten, not made" of the Father. God's eternal Fatherhood exists within the trinitarian relationship of Father, Son, and Holy Spirit. There is no eternal mother, however. Motherhood is part of creation. It was created by God as the means of bringing new life into the world.

Human motherhood begins when the father's seed is implanted within her and she conceives, but from there onward, the entire composition of the child's body comes from the mother. Adam was formed in the same way, though he did not have a human mother. God was his father, taking initiative to form the man from the "dust of the ground." The earth was a kind of mother to Adam, at least at the symbolic level, since God formed him from the dust of the ground. In fact, the words "matter" and "material" both come from the word for mother.[2] The Hebrew word for "ground" is *adamah,* which is related to *adam,* the word for man. Striking parallels between the woman and the earth can be found in Genesis and elsewhere in the Bible. Life comes from her, and life is bound to her. For example, in David's prayer of Psalm 139, he says, "you knitted me together in my mother's womb" (v. 13). Two verses later, he says, "My frame was not hidden from you, when I was being made in secret, intricately *woven in the depths of the earth*" (v. 15, emphasis mine). His mother's womb is associated with the depths of the earth. In other Scriptures, the reproductive power of women is often described in earthy ways, such as a fountain (Prov 5:18) or a garden (Song of Solomon 4:12ff). This sort of thinking might seem strange to us, but it was common in the ancient world. Some vestiges of this thinking still remain in notions such as "mother nature."

---

2. Alastair Roberts, "The Revolutionary Work of Motherhood," https://alastairad-versaria.com/2017/05/15/the-revolutionary-work-of-motherhood/ (Accessed July 22, 2022).

God is the eternal Father, and he created all things *ex nihilo.* He did not create from preexistent materials. He created from nothing. But when he made man, He created him from the ground, from earthy materials that were already there, and breathed life into them. Adam's creation was mediated by the ground. There's a theological point in all this. Adam was created *from* the ground because God created him *for* the ground. Likewise, Eve was created *from* the man because God created her *for* the man. What each was created from indicates what each was created for. Reflecting on the Genesis account, Paul wrote, "For man was not made from woman, but woman from man. Neither was man created for woman, but woman for man… Nevertheless, in the Lord woman is not independent of man nor man of woman; for as woman was made from man, so man is now born of woman. And all things are from God" (1 Cor 11:8-12). In this text, Paul is writing about the interdependent nature of the sexes. Man is dependent on woman because all men come from a mother. Woman is dependent on man because the first woman came from a man. Everyone came from God and are dependent upon God who ordered them in this way.

What Genesis teaches (and Paul reflects upon in 1 Corinthians) is the fact that there is a relational pattern between the sexes that God built into the created order. The way God relates to his cosmic household is a relational pattern for humans to follow. He designed it that way. God wrote a masculine-feminine relational pattern into the created order to reflect a cosmic reality. Of course, these are symbolic realities, and symbols have limited use. But the symbols can help us learn what masculine and feminine mean and what God made them for. Male and female are not merely biological traits, and masculinity and femininity are not merely social constructs. God, in his matchless wisdom and goodness, designed humanity this way to reveal delightful truths about himself and human nature. God is distinct from his creation yet made it to dwell with him in love and glory. In the same way, woman is distinct from man yet made to dwell with him in love and glory (this should not be taken to mean woman is ontologically subordinate to man, a point that will be developed later).[3]

The Fatherhood of God

When we speak of God's Fatherhood, one might be tempted to think it's an anthropomorphism. An anthropomorphism is a description of God in human terms that helps us understand him better, such as "the mighty hand of God" (1 Peter 5:6) or "the eyes of the Lord" (Prov 15:3). God's Fatherhood is not an anthropomorphism, however. In Paul's prayer in Ephesians 3, for example, he says, "For this reason I bow my knees before the Father, from whom every family in heaven and on earth is named" (vv. 14-15). There is a word play in Greek that is not obvious in English. The Greek word for "family" in this text is *patria*, which is related to the word "Father" (*pater*). In other words, Paul says he bows his knees before *the Father*, from whom *all fatherhood* in heaven and on earth is named.[4]

Therefore, when we think of God as our Father, we should not imagine a human father and think, "Oh I get it, God is like my dad," because that would be an anthropomorphism and we are not taught to deify our earthly fathers. Rather, human fatherhood is theomorphic. It is a human form that reflects the divine reality.[5]

---

3. William E. Mouser and Barbara Mouser, *The Story of Sex in Scripture* (Waxahachie, TX: International Council on Gender Studies, 2006), 4.

4. Tim Bayly, *Daddy Tried: Overcoming the Failures of Fatherhood* (Bloomington, IN: Warhorn Publishing, 2016), 77.

5. Mouser and Mouser, *The Story of Sex*, 53–54.

Human fatherhood is derivative of God's perfect Fatherhood. God the Father is the original. Human fathers are modeled after him. Human fathers were made to imitate God's Fatherly authority, initiative, and self-sacrifice. Fatherhood is also where households begin, which will be explored later in this book.

This does not mean, however, that men are more like God than women, or that women are less like God than men. Nor does it mean that men who have become natural fathers are more like God than those who have not. Rather, to those men who have been given this gift, fatherhood is an opportunity to glorify and imitate God in a particular way. To those who have not been given this gift, they can nevertheless pursue the virtues of fatherhood in their current circumstances. We'll talk more about these virtues in chapter 5.

Resisting God's Fatherhood

Some people resist the notion of God as Father because they project the failures of their own fathers back onto God. These are called "father wounds," which can affect our theology in ways that we don't realize. I once heard the story of Stephanie, a former exotic dancer, who was talking in an interview about her dad. She said, "from your father you learn how a man is going to treat you, love you, how you see authority, and how you react to authority. When there's not that male influence, there's this void, this hunger for male attention. I definitely needed that and wanted that in my life."[6] As she pointed out, there is a natural association between fatherhood and authority. In its essence, authority is life-giving.

6. I heard this story years ago and wrote down Stephanie's quote but have not been able to track down the precise citation since then.

It is generative in nature. The author of a book is one who creates something new. Yet the authority of a father is not limited to the fact that he has "authored" a new life, but that he takes responsibility to protect and provide for that person. In Scripture, authority is regarded as a good gift that can easily be abused. Bad authority can be cruel and tyrannical, while good authority can be delightful and freeing. God always exercises his Fatherly authority for his glory and for our good.

Many young girls like Stephanie never received healthy love or affection from their dads. Naturally, when a young girl lacks a fatherly presence to model what healthy, masculine affection looks like, she may easily internalize the world's message that sex is how you get a man to love you. Some women even end up objectifying themselves sexually to gain the love and attention from men that they should have received from their fathers.

To give another example, actor David Spade tells a story about a heartbreaking experience with his dad when he was growing up in the suburbs with his two older brothers. "One day," he said, "I was playing football with my dad. He told me to go out for a pass and shouted, 'go deeper!'" David did as he was told and ran hard to catch the pass. As he turned around to look for the ball, he saw his father jump into a car and leave. He never came back. His dad left the family because the pressure of having a wife, kids, and a job was too much for him.[7] Spade learned to mask his pain with humor, as many comedians do. Wounds like this run deep, because God created us to be secure in the love of our heavenly Father. By God's design, earthly fathers function as a proxy for God. Psychologists have long recognized that people form their thoughts about God from their dads.

---

7. *Parade Magazine*, 2001, March 4. I have not been able to locate the title or author of this article.

Every human needs to experience love, attention, and affection from a masculine authority. When the failures of our human fathers are projected back onto our heavenly Father, we end up with a distorted view of God. But in Christ, we can truly see who our Father is. Jesus said, "whoever has seen me has seen the Father" (John 14:9). This is the gift we receive in the gospel through faith in Christ. Not only does God forgive our sins and give us eternal life, but we are also adopted into his family as children of God (John 1:12). Through faith in Christ, we are reconciled and restored to our heavenly Father. This eternal gift is available to all people through faith, whether they had a wonderful earthly father or a terrible one.

The Masculinity of God

To state the obvious, fatherhood is a masculine concept, and Scripture consistently describes God in masculine terms. Of course, the Fatherhood of God does not imply that men are ontologically superior to women, or that women are ontologically inferior to men. Further, although God reveals himself with masculine language, it is not appropriate to say God is a male, because maleness is a created, biological reality, and God is spirit (John 4:24). The Father, Son, and Spirit are all described with masculine language (John 16:7-8, 13-15). It is therefore blasphemous to speak of God as mother.

Christians have long pondered what the Fatherhood of God means for women since men and women are both created in God's image. This troubles some Christians who feel that this excludes or even devalues women, as though women bear God's image in a lesser way. Others think that the Bible's masculine language for

God is an outdated remnant of the ancient patriarchal culture that should be remedied by using more feminine, motherly language for God. This desire can be especially pronounced if one grew up with an abusive or distant father. In cases like this, a more feminine deity seems safer, more approachable, and more loving.

Some people take a more philosophical approach. I spoke with a young man named John once in a small group at my house. John had spoken with a homosexual friend who planted doubts in his mind about Jesus' sexuality. As John reasoned through it, he began to wonder if Jesus had a "feminine side." The way he saw it, since women are created in God's image, then God must have a feminine side as well. And by this logic, Jesus must also have had a feminine side. John's error is common.

His thinking reflects the intrusion of Eastern pantheism into the Christian faith. Eastern religions see God and creation as part of a seamless whole. They believe that all of creation is in some way an expression of the divine, and the ultimate goal of all existence is to become one with the universe. When this thinking makes its way into popular level Christianity, you end up with bizarre contradictions. In John's case, his homosexual friend convinced him that human femininity must be a reflection of some kind of divine femininity. But since Christians only believe in one God (in three persons), then God himself must be both masculine and feminine.

This thinking is wrongheaded and pagan. Christianity teaches that God is distinct from his creation, a point which is emphasized in the creation account of Genesis 1. The creator-creature distinction is an important concept in Christian theology. God created a universe that was distinct from him. And yet, God created it to be united to him. This creator-creature distinction is mirrored in the sexual differences between men and women. Man and woman are distinct from one another yet created to be united to one another.

In other words, God is perfectly capable of creating a feminine human, in his image, without himself being a feminine God. Remember, the image of God is both an identity ("male and female") and an activity ("be fruitful and multiply"). Therefore, human masculinity and femininity were created to relate to one another according to a glorious, cosmic pattern of how God relates to his creation. Men and women are both created in God's image, and both are called to glorify God by imitating his character (1 Cor 11:1). God also created us distinct from one another, so we might glorify him by relating to one another in masculine and feminine ways. We should not regard our masculinity and femininity as a cage we are trapped in, but the prism through which the light of God's nature and character is illuminated.

Objection: Isn't Masculinity Toxic and Harmful to Women?

Some people are uncomfortable with the masculinity of God because they perceive masculinity as toxic and threatening. There are plenty of examples of men using their masculine aggression and strength in cruel and harmful ways, but masculinity itself is not evil. God is not like a human man with divine attributes. The opposite is true. Men are created in God's image to uniquely reflect God's attributes in a holy way.

For example, God gives men greater physical strength so they can take responsibility for their households and exercise godly authority over them. Men are called to image God's holy and just masculinity, using their superior strength and skill to lead, provide for, and protect others. God also gives women a nurturing and life-giving strength to complement man's masculine strength. Her feminine strength was given to complement man's strength, not compete with it.

Contrary to what you might have heard, the Bible never describes God's being with feminine language. God may *do* things that seem more feminine, but God's *being* is never described that way. For example, Jesus lamented over Jerusalem in Matthew 23:37 by saying, "O Jerusalem, Jerusalem, the city that kills the prophets and stones those who are sent to it! How often would I have gathered your children together as a hen gathers her brood under her wings, and you were not willing!" In this text, Jesus was not saying that he is a mother, but rather his love for his people is strong and protective, like the love of a mother. He was using a mother-hen metaphor to describe his desire to gather his unwilling people together.

Here's another example. In Deuteronomy 32:18, God says, "You were unmindful of the Rock that bore you, and you forgot the God who gave you birth." Does this text mean that God is a mother? No, because a few verses earlier in the same text, God calls himself their "father." Verse 6 says,

> Do you thus repay the Lord,
> you foolish and senseless people?
> Is not he your father, who created you,
> who made you and established you?

In verse 6, God was the "father" who created them, but in verse 18, God's people had forgotten God who gave them birth. This text is talking about how Israel rebelled against God in the wilderness after God rescued them from Egypt. Their deliverance through the Red Sea was like a birth. In this sense, God gave birth to his people by saving them from Pharaoh.

To be sure, God may do motherly things, but God is never called a mother in Scripture. When Scripture describes God's *being*, it uses masculine terms. When Scripture describes God's *actions*, a variety of words, metaphors, and images are used. The feminine images that describe God's actions do not diminish the masculinity of God but rather highlight it. For example, if a mother cuddles her infant child, it is unremarkable because women are more naturally attuned to nurturing. But if a man cuddles an infant in his arms, someone might say, "Look, he's tender with her like a mother!" This statement does not diminish his masculinity but rather highlights it. The motherly language to describe God's actions demonstrates the remarkable range of God's love. William and Barbara Mouser said it well: "Christ is a son, but never a daughter. Christ is a brother, never a sister. Christ is a bridegroom, never a bride. Christ is a husband, never a wife. Christ is a king, never a queen."[8]

Is a masculine God bad for women? The answer is an emphatic "no!" The masculinity of God is not bad news for women. Rather, it is good news for women as well as men. To make this clear, I'll use an admittedly bizarre example. This example is offered only to illustrate a point, not to be irreverent. Let's suppose for the moment that I've gotten this all wrong and God is both feminine and masculine. If that were the case, what would prevent Jesus from being born as a girl? Again, I'm not saying this to be edgy. I'm making a theological point. If that were the case, *Jesus* could have been born as *Jessica*. Let's apply the same logic a step further. In this scenario, could Jessica lead a sisterhood of twelve female disciples? Could she have been the one who was crucified for the sins of the world and raised on the third day? Hopefully, something within

---

8. Mouser and Mouser, *The Story of Sex*, 21.

you recoils at these ideas and you think, "that's blasphemy." If you react in that way, that's good, because it is blasphemy to believe such a thing. But can you say *why* it's blasphemy? Can you articulate a reason why it's blasphemous? Or does it just seem odd and unfamiliar? Is there something deeper that tells us that Jesus *must* have been male? Yes, there is, and it's the doctrine of headship.

Headship Is a Masculine Calling

The doctrine of headship is important because it reveals something about the nature of masculinity and femininity. In creation, God, who has all authority over all things, delegated a measure of his authority to Adam as the head over creation. God then commanded Adam to establish a household with Eve and they would rule over creation together. This is the pattern for all rule and authority. Further, every household has a head who takes responsibility and exercises authority over the house. Headship is a masculine calling because God created it to reflect his own headship. First Corinthians 11:3 says, "But I want you to understand that the head of every man is Christ, the head of a wife is her husband, and the head of Christ is God."[9]

At the heart of it, headship is about taking responsibility for others. In Eden, even though Eve was the first to commit a sin, Adam was held accountable since he was the head (Gen 3:9). Eve was held accountable for her sin, but Adam was held accountable for both of their sins because he was the head of his house. This is why Romans 5:12 says, "just as sin came into the world through one man, and death through sin, and so death spread to all men

---

9. The ESV translation of this text is not very literal. The Greek literally reads, "Christ is the head of every man, and the man is the head of a woman, and God is the head of Christ." The ESV interprets the words for "woman" and "man" as "wife" and "husband."

because all sinned." Thus, humanity fell under a curse, and every human being after Adam and Eve were born in sin. You and I were born in sin because of Adam's sin, not Eve's, because Adam was the head of his house. This principle applies to every marriage. Every man becomes the head of a new house when he gets married (Eph 5:23). He bears a unique responsibility for his entire household.

This is where the good news of the gospel comes in. Adam's sinful household was replaced by Christ's righteous household. First Corinthians 15:22 says, "as in Adam all die, so also in Christ shall all be made alive." Adam's household had grown to become a kingdom of darkness, but Christ, through his death and resurrection, established a new, righteous kingdom. Colossians 1:13 says, "He has delivered us from the domain of darkness and transferred us to the kingdom of his beloved Son, in whom we have redemption, the forgiveness of sins." First Corinthians 15:45 says, "Thus it is written, 'The first man Adam became a living being'; the last Adam became a life-giving spirit." Every human being belongs to one of two human households. We are either in Adam, the head of a fallen house, or in Christ, the head of righteous house. Those who are in Adam are lost, those who are in Christ become "sons of God through faith" (Gal 3:26). This is what it means to be "in Christ," a phrase used over 80 times in the New Testament. Being "in Christ" means we belong to a new household—and this changes everything. Therefore, "if anyone is in Christ, he is a new creation. The old has passed away; behold, the new has come" (2 Cor 5:17).

This is why there could not have been a Jessica Christ. Headship is a masculine calling, beginning with God's cosmic household, continuing through Adam's fallen house, and ending with the righteous house of Christ. And this pattern of masculine headship was written into the created order. Therefore, when the time came for God the Son to take on a human body forever, God did not have two equally suitable genders to choose from. Rather, a masculine God could only be incarnated in a masculine body. Jesus Christ was born as a boy, not a girl, because only a man could have secured our redemption as the covenant head of a redeemed house.

There are at least three conclusions we can draw at this point. First, headship is an essential feature of the gospel. Christ's victory is a victory of headship. Christians are not saved because we are righteous, but we are saved because our covenant head is righteous. Second, headship is masculine. God's ultimate headship was written into the created order. The heavenly father delegates authority to human fathers and expects them to exercise authority in God honoring ways. Third, Jesus is the model of true masculinity. Since headship is about taking responsibility for others, God created men to bear this burden. Doug Wilson defines masculinity as "the glad assumption of sacrificial responsibility."[10] Christ embodied this perfectly. Christ assumed sacrificial responsibility for others, laying down his life for them (Eph 5:25, John 10:11). In Christ, the Father has revealed the "breadth, length, height, and depth" of his love for his people (Eph 3:18). Thus Paul's prayer was that we would all "know the love of Christ that surpasses knowledge, that you be filled with all the fullness of God" (Eph 3:19). Christ is the model for how men should relate to women. Women are not to be harmed or abused, but they are to be led, cherished, and protected. Men are not to be tyrannical or cruel, but they are to lead in sacrificial ways, with humility, strength, and love. True masculinity is good for men and women.

---

10. Douglas Wilson, *Father Hunger: Why God Calls Men to Love and Lead their Families* (New York, NY: Harper Collins, 2012), 41.

Conclusion

God is the eternal Father, and he reveals himself with masculine terms. He is the eternal reality upon which all other reality is built. He is the source of everything good and right; he is reality and truth. God relates to his redeemed creation as a husband relates to a bride. In Revelation 21:3, redeemed creation is called the "New Jerusalem," which is a "bride adorned for her husband." God's masculinity in no way diminishes women or femininity because it is for his bride that Christ gave his life. Also, this in no way exalts men to a higher status than women because both men and women comprise the bride of Christ together equally (Gal 3:28). In God's household, the masculine and feminine are distinct from one another, yet united to each other in joyful harmony.

CHAPTER 2

Embodied Souls

"There are no ordinary people. You have never talked to a mere mortal." [1]

C. S. LEWIS

"And the LORD God formed man of the dust of the ground, and breathed into his nostrils the breath of life; and man became a living soul."

GENESIS 2:7 (KJV)

Introduction

Some truths are so beautiful and profound that they awaken within us a longing for God and eternity. No doubt we have all had profound experiences of being moved by a sublime truth about God—who he is, what he's done, and how his world operates. One of my favorite things to do is to go away for a couple of days at a time to be alone in nature. For me, nothing compares to the experience of hiking out on

---

1. C. S. Lewis, *The Weight of Glory: And Other Addresses* (HarperOne, Kindle Edition, 2009), 47.

some wilderness trail or on some mountain and looking out upon the grandeur of creation. There is something delightfully humbling about experiencing my own smallness in such a powerful way. It reminds me that such beauty was made by a beautiful God.

God's essence is true, good, and beautiful. And all truth, goodness, and beauty come down from him as a perfect gift (James 1:17). When God created man and woman, he left his signature on them, granting them dignity as creatures made in his image. Having been crafted in this way, we have the unique ability to perceive real beauty, to truly enjoy and delight in the Father, and to reflect his perfections back to him. The beauty we experience all around us can stir up desire for God, who is the source of all beauty. And one of the most profound ways God has written his beauty into creation is through human sexuality. He has woven the story of sex into the created order and written it into the pages of Scripture to reveal his nature and the mystery of the gospel.

The story is there in the beginning, when God originally created the universe by separating things into complementary pairs (Gen 1). He separated light from darkness (v. 4), the heavens above from the waters below (vv. 6-8), the seas from the land (vv. 9-10), and the greater light from the lesser (vv. 14-18). Then he populated the sea and the land with life that would thrive in each environment (vv. 20-21, 24-25). And it was good. This pattern culminated in God creating man as male and female. And it was *very* good.

Catholic theologian Peter Kreeft points out that in all these complementary pairs, the points of greatest contrast are points of most profound beauty.[2] Sunsets are beautiful because that's the point when day touches night. Beaches are popular because that's where the sea touches land. Fall is evocative because it marks the

---

2. CanaVox, 2021, "Episode 3: Understanding Man & Woman." YouTube, August 31, 2021. https://www.youtube.com/watch?v=TU6ITOi3EtM.

contrast between summer and winter. In the same way, human sexuality is wonderfully fascinating and mysterious because it marks the contrast between two kinds of people who were both uniquely created to bear his image. God revealed his goodness to us in the wonderful, mysterious, complementary, and often comical pairing of the sexes. As the Proverbs says, "three things are too wonderful for me; four I do not understand: the way of an eagle in the sky, the way of a serpent on a rock, the way of a ship on the high seas, and the way of a man with a virgin" (Prov 30:19).

In this chapter, we will look at the beauty of God's design for sexuality. Male and female bodies are not incidental. The differences between men and women were created by God to fulfill the distinct, God-honoring purpose of establishing multiplying households through which God would rule over the earth. The sexual functions of our bodies tell a story about how God creates life for his honor and glory. Correspondingly, male and female is not merely a physical distinction because humans are a composite of both bodies and souls. To put it another way, we are embodied souls. Our bodies are sacred spaces, temples of the Holy Spirit, where the life of God lives in us, for beauty and glory, in our sexual distinctions.

The Image of God

The "image of God" is indispensable to our understanding of humanity because every human is created in his image and every image bearer is either male or female (Gen 1:27; Gen 9:6). As divine image bearers, men and women are the crown of creation. Our value is derived from the image we bear, the signature of the divine, written on every soul like an artist signing his masterpiece.

As stated previously, the image of God is both a human identity and a human activity. As a human identity, the doctrine of the image of God establishes the fact that humans have inestimable value to God. The basic assertion that women have equal value to men did not come from the feminists but from the Bible. This is because God made them both in his image, and the cost of redemption was the same for both. Jesus did not purchase the souls of women at a discount, and every redeemed soul is saved on the basis of the shed blood of Christ. God makes no distinctions (Gal 3:28). Even though some people have sinfully twisted the Bible to oppress women, they do so in rebellion against God. Obedience to God leads to treating women better, not worse. As Rebekah Merkle said, "Unconverted societies never treat women well, and that is extraordinarily easy to document. Women being treated with respect is fruit that grows on one kind of tree, and that tree is a cross."[3]

The problem that often finds its way into discussions like this is a misunderstanding of what equality means. Equality doesn't mean sameness. Sameness is bland and boring, like an ice cream shop that only sells vanilla. God is more creative than that. God can create endless variety and distinction without altering the value. Christian equality means equal worth before God while recognizing the wonder of our differences. Men and women have different bodies, natures, abilities, aptitudes, interests, and callings.

The feminist vision of equality flattens out our good and necessary differences with the goal of ensuring that women and men are equally represented at every level of society in every way. But our physical and psychological differences guarantee that this will never happen the way they want. God designed our differences to

---

3. Rebekah Merkle, "Throw like a Girl: Why Feminism Insults Real Women," https://www.desiringgod.org/articles/throw-like-a-girl (Accessed July 22, 2022).

increase interdependence on one another, not unlike the various gifts in the church (1 Cor 12:12-31).

Although the Bible teaches the equal value of men and women, the whole story of Scripture moves to highlight, glorify, and even exaggerate our distinctions.[4] The vision of the Creation Mandate began with the marriage of a single human pair that would produce an incredibly diverse global civilization for the glory of God. Despite the disruption of sin, this redeemed vision will be fulfilled at the end of the story, when new Jerusalem will come down out of heaven, prepared as a bride adorned for her husband (Rev 21:2). But this civilization-building work cannot be accomplished if everyone is the same. This is the point of several New Testament texts that liken the church to a body where each part contributes to the whole, and all are valuable (1 Cor 12:1-31, Rom 12:3-8). Distinctions are part of the design to create interdependence, a division of labor, and a diversity of output, for everyone's mutual benefit. The interplay between male and female is the stuff of romance, comedy, drama, art, music, and poetry. These glorious and mysterious differences affect every part of who we are, body, mind, and soul.

As a human activity, the image of God indicates that God created men and women to rule. The sequence of events in Genesis 1:26-28 reveals a divine pattern that links the image of God to exercising dominion. In verse 26, God says, "Let us make man in our image," followed by "let them have dominion." Then, verse 27 says, "God created man in his own image, in the image of God he created him; male and female he created them," followed by this statement in verse 28, "Be fruitful and multiply and fill the earth and subdue it, and have dominion…" The pattern in these verses is

---

4. Mouser and Mouser, *The Story of Sex*, 11.

clear: image, dominion, image, dominion. Zachary Garris writes, "The description of man being made in God's image is sandwiched between the two dominion references. Together a man and woman carry out this dominion mandate through marriage and reproduction… Even this command assumes differing gender roles based on the different bodies and reproductive roles of men and women."[5] Men and women, created in the image of God, are called to exercise dominion over the earth together.

Herman Bavinck put it this way: "dominion over the earth is an unfolding of the image of God in humanity… Dominion is inseparable from the image of God according to which people were created. Sin did indeed introduce an immense change in the image of God, but insofar as human beings still display the image of God, they also retain the calling and the power to subdue the earth."[6] Therefore, God's original creation of man and woman at the beginning of the story contained the seeds that would sprout and bloom at the end of the story. Everything in between was propelled by thousands of generations of men and women whose distinctions work together to fulfill this divine purpose.

Bodies and Souls

Men and women have different bodies which correspond to their differing natures. Sexual differences are imprinted onto every human soul, and as such, the differences are gloriously eternal. When God first created Adam, Genesis 2:7 says that "the LORD God formed the man of dust from the ground and breathed into his nostrils the breath of life, and the man became a living creature."

---

5. Zachary M. Garris, *Masculine Christianity*, rev. ed. (Ann Arbor, MI: Reformation Zion Publishing, 2021), 104.

6. Bavinck, *The Christian Family*, 117.

The Hebrew word for "living creature" is *nephesh*, which indicates a psychosomatic unity of body and spirit. Every human being is an embodied soul, a composite of spirit and flesh, uniquely knit together in each individual.

The human body is a work of art. Even in its current, fallen form, corrupt with sin, its design is masterfully wondrous. Every hair follicle, blood vessel, brain cell, and DNA strand has an assigned purpose given by the Creator. C. S. Lewis once said, "Christianity is almost the only one of the great religions which thoroughly approves of the body—which believes that matter is good, that God Himself once took on a human body, that some kind of body is going to be given to us even in Heaven and is going to be an essential part of our happiness, our beauty, and our energy."[7]

God's good design is sexual. We are not androgynous carbon units. Manhood and womanhood are not suits of clothes. Gender cannot be assigned, only acknowledged. Sexuality isn't merely a physical characteristic, but characterizes the entire person, including the soul. God created Adam with a male body and a masculine soul. Eve was created differently. She was formed from Adam's side with a female body and a feminine soul.[8] As J. Budziszewski put it, "Human beings aren't one thing but two things together,

---

7. C. S. Lewis, *Mere Christianity* (London, England: William Collins, 2012), 77.

8. Some people claim that the existence of intersex people should lead to the rejection of the gender binary. Intersex, and related conditions, such as Swyer's syndrome, is a physical condition where a person has ambiguous genitalia, exhibiting characteristics of both male and female. This is a very rare phenomena, occurring in roughly 0.018% of the population (according to Wikipedia). Intersex does not negate the rule but proves it. In other words, the existence of intersex does not require the recognition of a third gender, but the acknowledgement that this condition is a rare deviation from the pattern and is the result of the fall.

composites of physical body and rational soul, each element equally personal and equally part of what we are."[9]

Male bodies have masculine souls with a masculine nature. Female bodies have feminine souls with a feminine nature. Male and female bodies are similar in most respects, having the same organs and body functions. These God-given differences are gifts that bring beauty, wonder, excitement, and mystery into our human experience. When Adam first sees his wife, she is naked, and he notices that she is physically different—and he immediately burst into song. "This at last is bone of my bones and flesh of my flesh," which is a statement of equality. She and he are alike. But he goes on, saying, "she shall be called Woman, because she was taken out of Man." This is a statement of distinction and purpose. She and he are different. There was something delightfully similar about her, yet something curiously different, which triggered the first love song in the Bible (Gen 2:23). What he observed on the outside was only the beginning of his exploration of all the delightful differences contained within.

The gnostic understanding of human beings which is so common in the modern world does the opposite. The essence of a person, some say, is what's on the inside. What one *feels* like is who he or she truly *is*. The body is incidental, maybe even incorrect. For a man to say he feels like a woman trapped in a man's body reflects this neo-gnostic attitude because it is believed that the body has nothing to do with one's gender. Gender is merely a matter of feelings. To an extent, we are conditioned to think this way. For the last generation or so, a large number of people form significant relationships online. In some video games, players choose an avatar and play the game as someone other than themselves.

---

9. Budziszewski, J., *On the Meaning of Sex* (Wilmington, NC: ISI Books, 2014), 40–41.

They play a role, enacting a game-world fantasy. One's avatar can be male, female, or a different species of being altogether. In the make-believe world of video games, it's simply entertainment. But it can subconsciously reward gnostic thinking, where the player sees himself as something other than what his body says. Further, he can find more gratification in an online gaming "community" than in reality. His gaming avatar is more exciting, skilled, powerful, and attractive than anything in his real life. It's a disembodied experience that gratifies a gnostic desire to escape the body. If a man imagines himself a young, desirable female character, he can become that by clicking the settings icon. Simple. And gnostic. In the gaming world, the body is irrelevant (except for the thumbs).

The Scriptures remind us that the body matters. For example, John wrote in his letter, "I had much to write to you, but I would rather not write with pen and ink. I hope to see you soon, and we will talk face to face" (3 John 13-14). John recognized the need for an embodied, face to face interaction. German theologian Werner Neuer once said, "Soul and body form an inseparable unity, being male or female characterizes the whole person and not only his or her body… Sex is therefore not just one personal characteristic among others, but a mode of being which determines one's whole life. 'Sexuality is the ultimate, irremovable and irreplaceable mode, which makes a person the kind of person he or she is.'"[10] As embodied souls, we are not spiritually androgynous, but our souls correspond to our bodies. Sex encompasses our whole person, both outward and inward.

Since our bodies are eternal, sexuality is also eternal. Sexuality is the reality through which we experience both this life and the life to come. At his return, Christ will "transform our lowly body to be

---

10. Neuer, *Man and Woman*, 27. In this quote from Neuer's book, he is quoting Catholic philosopher and theologian Fritz Leist.

like his glorious body, by the power that enables him even to subject all things to himself" (Phil 3:20-21). The "glorious body" referred to here is Christ's resurrection body. The resurrection body of Jesus was not androgynous. It was male, as it was from his birth. Since Christ ascended to heaven bodily, the maleness of that body is eternal. This means that we, too, will not experience eternity as disembodied, floating spirits, but as men and women with glorified bodies.

Natural Law

Most cultures believe in some version of an unseen, spiritual order that is linked to the visible, natural order. Though they occupy separate realms, they are connected in some kind of mysterious harmony. In the modern, western world, however, we have separated the two. The natural realm is all about scientifically observable facts. The spiritual realm, if it even exists at all, has nothing to do with the natural realm.

This is not what Christianity teaches, however. Francis Bacon, 17th-century scientist and devout Christian, is regarded as the father of experimental science and pioneer of the scientific method. Yet his pursuit of science was based on his belief that God created an orderly universe and he invites us to explore it.[11] Bacon recognized that nature reveals the Creator because God created it too. Psalm 19:1-2 says,

> The heavens declare the glory of God,
> and the sky above proclaims his handiwork.
> Day to day pours out speech,
> and night to night reveals knowledge.

---

11. Bacon, Francis, *The Advancement of Learning*, transcribed from the 1893 Cassell & Company edition by David Price (Kindle Edition).

In this Psalm, David says God, the Creator, reveals himself through his creation. We may not always observe or understand it properly, but nature doesn't lie to us. It is what it is. When we do understand nature properly, it is a wonderful teacher. For example, ants can teach us about hard work, independence, and being prepared (Prov 6:6-8). The heavens "declare" something true about God. The sky "proclaims" the works of God. Every day and every night, nature "pours out speech" and "reveals knowledge" about God.

In theological terms, this is called general revelation. God reveals himself in a general way through the created order. God has also revealed himself in a special way through his Word, which is called special revelation. The special revelation of God's word is the ultimate authority, which guides us into a proper understanding of what God has revealed about himself in nature through general revelation. Together, special revelation and general revelation help us move along with the grain of God's design. The conclusions we make from this combination is called natural law. Natural law assumes that God designed the world with a moral structure that can and should be followed. When an observation about what "is" leads to a conclusion about what "ought" to be, that's natural law.

To be clear on this point, natural law doesn't have the same authority as Scripture, but that doesn't make it unimportant. For example, there are no explicit Bible verses telling us not to eat dirt, stick forks in our eyes, or amputate healthy body parts. There are lots of things we believe to be right and wrong because we know it from nature. Protestant Christians are committed to Scripture as our *highest* authority, but Scripture is not our *only* authority. Nature has its own kind of authority as well.

In his book, *On the Meaning of Sex*, Catholic thinker J. Budziszewski writes this about the value of natural law: "Although the natural law tradition is unfamiliar to most people today, it has been the main axis of Western ethical thought for twenty-three centuries." As this applies to sexuality, "human beings really do have a design, and I mean that term in the broadest sense: not merely mechanical design (this part goes here, this part goes there), but what kind of being we are. Because the design is not merely biological, but also emotional, intellectual, and spiritual, the languages of natural law, natural design, natural meanings, and natural purposes are intertranslatable, and most of the time interchangeable. Some ways of living comport with our design. Others don't."[12]

Natural theology recognizes that some truths are self-evident and entail moral obligations. The apostle Paul gives an example of this in Romans 1 when he says that homosexual intercourse is *always sinful* because it is *always unnatural.* How so? Between two men, homosexual intercourse is consummated in the part of the body designed to expel waste. That act is "contrary to nature" (Rom 1:26) and it testifies to death. Nature, on the other hand, teaches that sex between a man and woman creates new life. If we reflect on God's design, we recognize that nature speaks. It tells a story. Nature testifies that man was designed to beget children and woman was designed to bear them. Of course, this doesn't mean *all* heterosexual sex is good. Fornication and adultery are sinful also. Only Scripture can explain the full meaning and design for sex. But nature has a voice in the matter too. Sex has a built-in logic that is obvious to anyone who isn't trying to suppress it.

The reason I'm making this point about natural law is to encourage us to reflect on the meaning of God's design of our bodies, and what this might teach us about how to glorify God with our sexuality. The Scriptures do not spell out with chapter and verse every

---

12. Budziszewski, *On the Meaning of Sex*, 21.

single thing that men and women may do or not do with their bodies. That's not how wisdom works. Wisdom is gained by paying attention to what God has revealed in both Scripture and nature and living in line with it. Let me say it another way. One of the recurring themes of this book is that God's design for sexuality is revealed in both Scripture and nature. The "is" of God's design for sexuality implies an "ought" about how to live. That's natural law. Natural law acknowledges that God has embedded principles and meaning into the created order. Natural law does not undermine the authority of Scripture but honors the Scripture's invitation to observe what God has revealed in creation. It may not tell us everything about how to live, but it certainly can tell us some things about how to live. The Bible speaks Truth with a capital "T," and nature speaks truth with a lowercase "t." It is perilous to ignore the testimony of either.

Therefore, if God designed sex with any goals in mind, we should expect them to be revealed in Scripture and evident in nature. J. Budziszewski argues that the two primary purposes of sex are procreation and union.[13] Both of these purposes are mutually reinforcing—a union of two people is necessary for procreation and raising the child they create together requires an ongoing union. When God joins them together in the covenant of marriage, they consummate their marriage sexually in a "one flesh" union (Gen 2:24). The pleasure of their intimacy sustains their love and produces new life. Since they are embodied souls, their bodies and minds harmonize and correspond to one another. God designed both male and female with a potentiality that is fulfilled when they marry and have children. Both mother and father are needed to raise the child, and this is because boys and girls need models of their own sex who demonstrate how to live and relate to the other sex.

---

13. Budziszewski, *On the Meaning of Sex*, 24.

The Meaning of Male and Female

This leads us to the meaning of male and female. Of course, the full scope of what manhood and womanhood means cannot be contained by definitions. We are far too complicated for such reductionism. And yet, we must still attempt to define them for the modern world that is so eager to eliminate sexual distinctions altogether. So, I offer these definitions from J. Budziszewski as a starting point, not the finish line. He says, "Sanity begins with the fact that men are potentially fathers, and women potentially mothers. This is not just a fact about what kind of thing they might or might not do some day, but about what kind of being they are inwardly aimed at becoming."[14]

He goes on to make a helpful distinction between potentiality and possibility. The design for womanhood includes the potentiality for motherhood, even though, for various reasons, motherhood is not possible for some women. In other words, what most fundamentally distinguishes woman from man is her potential for motherhood, even though it may not always be possible. Budziszewski says, "A potentiality is something like a calling. It wants, so to speak, to develop; it demands, so to speak, a response. Of course, this is figurative language because a potentiality has no will of its own. Yet it really is directed to fruition. The potentiality for motherhood is like an arrow, cocked in the string and aimed at the target, even if it never takes flight. It intimates an inbuilt meaning, and expresses an inbuilt purpose, which cannot help but influence the mind and will of every person imbued with them."[15] The potentiality for motherhood goes beyond the physical aspects of giving birth. Since she is an embodied soul, her potentiality for

---

14. Budziszewski, *On the Meaning of Sex*, 54.
15. Budziszewski, *On the Meaning of Sex*, 55–56.

motherhood encompasses her whole being. Similarly, an adoptive mother who has not physically given birth is no less a mother, as she is expressing the potentiality she was designed for.

The potentialities of manhood and womanhood find expression in the institution of marriage, where the sexual purposes of union and procreation are fulfilled. J. Budziszewski said the reason is that "children change us in a way we desperately need to be changed. They wake us up, they wet their diapers, they depend on us utterly. Willy-nilly, they knock us out of our selfish habits and force us to live sacrificially for others; they are the necessary and natural continuation of the shock to our selfishness which is initiated by matrimony itself. By seeking the unity but deliberately refusing the gift of children, we still get a kind of unity, but it goes bad. Because it turns inward, it ferments, turns sour, and begins to stink. The decisive factor is not sterility, which is nobody's fault, but deliberate rejection of fertility. If we willfully refuse the procreative meaning of union, then union itself is stunted. We merely change from a pair of selfish ME to a single selfish US."[16]

Conclusion

The implications of this will be developed throughout this book, so I will conclude this chapter by summarizing a few points made so far. Every human being is either male or female, created in God's image, with equal value and dignity. Men and women have different bodies and natures since every human is also a composite of both body and soul. These differences are for God's glory and our good. God created them for the purpose of union and procreation in the covenant of marriage. Thus, what it means to be

---

16. Budziszewski, *On the Meaning of Sex*, 31.

male or female entails the inherent potentialities of fatherhood and motherhood.

Grace doesn't overturn nature. It restores it. It is not legalism to conform to our sexual nature. With the Spirit-led eyes of faith, under the authority of Scripture, we can observe God's design in nature, draw ethical conclusions based on that design, and be empowered to live within those moral parameters. The modern, gnostic tendency is to see our bodies and natures as plastic and malleable, incidental to who we truly are on the inside. That is a mistake. Men are not women and women are not men. Men have male bodies, masculine souls, and masculine duties that God calls them to embrace. Women have female bodies, feminine souls, and feminine duties that God calls them to embrace. God's creation is good, and we need to receive his gift of sexuality with humility and gratitude. The grace of Jesus Christ redeems and restores that which was marred by the fall.

CHAPTER 3

Men and Women Are Different

"Sexuality is a window into someone's soul."

ALAN BALL

(WRITER, DIRECTOR, AND PRODUCER FOR
TELEVISION, FILM, AND THEATER)

"This at last is bone of my bones and flesh of my flesh; she shall be called Woman, because she was taken out of Man."

GENESIS 2:23

Introduction

Stereotypes have fallen on hard times these days. Some would say that all stereotypes are wrong because characteristics observed from the group do not always apply to every individual. Thus, they claim, stereotypes are harmful because they mischaracterize individuals. In other words, general rules are invalidated by exceptions.

I disagree. What we call stereotyping is simply pattern recognition, which is necessary for wisdom. Wisdom is the art of observing typical patterns, categorizing them, and drawing general conclusions from them. This is necessary to engage in any kind of rational thought. Stereotypes always have exceptions because they are, by definition, general truths. When a truth never has an exception, then it's simply a fact, not a stereotype. Facts never have exceptions, but stereotypes always do. A society that chooses to not recognize stereotypes is a society that chooses to not see the way things are. It's a society that cannot develop wisdom because it has chosen blindness. And we choose blindness when the truth is too uncomfortable to see.

In the modern world, the impulse towards expressive individualism is so strong that we are pressured to ignore the patterns. Whenever a stereotypical pattern is observed, someone will come along and point out an exception that is assumed to disprove the observation. Yet the differences between men and women are obvious to anyone willing to see them. Take physical strength, for example. God made men to be physically stronger than women. But in saying this, someone might object that this is an unfair stereotype because there are many strong women and many weak men. Do these exceptions make the observation unfair? Of course not. It's a stereotype, and stereotypes always have exceptions.

Further, stereotypes rely on subjective distinctions. The lines are often blurry. This is called the "fallacy of the beard." The fallacy of the beard gets its name from the fact that one cannot precisely define how many whiskers constitute a true beard. If you shave off one whisker, does it cease to be a beard? How about ten whiskers? One hundred whiskers? We know what beards are even though we cannot precisely identify the line between beard and non-beard. The distinction is imprecise and subjective. But an imprecise distinction doesn't mean beards don't exist.

We make imprecise, subjective distinctions every day. For example, when does a child become an adult? Nothing magical happens on the 18th birthday, although that's when one is legally considered an adult in the United States. The line between adult and child is quite blurry, but that doesn't mean the distinction is meaningless. Since there aren't precise lines between masculine or feminine characteristics, some deny the value of any such categorizations. If a woman can be found who is physically stronger than most men, then, we are told, physical strength should no longer be considered a masculine trait. But this is illogical. Generalizations assume exceptions. That's what makes them useful. Every day we observe clear distinctions that have blurry boundaries, such as short versus tall or rich versus poor. We need to recognize these general distinctions between men and women to live wisely with each other.

The Bible is full of stereotypes. Proverbs is considered a book of wisdom because it tells us about the way the world generally is. Proverbs observes and labels different behavior patterns, such as that of the wicked, the righteous, the fool, the poor, the friend, the ruler, the rich, the adulteress, the sluggard, and the scoffer, just to name a few. By noting behavior patterns in different kinds of people and naming them, we can learn which patterns to follow and which ones to avoid. Proverbs 15:1 says, "A soft answer turns away wrath, but a harsh word stirs up anger." This is a general pattern. As a general rule, you can expect conflicts to go better when you speak calmly and gently. But there are exceptions. Sometimes, people won't listen to you no matter how reasonable you are. Proverbs accounts for this, too (Prov 26:4, 5). Proverbs teaches the general rule and the exceptions to the rule. That's how wisdom works. Fools, on the other hand, refuse to see how the world works and try to live in fantasy land instead. By refusing to see how things really are, they render themselves incapable of attaining wisdom. Even though God has created men and women wondrously different from one another, in the modern world, it has become taboo to observe them or talk about them. This is the way of fools. But we will leave foolish ways behind and pursue wisdom instead.

Sexual Stereotypes

No discussion of sexuality can happen at all without observing what men and women are generally like and drawing conclusions about them. It's unavoidable. For example, we cannot know what "men" are like in general without disregarding each man's individuality to a degree, observing patterns common to most men, and drawing conclusions from the aggregated data. When closely observing human bodies and behaviors, and when these characteristics are grouped into categories we associate with masculine or feminine, we quickly find a great deal of overlap between the sexes. Almost every man will have some feminine characteristics, such as sensitivity, nurture, or compassion; and almost every woman will have some masculine characteristics, such as aggressiveness, directness, or competitiveness. Macro-level observations are not invalidated by the uniqueness of individuals. In other words, if we observe that men are generally stronger than women physically, we need not draw the conclusion that a man who happens to be physically weaker is a lesser man. Or if we observe that women are generally more sensitive than men in temperament, we need not draw the conclusion that a woman who is not as sensitive is a lesser woman. We will save the discussion on gendered virtue for chapter 5.

In the modern world, acknowledging differences between men and women is seen as restrictive and stifling to individual self-expression. But this has not always been the case. Other cultures around the world (not to mention in the past) have typically celebrated sexual differences by developing their own customs, forms, norms, and traditions to highlight those differences. Other cultures have been more prone to see sexual differences as beautiful, meaningful, and even liberating manifestations of transcendent realities.[1]

This doesn't mean there aren't some potential hazards when stereotyping men and women. I'll note three errors in particular. The first error is to make too much of the observations. I'm not interested in promoting unbiblical, rigid, and culturally determined gender norms. Nor do I want to bind anyone's conscience where Christ has given us liberty (Rom 14:1-12). Sexual stereotypes are more useful in describing behavior than prescribing it. The second error is to make too little of the observations. The patterns we observe about men and women can teach us something about God's purpose for sexuality. We need wisdom to draw the right conclusions. The third error is to disregard historical and cultural factors. Throughout human history, cultures have developed sexual norms and taboos to govern behavior and maintain order. For example, there is a big difference between a man wearing a Scottish kilt and an evening gown. A man in a kilt is conforming to a cultural expectation of masculinity. His kilt is part of the masculine uniform, and he wears it as part of the brotherhood of men. A skirt may be similar to a kilt in some ways, but the man wearing a skirt is signaling something different from the man wearing a kilt. He's openly defying a cultural expectation of masculinity. By committing this taboo, he is declaring his independence from such

---

1. Alistair Roberts, "Man and Woman in Creation (Genesis 1 and 2)," https://www.9marks.org/article/man-and-woman-in-creation-genesis-1-and-2/ (Accessed July 7, 2022).

expectations. To be sure, expressions of masculinity and femininity can vary across time and culture, and these variances need to be taken into account, but these variations do not render the cultural expectations meaningless.

Basic Differences Between the Sexes

It is foolish to disregard the differences between men and women. As Herman Bavinck observed, men and women are different "in terms of the body and all of its organs. Difference in the size of the head, in the development and weight of the brain, in the tint of the skin, in the growth of hair, in the shape of breast and stomach, in the form of the hands and feet. Difference also with regard to the strength and tone of the muscles, the sensitivity of the nervous system, the gracefulness of movements, the color of the blood, the flow of tears, the pulse rate, the sound of the voice, the multiplicity of needs, the capacity to suffer, the weight and strength of the body. In her entire development, the woman… reaches full adulthood sooner than the man."[2]

At the genetic level, every cell has a sex. Men carry XY chromosomes and women carry XX chromosomes. The human body has an estimated 37 trillion cells, and all of them are "sexed."[3] For example, a woman's heart tissue has female heart cells, and a man's heart tissue has male heart cells. To put it another way, all 37 trillion cells in your body testify in unison that you are either male or

---

2. Bavinck, *The Christian Family*, 67.
3. Institute of Medicine (US) Committee on Understanding the Biology of Sex and Gender Differences; Wizemann TM, Pardue ML, editors. Exploring the Biological Contributions to Human Health: Does Sex Matter? Washington (DC): National Academies Press (US); 2001. 2, Every Cell Has a Sex. Available from: https://www.ncbi.nlm.nih.gov/books/NBK222291/

female.[4] Feminist scholar and lesbian activist Camile Pagila agrees. She said, "The cold biological truth is that sex changes are impossible. Every single cell of the human body remains coded with one's birth gender for life."[5] One day, long after you've been dead, some archaeologist could dig up your bones and say, "this was a male" or "this was a female" regardless of what you "identified" as during your lifetime.

One neuroscientist said sexual differences are "marked, pervasive, and consistent."[6] Even though our bodies are different, it would seem as though our brains are even more different. Our differences reveal the genius of God's design, because we are different in corresponding and complementary ways. J. Budziszewski says, "Large parts of the brain cortex are thicker in women than in men. Ratios of gray to white matter vary, too. The hippocampus, which plays a role in memory and spatial navigation, takes up a greater proportion of the female brain than of the male brain. On the other hand, the CA1 region of the hippocampus is larger in the male. A variety of neurotransmitter systems work differently in men and women; neurotransmitters are the chemicals that carry nerve impulses across the synapses. Sex hormones, obviously different in men and women, influence not only the excitability of hippocampus cells, but also various aspects of their structure."[7]

Additionally, "The right and left hemispheres are more interconnected in female brains than in male ones, and the corpus callosum, which links them together, is larger. The amygdala,

---

4. See the footnote in chapter two that acknowledges the reality of intersex. In a fallen world, there are exceptional cases, but these do not negate the rule.

5. Scott Jaschik, n.d., "University of the Arts Rejects Calls to Fire Camille Paglia," Insidehighered.com, https://www.insidehighered.com/news/2019/04/17/university-arts-rejects-calls-fire-camille-paglia (Accessed December 17, 2022).

6. Budziszewski, *On the Meaning of Sex*, 38. Budziszewski was citing the work of neuroscientist Larry Cahill.

7. Budziszewski, *On the Meaning of Sex*, 38.

involved in emotion and emotional memory, is larger in men, but the deep limbic system, which is also involved in emotion, is larger in women. Across a spectrum of different functions, which side of the amygdala controls which function is reversed in men and women. Sex-related differences between the hemispheres exist for other brain regions as well, including the prefrontal cortex, involved in personality, cognition, and other executive functions, and the hypothalamus, which links the nervous system with the endocrine system and has some connection with maternal behavior. External circumstances, such as chronic stress, act on male brains differently than on female. Brain diseases also diverge in men and women, not only in their frequency, but in their age of onset, duration, and the way they manifest themselves. Even the neurological aspects of addiction differ between the two sexes."[8]

Bavinck goes on to describe the inner differences between the sexes—differences in our basic natures, differences "in the life of the soul," as he calls them. He writes, "the woman acquires sense impressions more quickly and retains them longer and more deeply than the man. Her imagination is characterized by greater liveliness and quicker connectivity. Her thinking and evaluating are characteristically more visual than analytic, attaching more value to the amenities of life than to abstract principles and rules. She seeks truth preferably along the route of an idealizing view of reality, rather than by the method of conceptual analysis. With the man, the volitional capacity is more logical, more capable of persistence, more persevering in striving for a goal, but the woman surpasses him in forbearance and patience, in the capacities for suffering and adapting."[9]

---

8. Budziszewski, *On the Meaning of Sex*, 39.
9. Bavinck, *The Christian Family*, 68.

J. Budziszewski describes how the physiological differences in our brains produce more obvious differences in how we relate to the world. Citing Edith Stein, a German Jewish philosopher who converted to Catholicism and became a nun, Budziszewski writes, "men are more prone to abstraction, and women more prone to focus on the concrete. Men don't mind what is impersonal; women are more attuned to the nuances of relationships, and to what is going on in other people. A man tends to be a specialist and single-tasker; he develops certain qualities to an unusually high pitch, using them to do things in the world. A woman tends to be a generalist and multitasker; she inclines to a more rounded development of her abilities, using them to nurture the life around her. The woman's potentiality for motherhood ties all her qualities together and makes sense of her contrast with men. Consider just that multitasking capacity. In view of what it takes to run a home, doesn't it make sense for her to have it? A woman must be a center of peace for her family, even though a hundred things are happening at once."[10]

These differences are not merely incidental. They mean something. Each difference has a God-ordained purpose, or goal, for which that difference was created. "Manhood in general is outward-directed, and womanhood inward-directed."[11] True Christian virtue comes from living in line with God's design, not against it.

---

10. Budziszewski, *On the Meaning of Sex*, 57.
11. Budziszewski, *On the Meaning of Sex*, 59.

The Design of Men

Physiological, Intellectual, Temperamental, and Hormonal Distinctions

Male bodies are more utilitarian and adaptable. Unlike women, whose vocation of motherhood is biologically integrated, male bodies are more versatile and suitable for a wider variety of physical tasks. To put it another way, men are more naturally designed for hard, physical labor. Men are taller and faster than women. Women's world record speeds are only about 90% as fast compared to men. Men have more twitch muscle fibers, giving them more athletic explosiveness. The strongest 10% of women can only beat the bottom 10% of men in hand grip tests, which is one of the most widely used indicators of overall strength. Men have 66% more upper body muscle and 50% more lower body muscle than women. Men have larger hearts and lungs, allowing their bodies to pump more blood to the body and for bodily tissues to receive more oxygen. Men have bigger and stronger bones, giving them superior physical leverage. Men tend to have an overall higher pain tolerance than women.[12]

These characteristics make men better suited for being protectors and providers in the family and in society. Protecting others is a combative role. Men are better equipped for combat because of their physical strength and speed combined with their greater affinity for anger and aggression. Even though these tendencies have sinful out-workings, they are not sinful in themselves. Masculine aggressiveness can be expressed in God honoring ways.

In an unpublished work entitled "A Biblical Theory of Sexual Attraction," my friend Michael Foster wrote, "Males tend to be

---

12. Michael Foster, "A Biblical Theory of Sexual Attraction," unpublished. This was provided by personal correspondence.

more oriented towards the world of 'things.' Males are superior to females in logical consistency, abstract reasoning, and spatial conceptualization (e.g. STEM)."[13] Men have the unique ability to look at the unshaped world around them and determine how to shape it into something good and useful. The technological innovations of the modern world were overwhelmingly pioneered by men.

Men tend to be more competitive, more fearless, more prone to violence, more confident, and more self-assured than women. These characteristics can be sinfully expressed as domineering, angry, sexually promiscuous, contentious, divisive, or lazy. As Michael Foster said, "Males are hormonally wired (i.e., testosterone) to be more aggressive than their female counterparts. Males are more apt than females to take both intellectual and physicals risks... Males tend to 'partition' their feelings from their reasoning. Males are more rule-conscious. The design of the male sexual organ and the male reproductive cell demonstrates that man is equipped to be an initiator... In summary, men are uniquely equipped to engage in conflict and establish structures."[14] In summary, men are physically, intellectually, and temperamentally equipped to structure society.

In groups, males often organize themselves into social hierarchies to achieve a common purpose. Male groups are characterized by competition, aggression, and conflict. Men more naturally develop organizations and chains of command. Since competence and skill are a form of social currency for men, who tend to either submit to or compete with other men until order is established, masculine organizations tend to have strong leadership, clear objectives, and chains of command. Both men and women can thrive

---

13. Michael Foster, unpublished correspondence.
14. Michael Foster, unpublished correspondence.

in this environment because virtuous male leadership provides the structure and discipline needed for everyone to excel.

Men Go to Extremes

Men tend to go to extremes, whereas women are more prone to moderation. While men are driven to achieve higher and higher levels of excellence in every level of society, they are also disproportionately found on the bottom end of the spectrum. Men are more likely to be found on the extreme ends of poverty and power. Men are more likely to be criminals, murderers, or prisoners, as well as more likely to be CEOs, inventors, or rulers. In fact, Alistair Roberts observed that men "commit practically every crime at a higher rate than women. Across human societies, men are directly responsible for almost all serious violence and war."[15] For example, the aggressiveness and combativeness of a man when applied in a sinful manner may lead him to abuse his wife, but these are the same traits that would lead him to die to protect her. Man can indulge in great evil in his own life or conquer great evil he encounters in the world. The greatest achievements of mankind will be performed mostly by men, and the greatest and most vile evils will be performed mostly by men.

Men and Society

Herman Bavinck observes, "In the formal sense, ... a feminocracy never existed anywhere. Naturally the woman never lacked power and influence over her children, her husband, and her entire

---

15. Alistair Roberts, Calvinistinternational.com, https://calvinistinternational.com/2016/09/13/natural-complementarians-men-women/ (Accessed July 7, 2022).

family. Here and there she was even called to fill important and dignified posts, so that from time to time queens have governed among various nations. But this is exceptional."[16] Why? Because God designed men to rule. Men have the more natural inclinations and strength to govern. Since men will inevitably rule every society, a society needs virtuous men to fight and oppose the tyranny of evil men.

Men of virtue need the power of the Spirit to honor God in their calling. God gave men bodies and natures suited to this task, and they need God's power at work in them to truly succeed. Men who recognize that their masculine strength is needed in their homes, churches, and society will often rise to the challenge because the weight of these responsibilities draw out the strength needed to fulfill them. Men tend to thrive when they are given a great and noble goal to pursue that demands total sacrifice and commitment.

Unfortunately, our society does not properly recognize its need for strong, holy masculinity. The modern world too often regards masculinity as harmful or even "toxic." In fact, the world often judges masculinity by feminine standards. When toxic men are seen as defective women, the usual antidote is to try to make them more feminine. Our society has produced generations of "nice guys" who are shriveling up on the inside, dying of boredom, and are afraid of or even ashamed of their masculinity. Although God has given them natural strength, many of them lack the purpose and direction to use it in a God honoring way.

If God has designed and equipped men for the task of being the leaders, providers, and protectors of society, then emasculating and feminizing them will not only weaken them, but also society as a whole. Evil men will use their masculine strength to tyrannize,

---

16. Bavinck, *The Christian Family*, 26.

and godly men will lack the strength to resist. The strength of tyrants and bullies in the world can only be stopped by the greater strength of masculine virtue. Men who deny their masculinity and embrace passivity are not capable of protecting others. Evil men will exploit their error.

Our fallen world needs the strong masculinity of holy men, whose love of risk, adventure, and courage is needed and put to good use. Masculine aggression, combativeness, and the desire for conquest are glorious and noble when dedicated to the Lord.

Christ and Masculinity

Jesus Christ is the embodiment of perfect, glorious, and holy masculinity. Jesus was not passive or weak, but he was strong, courageous, faithful, and true. Jesus said, "no one can enter a strong man's house and plunder his goods, unless he first binds the strong man. Then indeed he may plunder his house" (Mark 3:27). The strong man is Satan, and Satan will not be defeated by weakness and passivity. No, Satan is defeated in the masculine strength of Christ, the "stronger man," who bound him and plundered his house. Even in his crucifixion and death, Christ was not a passive victim. He said, "I lay down my life that I may take it up again. No one takes it from me, but I lay it down of my own accord. I have authority to lay it down, and I have authority to take it up again" (John 10:17-18). When Christ died on the cross, he did so willingly in the ultimate demonstration of masculine strength and virtue.

The Design of Women

Physiological, Intellectual, Temperamental, and Hormonal Distinctions

Female bodies are not as versatile as male bodies. Male bodies are utilitarian and have the versatility to excel at a number of tasks, but the female body is clearly designed for the specific purpose of bearing and nurturing children. Foster wrote, "Female bone structure tends to be smaller, rounder, and less sharply formed. The female pelvis is wider, longer, and held together by ligaments that soften during pregnancy, allowing the two halves to slide apart. Females have a longer torso to accommodate extra reproductive organs and finds space to push things out of the way during pregnancy. Females have much less muscle mass and higher body fat. Female skin has a greater sensitivity. Females have a womb and breasts necessary to bear and nurture children. In summary, women are uniquely equipped to carefully respond to the nearest and most intimate things. Also, it must be noted that females are clearly and overwhelmingly designed for motherhood."[17] The physical characteristics of women are more holistically oriented towards motherhood than the characteristics of men towards fatherhood. The implications of this will be more fully explored later.

Foster wrote, "Females tend to be more oriented towards the world of 'people.' Females are superior to males in linguistics, verbal communication, and in fields/activities requiring a high level of empathy." In short, while men are uniquely equipped to structure society at large, "women are uniquely equipped to nurture and manage structured community."[18]

---

17. Foster, unpublished.
18. Foster, unpublished.

While men tend to be outwardly oriented, toward the world, women tend to be inwardly oriented, toward the home. Women are more nurturing, warm, and compassionate than men. Women are more relationally wired, having a strong impulse towards equality, togetherness, hospitality, and community. These characteristics can be sinfully expressed when women are immodest, brash, manipulative, or demanding. Women are physically, intellectually, sexually, and temperamentally equipped to help, nurture, and refine society. Thus, women tend to be multipliers, refiners, nurturers, and followers.

Foster wrote, "Females are more agreeable than their male counterparts. Females are more apt to seek out the company of others for simply the pleasure of the company. Female reasoning is more emotionally integrated. Females react to any stimulus in a more lively and complete way than a male. Females possess a greater social adaptability. The design of the female sex organ and female reproductive cell demonstrate that woman is equipped to be a recipient (i.e. the woman receives the man, the ovum receives the sperm). In summary, women are uniquely equipped to provide care/nurture and be responsive to leadership."[19]

Since women are more relationally attuned, nurturing, compassionate, and hospitable, women naturally transform their surroundings into home-like environments for gathering and fellowship. While men are usually better at conquering and subduing, women are usually better at domesticating and beautifying.

---

19. Foster, unpublished.

Women in Groups

Female groups tend to be smaller, egalitarian, conflict averse, verbal, and oriented around people more than things. The maternal instincts of women cause them to more readily notice others who feel hurt or excluded, which is one reason why women will often be champions of diversity and inclusion initiatives. Men tend to create hierarchies, which are good for pursuing goals and accomplishing tasks, but that's not how women most naturally relate. Men relate in triangular formation with the chief at the top, women relate in circular formation where everyone is equal and every voice is heard. As women's voices become more prominent in business and the marketplace, sharp hierarchies tend to flatten out and a spirit of cooperation and teamwork emerges. These feminine influences can bring much needed corrections to organizations where power is concentrated in the hands of a few, which can tend toward corruption. The listening and empathetic skills of women can be good for an organization, as their presence tends to be more "motherly," and men respond accordingly to their gentle presence. God has gifted women with the ability to transform their environments into homes, places of warmth and hospitality, where people are welcomed and feel loved. In short, men excel at making things *functional* and women excel at making them *pleasant*.

Women and Motherhood

In the home, although raising a family is a team effort of both husband and wife, the role of the mother in carrying, giving birth, and nursing an infant child is disproportionate to the father's. There is simply no substitute for a mother's care. She is irreplaceable. It has been said that the father is the head of the home but the mother is the heart. Those who have been blessed with good mothers know that if anything, this understates the mother's importance. She is much more than the heart. In very real and tangible ways, she *is* the home. From the moment of conception, her body transforms itself into a home for her child. Throughout childhood and adolescence, she is more likely to be at the center of all the activities of the home, from managing schedules, providing meals, celebrating birthdays, and ensuring that everyone feels secure and loved. Even in healthy homes, children typically have a better relationship with their mother than with their father, though they love both the same. I have noticed that when many people speak of their parents, they often speak of "mom and dad," mentioning the mother first.

Different Potentialities

This brings us, once again, to the *teleology* of manhood and womanhood. The differences between them go beyond complementarity. The distinctions are not limited to how body parts fit together, or how temperaments can gel in harmonious ways. Ultimately, the purpose of these distinctions is to create new life. Manhood and womanhood are defined by the goal for which they were made, which is procreation. But we must press further, because men and women do not play equal roles in this endeavor. Manhood and womanhood are defined by their respective potentialities of fatherhood and motherhood, which reflect the fact that men and women have different natures.

It is undeniable that the woman's vocation of motherhood is more biologically integrated than the man's vocation of fatherhood. Her entire body is designed for and oriented towards reproduction. Her brain, hormones, joints, bones, cardiovascular system, immune system, breasts, and reproductive organs are all designed for the bearing and nurturing of children. This fact has angered and animated feminists, who see this disparity as a source of oppression and need for liberation, but this is regarded as a blessed and high calling in Scripture.

Another undeniable reality is that men can be more sexually promiscuous because, biologically speaking, reproduction doesn't cost them anything. Men are free to have sex whenever they want without ever personally facing the consequences of conception. Neuer wrote, "the physical contribution of the man is… fleeting in comparison with the bodily processes which the woman undertakes in motherhood. While a man simply becomes a father through begetting, conception is for the woman only the beginning of a period of far-reaching burdens and demands."[20] Therefore, "the woman's body is far more determined by her potential mother-hood than a man's is by his potential fatherhood." This is no small thing, and it shapes the vocations of women in incalculable ways. This is not to say that the potentiality for motherhood encom-passes the entirety of what it means to be woman, but neither can womanhood be properly understood apart from it.

Budziszewski says, "This explains the beauty of someone like Teresa of Calcutta. It is no accident that she was called 'Mother' Teresa. Though she set aside the whole business of erotic love, marriage, and physical conception, her beauty was that of a holy woman, distinct from the beauty of a holy man; the qualities that distinguish women from men were distilled, concentrated, and spiritualized in her. This kind of beauty also has its signs, its radi-ance, and its glory, and it is utterly womanly."[21]

---

20. Neuer, *Man and Woman*, 39.
21. Budziszewski, *On the Meaning of Sex*, 97–98.

The Balance of the Sexes

From these observations, it seems as though God has ordered the sexes with a kind of "protology" and "eschatology." Masculinity seems to be more *protological*, having to do with the beginning of things, such as building, inventing, and creating. Thus, men tend to be initiators, conquerors, and explorers. Similarly, femininity seems to be more *eschatological*, having to do with the end of things. Women, therefore, tend to be more refined and nurturing, excelling at domesticating and beautifying their environments. Women also tend to be custodians of civility and social harmony.[22] Neuer said that the man is "more strongly equipped for creative or destructive remodeling of his environment," and "the woman is more strongly equipped for arranging what the man has acquired for her or she has received from him."[23]

These aggregated observations point to a basic blueprint of God's design for men and women, with broader implications for the household. Men and women are complementary and interdependent, both physically and mentally, which is directed towards establishing productive households. Put simply, God's design for men and women at least implies a household structure that would be mutually beneficial for them and their children. This is taught in Scripture and is also evident in nature.

In the household, the masculine leadership of the father and the nurturing tendencies of the mother bring a sense of balance and stability. A common conflict in many families occurs when the mother complains that her husband is "too hard" on the kids, and he complains she is "too soft." These sorts of conflicts may indicate a healthy home, as mother and father are balancing each other out.

---

22. Credit to G. Shane Morris who made this point on a podcast.
23. Neuer, *Man and Woman*, 38.

The mother loves with nurturing care and the father loves with firm accountability. Both are needed. For example, if a boy wrecks his bike and starts crying, his mother will immediately rush over to him to comfort him and tend to his wounds. The father, wanting to prepare the child for difficult challenges that lie ahead in life, may instead say, "leave him be; he'll be just fine." The mother's desire for comfort and care is balanced by the father's desire for strength and toughness. The father wants his son to be tough and strong because life is hard. The mother wants to comfort and heal her child for the same reason—life is hard! As J. Budziszewski put it, "A wise father teaches his wife and family that in order to love you must be strong; a wise mother teaches her husband and family that in order to be strong you must love."[24]

Households can become unhealthy when the gifts and strengths of both sexes are not functioning fully and in an orderly way. For example, children that are over-fathered can become exasperated, feeling as though his high standards are always beyond their reach (Col 3:21; Eph 6:4). Fathers may discipline too harshly and with anger out of a good desire for his children to develop skill and excellence, but ultimately do them harm. Similarly, children that are over-mothered can become emotionally fragile and weak, often due to lack of exposure to the risks, dangers, and obstacles needed to become strong and resilient. Mothers who go soft with discipline often do so because discipline inflicts pain on the child and mothers will naturally resist this, even when it is for their good.

Scripture presents discipline primarily as the father's domain (Heb 12:5-8). Fathers tend to have a more commanding presence but can be less sympathetic and more emotionally detached. This is why a mother can say, "just wait till your father gets home!" and

---

24. Budziszewski, *On the Meaning of Sex*, 61.

strike fear in the hearts of her children. Nevertheless, the mother's tender touch can soften the father's rough edges and ensure he doesn't exasperate the children. This balance between masculine and feminine strengths is a design feature of godly households, which is the optimal environment for these strengths to be expressed.

Conclusion

The biological differences between men and women are incontestable, and most of the social differences are undeniable, even if some are uncomfortable to acknowledge in the modern world. Nevertheless, we must realize that the cost of denying the manifest differences between men and women is unimaginably steep. We cannot exchange reality for fiction without yielding massive collateral damage. Trying to pretend the sexes are identical or interchangeable is like trying to level Mount Everest by hitting it with a spoon. Men and women are gloriously different, crafted that way by a masterful maker.

CHAPTER 4

The Blueprint for
the Household

"Heaven and Earth are separate but connected realms. God's households operate in tandem toward a mutual destiny."[1]

MICHAEL HEISER

"Unless the LORD builds the house, those who build it labor in vain."

PSALM 127:1

Introduction

My dad designed and built his house in 1980 in the outskirts of Kenova, West Virginia. He still lives there with my stepmother. Since I live in an urban setting in Cincinnati, taking my wife and kids back to the rural house I grew up in brings back a lot of memories. My dad loves keeping a neatly trimmed lawn, and probably

---

1. Michael S. Heiser, *The Unseen Realm: Recovering the Supernatural Worldview of the Bible*, First Edition (Bellingham, WA: Lexham Press, 2015), 68.

loves having the right tools for the job even more. When my kids were little, he would load them all up in a cart behind his John Deere tractor and take them on a tractor ride. It was always the highlight of our visits. The older ones would sit on his lap, and he'd let them steer, while discretely keeping his hand on the underside of the wheel just in case.

Dad was an electrician by trade before he retired, but he also has a lot of carpentry and design skills. He's thorough and attentive to details, like he was taught in the Navy. He's the kind of man that had a pegboard in the garage with outlines drawn in for every wrench, hammer, and screwdriver. Everything in its proper place. When I was little, I remember marveling at the blueprint he'd drawn up for his house. So much precision and forethought in every detail. Although he would not consider himself an artistic man, his creativity shines through in the little things he and my stepmother have continued to do with the house through the years.

The kids call them "Mimi and Grandpa." Their house is a special place for all of us. But it's not just the house, it's the *household*. The household is a package deal. It's the people, the experiences, the memories, and the routines. It's the way they greet us when we arrive. It's the micro-traditions that everyone looks forward to, such as "Mimi's pancakes." There's nothing special about the pancakes themselves. She just mixes them up from a box. But somehow, for my children, Mimi's pancakes have become iconic. Going to visit Mimi and Grandpa is much more than driving to a particular address and staying a couple of days. It's a bundle of experiences and emotions that bring joy and love into all of our lives.

My kids have said that they like being at Mimi and Grandpa's house better than their own house! My wife and I don't take offense to that at all. In fact, we wouldn't want it any other way. These joyful times are formative for our children, like a catechism of the soul. It trains them to delight in God, who gives us these good gifts. I'll admit that I'm nostalgic for things like this. I've already begun to imagine how my wife and I might create these kinds of experiences for our future grandchildren or great-grandchildren. I want to recapture the beauty of these times and bring them forward into the next generation like a family liturgy that resonates on an eternal frequency.

The Importance of the Household

I grew up hearing statements like, "the family is the building block of society." Even though that statement is correct, it's not as correct as it could be. The reason is that the word "family" as it is commonly used today is too small. In the modern world, we think of a family as dad, mom, the kids, and a minivan. If we were to expand our definition of family to include the extended family, we'd be getting closer. Extended families include more family members and a larger web of relationships that bind people together, but we're still missing something. The foundational building block of society is, in fact, the household. Sexuality cannot be properly understood apart from a proper understanding of the household, because the one-flesh union between man and woman is the fountainhead of the household.

The word "household" has fallen into relative obscurity, mostly appearing on legal documents and tax forms. The IRS uses it to refer to how many people live under the same roof as dependents. But the biblical meaning of household is much broader than that. The word "household" (or simply "house") is more precise. There is a lot of overlap between "family" and "household," but our modern usage of the word family is so plastic that it obscures the richness of the biblical meaning. "Family" has become a somewhat hallow concept, as the term can be used now to describe almost any group of people that have something in common. If you buy a new car, for example, the salesman could say "welcome to the Toyota family" as you drive away, even though he's already forgotten your name by the first stop light.

Household is a much richer concept.[2] As discussed in chapter two, the whole cosmos is like a household ruled by God as the supreme authority over it all. God placed man on the earth and commanded him to establish his own ruling house on the earth with the woman. Adam and Eve were created in God's image, which indicated their divine right as rulers. Adam and Eve were a king and a queen directly authorized by God to rule the earth, and they were given a divine mission to subdue the world by establishing and multiplying their household (Gen 1:26-30). They weren't simply commanded to get married, have a couple of kids, and drive around Eden in their Sienna.

Ancient rulers commonly regarded their households as an extension of a divine household. This was the typical view among the Canaanites, Egyptians, Romans, Greeks, and Chinese, who all understood their households on earth to be extensions of the divine household in the heavens. Of course, these were pagan religions, but they contain a kernel of truth that Scripture affirms. For example, in the book of Zechariah, the Lord told the high priest, "If you will walk in my ways and keep my charge, then *you shall rule my house* and *have charge of my courts*, and I will give you the right of access among those who are standing here" (Zech 3:6-7). God gave authority over his house to a human man. Perhaps the

---

2. C. R. Wiley, *The Household and the War for the Cosmos: Recovering a Christian Vision for the Family* (Moscow, ID: Canon Press, 2019), 54–55. Wiley has greatly influenced my thinking on matters discussed throughout this book, this section in particular.

clearest example is Psalm 2, where God speaks of the Messiah: "You are my Son; today I have begotten you. Ask of me, and I will make the nations your heritage, and the ends of the earth your possession" (vv. 7-8). The earth is God's household. It belongs to the Father who appointed his Son to rule over it.

In Scripture, the kingdom of God refers to God's kingdom ruled by the God-man, Jesus Christ. Even though Jesus was the first to use the phrase "kingdom of God," he wasn't introducing a new teaching. He was giving an old teaching a new coat of paint. Adam was the first king who failed to properly rule God's earthly house. Christ succeeded where Adam failed, thus restoring the kingdom of God, receiving all authority in heaven and on earth (Matt 28:18) and reestablishing his rule with the "sons of God,"[3] his ruling household.

In the ancient world, kingdoms were almost always ruling households. This is implied by the word itself. "Kingdom" is a compound word. The first half, "kin," implies a biological family.[4] The second half, "dom," is short for *domain*, or *dominion*, which is a place of rule. A related word is "domestic," which typically refers to matters of the home.[5] In other words, home is a place of dominion. Home is where you're in charge. Your home is your kingdom.

---

3. "Sons of God" is a technical term that includes both men and women, referring to them all having the status of God's first-born son. See Galatians 3:26, "in Christ Jesus you are all sons of God, through faith."

4. "Kingdom," Etymonline.com, https://www.etymonline.com/word/kingdom (Accessed July 7, 2022). "This is of uncertain origin. It is possibly related to Old English *cynn* 'family, race', making a *king* originally a 'leader of the people.' Or perhaps it is from a related prehistoric Germanic word meaning 'noble birth,' making a king etymologically 'one who descended from noble birth' (or 'the descendant of a divine race'). The sociological and ideological implications render this a topic of much debate. 'The exact notional relation of *king* with *kin* is undetermined, but the etymological relation is hardly to be doubted' [Century Dictionary]."

5. C. R. Wiley, *The Household and the War for the Cosmos: Recovering a Christian Vision for the Family* (Moscow, ID: Canon Press, 2019), 54.

In the biblical sense, a household would include at least four elements. The first element is *kinship*. The members of one's household were primarily members of the same family, often including multiple generations. A household could include grandparents, uncles, aunts, and cousins. They could also include widows, orphans, and sojourners, who were not biologically related, but could add value to the household as productive members. The second element is *authority*. God is the ultimate authority, the father of the household was under God's authority, and the rest of the house under his authority (1 Cor 11:3). The father and mother had authority over the children (Ex 20:12). Household servants were under authority as directed by the father (Eph 6:5). The third element is *work*. In the ancient world, most work was done by and for the household. People did not "go to work" at a job somewhere else, but they worked to provide for their own needs directly within their households (2 Thess 3:10). The needs *of* the household were mostly provided *by* the household. This included food, education, protection from threats, and medical care. The fourth element is *legacy*. A household could include dead relatives of prominence stretching back to past generations, as well as the benefits that would be passed on to future generations (Gen 30:30; 1 Tim 5:8).

So, biblically speaking, what is a household? A household can be defined as multiple generations of relatives who lived together, plus the servants who lived and worked with them, plus the work they did together, plus the possessions they owned, including their livestock and other tools of production, plus their status and honor in the broader community. In the ancient world, there were no police departments, fire departments, hospitals, or social services. Most children were educated in the household trade so they could develop skills to be productive within it. Few of them ever learned to read, but there wasn't much need to. They sustained themselves through the cooperative efforts of each member. They educated their own children, protected their own people, cared for their own elderly and infirm, and represented their own interests in the public square. Households were like mini kingdoms: places of kinship, authority, work, and legacy.

A clear example of this in Scripture is Abraham's household. Early in their story, Abraham and his wife, Sarah, did not have any children, yet God promised to establish through them a ruling house that would last forever. It's a stunning promise. Even though Abraham had no children of his own until he was very old, he was nevertheless considered the head of his household already, even commanding a militia of 318 fighting men that were "born in his house" (Gen 14:14). Abraham's "house" included his extended family, his flocks and herds, their various tents and other dwellings, the work they did together to sustain the household, and even their relationship to the surrounding nations.

Since God designed every household to begin with a marriage covenant and one-flesh union, sexuality cannot be properly understood without taking the ancient context of the household into account. God rules the earth through households. The household is at the heart of God's plan for the world. The household is where the mutual benefits of our sexual distinctions are most fully experienced. It is the organizing principle of all society. God created man and woman in his image, joined them together, and gave them a job to do. This fact touches all biblical teaching about sexuality, marriage, children, work, government, and family.

In what follows, I will go through some key Scriptures about the creation of the household, highlight some examples of how the household developed throughout the Old Testament era, and show how the household shapes much of the New Testament's teaching about Christian holiness.

The Household in Scripture

God Rules Through Households

The Scriptures teach that God rules through households. He rules the heavens through his heavenly household, which is comprised of the angelic realm (Ps 82:1). God's heavenly household includes the entire cosmos. Isaiah says, "Heaven is my throne, and the earth is my footstool; what is the house that you would build for me and what is the place of my rest? All these things my hand has made, and so all these things came to be, declares the LORD" (66:1-2).

Similarly, God rules the earth through his earthly household, which is comprised of human beings. Thus, the earthly household is a miniature copy (or micro-cosm) of his heavenly household. God rules both the heavenly realm and the earthly realm through households. Human households are theomorphic, scaled down versions of God's heavenly household. God has also set up his human household with the potential to expand. God's dominion over the earth grows as men and women establish households of their own and children are born into them. In other words, Christian marriage is not merely a sexual partnership, but it is a means of taking dominion for the glory of God. It's how we bring order to chaos. This makes all the difference for how we understand God's good design for human sexuality.

The Creation Mandate

Adam was the first human in God's household. The entire human household descends from Adam, "the son of God" (Luke 3:38). Genesis 1 describes what God did to create his household. Initially, the earth was "formless" and "void" (v. 2). God proceeded to *form it* by separating dark from light, the heavens from the waters, and the seas from dry land. Then, God *filled it* with life—vegetation, plants, trees, aquatic life, birds, land creatures, livestock, creeping animals. Finally, God completed his work by creating two kinds of human beings, a male kind, and a female kind, who would "image" God by raising up a household of their own.

Being created in God's image means more than having human dignity. The image of God implies dominion. Humans were created to rule, and rule is what we must do. When God commanded them to "be fruitful and multiply and fill the earth and subdue it, and have dominion" (v. 28), he was telling them *how* to image him. We rule by expanding God's household together. The man expands it by subduing the wild earth and making it into a suitable place to live. The woman expands it by making that place into a home and filling it with people. The man and woman were created to be creators, like God. Theologians call this command the "Creation Mandate," which is a very important concept for the story of the Bible. The Creation Mandate is the first command God gave to man and woman after He created them, and he created sexuality as the primary means of obeying that command.

Differing Responsibilities

Genesis 2:4 begins another account of creation that zooms in on the particulars. God commanded Adam to *form* the garden by working and keeping it (v. 15), but he could not *fill* it on his own. When God said, "it is not good that the man should be alone," he was not referring to man's loneliness, but to man's inability to reproduce by himself (v. 18). God solved this problem by creating Eve. When God created Adam, he formed him outside the garden (before it was planted), in the wild, away from the sanctuary of the garden (vv. 7-8). When God created Eve, he built her in the domesticated environment of the garden. It was a home.

Different Hebrew words are used to describe the creation of Adam and Eve. Adam was "formed" (Hebrew: *yatzar*) from the dust (Gen 2:7). Eve was "built" (Hebrew: *banah*) from Adam's rib (v. 22). Man was designed *from* the ground and *for* the ground. Woman was designed *from* the man and *for* the man. This teaching is echoed in 1 Corinthains 11:11-12, which says, "in the Lord woman is not independent of man nor man of woman; for as woman was made from man, so man is now born of woman. And all things are from God." God created Eve as Adam's equal partner (Gen 2:23), his delight, his commitment (v. 24), and his glory (1 Cor 11:7). He needed her just as she needed him, albeit in different ways. In one sense, she was a "weaker vessel" who needed his provision and protection. In another sense, she gave him a strength he lacked, the strength to create life. He owed her honor and understanding as a co-heir with him to the grace of life (1 Pet 3:7). She, in turn, owed him her loyalty and submission as his covenant partner in the Creation Mandate.

The Role of Helper

Before we move on, let's look at the word "helper" in biblical context. What does it mean that the woman is a "helper?" In modern usage, that might sound like an insult, but it isn't. God himself is described as a "helper" using the same Hebrew word *ezer* in many Old Testament passages. For example, in Psalm 20:2, David prays, "May he send you help [*ezer*] from the sanctuary and give you support from Zion." In Psalm 33:20, God is described as "our help [*ezer*] and our shield." God helps his people because they are weak and need his strength. Similarly, in the New Testament, Jesus describes the Holy Spirit as a helper (John 14:16-17). Describing someone as a helper doesn't relegate them to lesser status but highlights the need of the one being helped. The one helping brings fulfillment and completion to the one being helped. Therefore, the designation of "helper" is an affirmation of the woman's strength and value. It is not demeaning.

A feminist objection to this reasoning is that "helper" does not mean the woman is under her husband's authority, since God is also a helper and God is the authority over the man. This argument is unconvincing, because the woman's help is different from God's help. The help God provides is voluntary. He is not under a moral obligation to provide it, but does so mercifully as an act of divine grace. The woman is morally obligated to help her husband, since this is part of her created design. Zachary Garris writes, "*Woman's very being is wrapped up in her role as a helper.* This is never said of man, though a man obviously helps his wife in other ways. And though God is a 'helper' to His people, He is not a being created to help man."[6]

The first and most obvious way wives help their husbands is by managing their households. Women are more adept at the connecting and relational skills that are naturally within the domain of the household. Like a snowball growing larger as it rolls downhill, households can grow and expand over time. They are elastic. As children grow older, they take on more responsibilities and work alongside their parents and siblings to assist the household. A great biblical example of this is Proverbs 31. The matriarch of that household is incredibly productive, presiding over her domain

---

6. Garris, *Masculine Christianity*, 131.

with a thriving husband and children. But it doesn't stop there. Her influence extends well beyond the household as she engages in business while her husband takes on a leadership role at the gate of the city. She is not merely a mother to her own children, but she plays the role of mother within her community.

Division of Labor

Returning to the garden, we see Adam and Eve had work to do in this newly established household. They didn't go out to find jobs somewhere but they created their own work, which arose out of their need to provide for themselves. God gave the Creation Mandate to the man and woman together (Gen 1:26-28), and he equipped them with different bodies that would correspond to their respective tasks in fulfilling the mandate. God began the work and called humans to continue the work. The Creation Mandate's focus on establishing a new household implies a natural division of labor. Adam's vocation tended towards the "forming" tasks of the Creation Mandate: taking responsibility, leading, providing, and protecting. His body is optimized for initiative and dominance, which corresponds to the work he would do to subdue the earth. His sex organ testifies that God made him for initiative.

Eve's vocation would tend towards the "filling" tasks of the Creation Mandate: child-bearing, helping, beautifying, glorifying, nurturing, and establishing their home. God gave her a body and disposition for that kind of work. Her body, being smaller and weaker than the man's, testifies that God designed her to be gentler, more nurturing, more agreeable, and under his protection. She is optimized for response, reproduction, and cooperation. Her sex organs testify that God designed her for response, receptivity, multiplication, and sustenance. These features correspond to the work she would do to fill the earth.

Their vocations were not mutually exclusive, however. Adam was not excluded from nurturing children, just as Eve was not excluded from working the field. They did not work separate careers and then come home to eat dinner and watch TV. Rather, they worked together at a common task with a shared goal, specializing as needed. Eve's body told her what her specialty was. It was obvious. She alone could bear children, which is a defining feature of femininity. Adam's specialty, however, was not obvious. He would have to discover it as he ventured beyond the borders of Eden and encountered different challenges. Their respective specialties were cursed when they fell into sin. God later cursed her work as a helper and mother (Gen 3:16) and his work as provider (v. 17).

A few observations can be made at this point. The Creation Mandate established Adam as father and Eve as mother to the world. He gave them a mission that was bigger than themselves—a grand purpose that required their sexual distinctiveness to accomplish. The "one flesh" union does not merely refer to sexual pleasure, but it encompasses the comprehensive joining together of two lives, in mutual benefit, for a divine purpose. Adam's calling was more outwardly oriented, towards the earth, to subdue it. Eve's calling was more inwardly oriented, towards the home, where she expanded and filled the world with Adam's seed, nurturing and caring for them. As the man subdued the earth, the woman domesticated it, creating a place of refuge, community, love, and hospitality.

Thus, sexuality was created for the grand and glorious purpose of ruling the world by establishing a growing household. The division of labor evident in their own bodies teaches us something important. God did not make them merely different *from* each other but different *for* each other. They were created to be inter-dependent; called to love, serve, rely upon, and benefit from one another. Their sexual differences, chiefly expressed in the household, were made to reverberate outward from the household into their local communities and society at large. The household was the engine of the Creation Mandate.

Even though they fell into sin, God's plan of ruling the earth through multiplying households did not change. The Creation Mandate remained in effect. The image of God is directly linked to the Creation Mandate because establishing households is how people image God. The fall did not alter this. God's command for humans to continue forming and filling the earth by establishing legacies of faithful, multiplying households remained in effect after the fall. This meant having children, spreading out across the globe, diversifying tasks, learning specialties, and developing government as society grew.

Other Old Testament Households

After the human household fell into greater levels of sin and chaos in Genesis 1–11, God's plan to ultimately redeem humanity began with Abraham, where God made a covenant to give him a great household (Gen 15). This is one of the most important concepts in Scripture, and it drives the plotline of the Bible all the way to the end. God kept his promise and gave Abraham a son of his own, continuing Abraham's household legacy. Through successive generations, God kept his promise. Abraham fathered Isaac, who fathered Jacob, who fathered twelve sons. God was often identified to his people in the Old Testament as "the God of Abraham, Isaac, and Jacob." These are the patriarchs of God's ruling house. Jacob's twelve sons grew to become twelve tribes, which were twelve ruling households, or simply "houses" (Ex 2:1, Num 17:8, Josh 17:17, 2 Sam 2:4, 1 Kings 15:27, Ps 135:19, 2 Sam 3:6, Jer 2:4, Ob 18).

Many years later, after God's people moved into the land of Canaan, God established David as king and his house as the ruling dynasty over the nation. With David firmly established as king over Israel, he decided to build a "house" for God. What he had in mind was to build a temple for God in Jerusalem. But God doesn't dwell in houses made by men (1 Kings 8:27; Acts 7:48). Instead, God turned the tables and made a promise to build a house for David instead. The "house" God had in mind was not a physical house, but a household, an eternal, ruling dynasty (2 Sam 7:11-16).

The covenant with Abraham, and the household it established, was ultimately fulfilled in Christ. Matthew opens his Gospel with the genealogy of Jesus in order to establish that Jesus fit the Messianic pedigree as a descendant of David's ruling dynasty: "The book of the genealogy of Jesus Christ, the son of David, the son of Abraham" (Matt 1:1). Luke has a similar genealogy but works backwards, from end to the beginning, tracing the household of Jesus all the way back to "Adam, the son of God" (Luke 3:38).

The Creation Mandate and the Great Commission

After his resurrection, Jesus famously gave his disciples what is known as the Great Commission, where he sent them into the world to preach the gospel. He said, "All authority in heaven and on earth has been given to me. Go therefore and make disciples of all nations, baptizing them in the name of the Father and of the Son and of the Holy Spirit, teaching them to observe all that I have commanded you. And behold, I am with you always, to the end of the age" (Matt 28:18-20). Jesus begins with his claim to supreme authority. By his victory over death, he is now the ruling king over David's household. As the newly coronated king, his first command is strikingly similar to God's first command to Adam and Eve. That's because they both express the same desire. The Great Commission is none other than a redemptive republication of the Creation Mandate.

When Jesus spoke the words of the Great Commission, he was not announcing something new, but he was reinstituting something very, very old. God had not given up on his original plan. The Great Commission does not replace the Creation Mandate but renews and expands it in light of the finished work of Christ. They both have the same aim: God dwelling eternally on the earth with his human family. Two observations are in order here. First, the Creation Mandate remains in effect even now. It's a design feature; the trajectory built in from the beginning. Forming and filling the earth is as basic to the created order as water flowing down a mountain. God rules the world through households. He still calls his people to get married, have children, steward the earth's resources for good, and establish households for his glory. Second, the Great Commission answers how the Creation Mandate can be pursued in a fallen world. Every household must disciple their own children in the faith (Duet 6:4-8; Eph 6:1-4). If they do not, they become a divided household. Jesus said, "Every kingdom divided against itself is laid waste, and a divided household falls" (Luke 11:17). The seed of the gospel grows more easily in the fertile soil of a child's heart.

When Christ returns, he will usher in the eternal state, a "new heaven and a new earth," which includes the "holy city, new Jerusalem, coming down out of heaven from God, prepared as a bride adorned for her husband" (Rev 21:1-2). Then God's voice will boom forth, saying, "Behold, the dwelling place of God is with man. He will dwell with them, and they will be his people, and God himself will be with them as their God" (v. 3). This is what it will be like when the original vision of the Creation Mandate is accomplished. God ruling with his people over a renewed cosmos. In the heavens, God will eternally rule over his household on the earth. The seed of this vision was planted in Eden and will come into full bloom at the return of Christ.

From now until he returns, God's future rule is represented in Christian households: husbands and wives, fathers and mothers, parents and children, and brothers and sisters. The household codes of the NT tell us what that should look like in practice. By God's grace and in his strength, obedient Christian households embody the future reign of Christ.

Household Codes in the New Testament

Given the fact that God rules through households, it is not surprising that the NT nests its teaching about gendered relationships within the structure of the household. After all, the household was the primary context where sexual distinctions were expressed. Household codes are important because they show that redemption in Christ moves with the grain of how God created the world.

The central relationship of the household is the marriage. The husband is the head, and his wife submits to him (Eph 5:22-24; Col 3:18-19; 1 Pet 3:1-7). An authority structure also exists between parents and children, and between employers and employees (Eph 5:22-6:9; Col 3:18-4:1). In each of these relationships, Christian love is the governing principle.

It should be noted that marriage is only one among many ways that men and women can relate to each other in a household. In other words, marriage is not the paradigm for every male-female relationship. Marriage does not define how a son relates to his mother, for example. A son does not have authority over his mother, but she has authority over him, at least while he's young. Suppose a wife hires a contractor to do repairs in the home. She is the employer, which means she has the authority to hire whom she chooses and make sure the job is done the way she wants it done. Marital commands have nothing to do with that relationship. In other words, the Bible does not command *every woman* to submit to *every man*. That command applies to wives and husbands because they are in a covenant relationship.

In the modern world, we need Spirit-led wisdom to practically work out the principles we see in Scripture. This is because the Scriptures were written to ancient households that can be quite different from modern families. This wisdom can be gained by keeping the context of the ancient household in mind when applying the Scriptures.

The Problem with Gender Roles

Practically speaking, Scripture provides the blueprint for sexuality, yet many Christians sharply disagree about what that means. Contemporary debates about manhood and womanhood often focus too much on gender roles, particularly the roles of women in the home and the church. This has limited value because God's design for masculinity and femininity is not reducible to roles and rules. Masculinity and femininity aren't performative. There isn't an exact script to follow. Nor are they restricted to what each is allowed to do or not do. Rather, they represent two corresponding ways of being in the world where the strengths of each complement the other. The problem with how this debate usually plays out is that the marriage relationship gets most of the attention, because that's the way modern families are structured. This is where an understanding of the ancient household is helpful. In a household, men and women donate their respective strengths for the building up of the entire household, similar to how Scripture teaches the church to relate to one another as one body with many parts (1 Cor 12:12-26).

The structural flaw in the gender roles debate is an overemphasis on the modern nuclear family as the paradigmatic mode of relating between the sexes. In other words, there is a widespread tendency to define manhood and womanhood by means of the marriage relationship alone. Even though manhood and womanhood were created for the purpose of marriage, marriage cannot exhaustively account for all the wonder and complexity of various male-female relationships. Rather, Scripture defines manhood and womanhood in the context of the household, which includes the marriage relationship as well as a wide array of other ways men and women are bound together and relate to one other.

In modern families, it is easy for Christian husbands to use "headship and submission" verses to justify mistreating and controlling their wives, treating them like domestic servants. This is a caricature of God's good design. A godly husband who is wisely fulfilling his duties of headship will seek to increase his wife's productivity in ways that correspond to her gifts. After all, they were created to exercise dominion together. God gave woman to the man to rule *with him*. Simply put, the "headship and submission" texts should not turn husbands into tyrants and wives into domestic doormats. Homes should not become rigid, suffocating environments where the wife labors alone with her children, day after day, with little support or interaction with other grown-ups. This sort of environment would have been very rare in the ancient world. Ancient wives were connected to a household, which would have included brothers, sisters, grandparents, uncles, aunts, and cousins, living close together and working alongside one another. She would not have been alienated from other household members the way modern wives and mothers are.

The "headship and submission" verses in the Bible were written to households that included more male-female relationships than just the marriage. Take the household codes in the book of Ephesians, for example. Paul begins with instructions for marriage in 5:22-33, then moves to instructions for parents and children in 6:1-4, and concludes with instructions for household servants in 6:5-9. The instructions apply to all the various male-female relationships within the entire household. Therefore, when Paul says, "wives, submit to your own husbands, as to the Lord" (Eph 5:22) and "wives should submit in everything to their husbands" (Eph 5:24), that instruction was nested within a household context that could have included multiple generations, several marriages, many children, and other relatives.

The multigenerational aspect of household life can also be observed in 1 Timothy 5, where Paul instructs Christian households to take care of their widows and ensure they are meaningful participants in household life: "if a widow has children or grandchildren, let them first learn to show godliness to their own household and to make some return to their parents, for this is pleasing in the sight of God" (1 Tim 5:4). Paul goes on to say, "if anyone does not provide for his relatives, and especially for members of his household, he has denied the faith and is worse than an unbeliever" (v. 8). The household structure provided checks and balances that are often lacking in the modern family.

The wife's submission to her husband was part of a larger "household code," where both exercise dominion as king and queen together. God created them to be interdependent. Both need each another, serve each other, and benefit from each other's work. The interdependent relational context of the household is necessary to get beyond the rigidity of the "headship and submission" debate, because more factors are at play than simply "who's in charge." In other words, headship and submission become much more meaningful and helpful categories once we consider the productivity that was necessary for ancient households to survive (which will be developed further in chapter 6). When manhood and womanhood are defined according to the broader household, with all various relationships contained within, and not narrowly by the marriage in isolation, the authority structure of the marriage can be maintained without an absolutizing rigidity. Even though the modern household looks different from the ancient household, recognizing the structure of the household does account for greater complexity in how men and women relate to each other, without dismissing the authority structures taught in Scripture.

Understanding Christian Relationships as a Household

Scripture teaches in several places that the church is the bride of Christ, and marriage is a human picture of this reality. Yet when it comes to learning patterns of how men and women relate to one another in the church, marriage is an insufficient paradigm.[7] Men

---

7. Scott Swain, "More Thoughts on Theological Anthropology: Man as Male and Female," https://www.scottrswain.com/2020/05/14/more-thoughts-on-theological-anthropology-man-as-male-and-female/ (Accessed May 14, 2020).

and women are not called to relate to one another as husbands and wives, but as brothers and sisters. And yet, that is insufficient, because there are different lines of formal and informal authority that operate within a church. Since the church is itself the household of God, the natural household is the proper paradigm for understanding how men and women relate to one another in the church.

There are four potential household roles that men and woman can play in relation to one another. Men can be fathers, husbands, sons, and brothers. Similarly, women can be mothers, wives, daughters, and sisters. Some roles have a measure of formal or informal authority. The husband has formal authority in relationship to his wife, but not to all women in general. The father and mother have formal authority over their children, granted by God in the 5th Commandment (Ex 20:12). As children grow older, however, they become more independent and parental authority takes a different shape. When a young man gets married, for example, he must still honor his own mother, but not the same as when he was a child.

When Paul instructs Timothy about how to relate as a young pastor to the older saints in his church, he uses household language to make his point. First Timothy 5:1-2 says, "Do not rebuke an older man but encourage him as you would a father, younger men as brothers, older women as mothers, younger women as sisters, in all purity" (1 Tim 5:1-2). In other words, Timothy has formal authority as an elder in the church, but he needs to also recognize the honor due to the older men in the church. They have no direct authority over Timothy, but there is an informal, indirect authority they possess as older men who should be honored as such.

I've experienced this personally as a young pastor who planted my church when I was 33 years old. As is common in church plants, most of my church members were younger than me. Most of them saw me as a kind of big brother. A few of them even regarded me as a father figure. But there were some members who were much older than me, nearly twice my age, and I was responsible for shepherding their souls as well. One older woman came to me for counsel because she was going through a divorce after her husband had committed adultery multiple times over many years. She had sons of her own that were close to my age, and yet I had authority in her life as her pastor. How does a young pastor relate to an older woman he oversees? According to Paul, he treats her as a mother. He has authority over her as an elder in the church, but he exercises his oversight with the tenderness and care of a son with his mother. Even if he needs to correct her, he will do so with a degree of caution and deference that he may not show to someone younger.

Here's another example. I know a mature, young woman who was raised in the Christian faith from her childhood. She befriended a young man and ended up leading him to faith in Christ. She began relating to him initially as a mother in the faith. Even though they were of similar age, she nurtured his young faith and helped him grow. As he matured in his faith, they naturally related to one another as a brother and sister in Christ. Over time, as their friendship grew, they fell in love and got married. She who was once a mother and sister to him in the Lord became his wife. As a Christian husband, he needed to learn how to lead the woman who once led him to Christ in the first place. Even though her biblical knowledge and Christian maturity exceeded his, his duty was to lead her, and her duty to was follow his lead.

Dr. Scott Swain makes this observation: "There seems to be a built-in teleology to our sex identity. Husbands and wives become fathers and mothers. Fathers and mothers bear sons and daughters. Sons and daughters become brothers and sisters. Men and women are born. Men and women die. But this cycle is not circular. It is teleological. One day, they will no longer marry or be given in marriage (Matt 22:30). In that day, there will be no more husbands and wives and therefore there will be no more fathering and no more mothering. In that day, all will be sons of God (Rev 21:7) and all will be brothers and sisters of the one appointed to be the firstborn among many brothers and sisters (Rom 8:29). Learning to walk together as men and women therefore not only involves learning who God made us to be and living in accord with God's good design. Learning to walk together as men and women also involves learning who God has redeemed us to become and, in a manner appropriate to the overlap of the ages in which we live, learning what it means for all of us to be sons and daughters of the living God and brothers and sisters in Jesus Christ. The better we learn this lesson, the more beautifully we will grow into our social identity as the bride of Christ, which is the ultimate end of our life together."[8]

---

8. Scott Swain, "More Thoughts on Theological Anthropology: Man as Male and Female," https://www.scottrswain.com/2020/05/14/more-thoughts-on-theological-anthropology-man-as-male-and-female/ (Accessed May 14, 2020).

CHAPTER 5

Gendered Virtue

"The tyrant is the least free man, because he is slave to his desires."[1]

SOCRATES

"For this very reason, make every effort to supplement your faith with virtue, and virtue with knowledge, and knowledge with self-control, and self-control with steadfastness, and steadfastness with godliness, and godliness with brotherly affection, and brotherly affection with love."

2 PETER 1:5-7

Introduction

In the ancient world, virtue was a hot topic. What makes someone virtuous? Ancient Greeks believed that virtue was bound up with freedom, because freedom should always be directed towards the pursuit of virtue. Virtue was *teleological*, something beyond you that

---

1. Plato, *The Republic*, trans. H. D. P. Lee (Harlow, England: Penguin Books, 2003), Book IX. This is a popularized paraphrase of the original quote.

you were meant to pursue. People become virtuous by freely pursuing higher and more noble ideals for themselves and for society.

Although I could speak in terms of gendered "holiness," or gendered "piety," I prefer the word "virtue" because it evokes a sense of duty and the pursuit of excellence. Virtue is not so much about avoiding particular sins, although that's part of it. Since virtue is something freely expressed, the greater part of virtue is imaginative. It's a matter of prayerfully considering, "what kind of person does God want me to be?" Or more specifically, "what kind of man or woman am I becoming?" Or, "of all the possibilities that lie before me, what's the best version of myself?" In this chapter, I will make the case that the pursuit of virtue will be different for men and for women. Not in every way, but in many, important ways, because God designed our sexual differences to serve distinct purposes, and virtue corresponds to that created purpose. It is plain from Scripture that men and women obey God in different ways and sin in different ways. But there is more. The most virtuous version of ourselves will reflect the uniqueness of our sexual design.

This has become a controversial belief in recent years, due to our culture's constant messaging that men and women are mostly interchangeable. Unfortunately, the confusion of our culture has infiltrated the church. I have heard Christians say things like, "the fruit of the Spirit is the same for men and women." I agree; yes and amen. There is not one list for men and a different list for women. However, the individual fruits of the Spirit will find different expressions in men and women. Take love, for example, which heads the list of the fruit of the Spirit. A man's love is different than a woman's love. Both men and women express love, but their love will lead them to take different actions. This is a good thing, because the body of Christ benefits from both masculine and feminine love.

I once had a conversation with a church member who was the father of three girls and a son. Prompted by a recent news story, we were discussing the potential that girls might be required to register for the military draft to serve in active combat roles. This man told me that it would make no difference to him if his son or his daughters were drafted for active combat duty. In his mind, what's the difference? Boys and girls are basically the same, and both are equally suitable candidates for military combat. His opinion is common. After all, for decades movies and TV shows have depicted petite, warrior-like women fiercely defeating men in battle as though this were common. We've seen it so many times it's easy to forget how unrealistic this is. If "life imitates art," as it has been said, small wonder that women are now expected to be society's warriors and protectors in the same way as men. Personally, I have one daughter and three sons. In my view, it would be honorable for my sons to serve in active combat duty if called upon, but not my daughter. Why? Because my sons are designed for it, but not my daughter.

Men and women are different, and failure to recognize this basic fact causes real harm. We must live in the world as it truly is, not fantasy land. Of course, some girls are "tomboys" who like sports more than dolls. There is nothing wrong with that. Some boys are sensitive and bookish, that's fine too. In God's endless creativity, we have a vast range of ways we can express our humanity as men and women. Some women have a lot of stereotypical masculine traits, such as assertiveness or directness, and some men have a lot of stereotypical feminine traits, such as sensitivity or nurturing. That's fine, as far as it goes. God made us all unique. The question of virtue is what do we do with the unique personality God gave us? I am not saying that Christian virtue is different for men and women in every possible way, but our differences do matter. A gender-neutral vision for humanity is gnostic, not Christian.

Once we accept the premise that men and women were made differently, and for distinct purposes, a whole forest of implications arise. As William and Barbara Mouser once wrote, "Maleness and femaleness are written in our bodies, and masculinity and femininity are written in our souls. To be simply a 'good person' or a 'bad person' is not an option. If we are male, we must inevitably choose to be a good son, brother, man, husband, or father. If we are female, we must inevitably choose to be a good daughter, sister, woman, wife, or mother."[2] In other words, the creation order is renewed and redeemed in the Christian household, where grace restores and reorders what was corrupted by sin.

Androgyny Is Not Virtuous

Men and women have a basic nature, and we are designed to move with the grain of that nature, not against it. Yet the world is aggressively pushing us in the opposite direction. The lines between the sexes are being blurred or even eliminated altogether. We are told to reject the "gender binary" and embrace an ever-growing continuum of genders. Further, men and women are being encouraged to adopt patterns of behavior that more characterize the *opposite* sex. Men are encouraged to adopt more feminine patterns of behavior, while women are encouraged to adopt more masculine patterns of behavior. This creates a confusing cultural chaos as men and women increasingly deny their basic natures. We cannot pursue virtue if we deny our distinctions.

---

2. Mouser and Mouser, *The Story of Sex*, 113.

In the church, feminine character traits are often associated with virtue, while masculine traits are associated with vice. For example, strong-willed, independent, truth-oriented, and direct-speaking men are often considered arrogant, whereas passive, compliant, and egalitarian men are considered more Christlike.[3] This is evident in modern worship music, where churches sing romanticized love songs to Jesus. These songs express feminine sensibilities as the embodiment of true Christianity. Small wonder many men don't want to participate. Men don't like to sing love songs to other men. So they stand there, expressionless, arms crossed, with a thousand-yard stare.

Comparatively, the Psalms do not alienate men like modern worship songs can. The Psalms express the full range of human emotion, including exuberance, anger, sadness, anticipation, fear, dread, and sorrow. The "imprecatory Psalms" are famous because they express moral outrage against the evils and injustice of the world. Men can relate to these sorts of themes more easily than modern worship songs. Perhaps this is because God created men to be protectors of society. The Psalms give men language to express healthy outrage at evil while calling them to hope in God for justice.

David, who wrote most of the Psalms, was also Israel's greatest king. Even though he was called a man after God's own heart (1 Sam 13:14), the Psalms do not sound like love poems written by a heartsick emo band. He is known for his leadership, courage, and zeal for the Lord as much as he is for his music. In his zeal for God, David faced Goliath, the Philistine giant who defied the Lord's armies. David mustered his courage, confronted him, knocked him out with a shot from his sling, and victoriously decapitated him.

---

3. Leon J. Podles, *The Church Impotent: The Feminization of Christianity* (Spence Publishing Company, 2005). In his book, Podles demonstrates and documents this trend, going back centuries.

In the Old Testament at least, godly men demonstrated zeal for the Lord with courage in battle. The point here is not violence. Violence itself is not virtuous (1 Chron 28:3; Matt 26:52; 1 Tim 3:3). But masculine virtue is courageous and zealous for God. Virtuous men make hard decisions. Virtuous men stand for biblical truth no matter how unpopular. Virtuous men know how and when to fight. Virtuous men use their masculine strength to serve God and protect those who are vulnerable. Of course, the call for men to be strong does not imply a call for women to be weak. Virtuous women may also be strong, but their strength will be expressed differently.

In C. S. Lewis' classic children's book, *The Lion, the Witch, and the Wardrobe*, each of the Pevensie children receive gifts from Father Christmas that they will need in times of distress. Peter receives a sword and shield that he will later need for battle. Susan receives a bow and arrow and a magical horn that she will use to summon for help. But Lucy only receives a vial containing a magic healing potion and a small dagger. She feels slightly insulted. She questions why she isn't given a more glamorous gift like Peter's sword and shield. Father Christmas tells her that she will not be sent into battle. She was given a weapon only for self-defense. When the battle comes, she will be a healer. She will not be required to take another life in battle, she will be a *life-giver*. Feeling somewhat offended, she presses the matter further. But Father Christmas simply responds, "battles are ugly when women fight."[4] Father Christmas was not insulting her, he was honoring her by respecting her feminine nature.

A woman's zeal for the Lord is not demonstrated by courageous feats on the battlefield, but by her uniquely feminine ability to give

---

4. C. S. Lewis, *The Chronicles of Narnia* (New York: Harpertrophy, 2002), 119.

life. When Pharaoh wanted to murder the Hebrew boys in Exodus 1, the Hebrew midwives "feared God and did not do as the king of Egypt commanded them, but let the male children live" (Ex 1:17). They put their own lives on the line as mothers, protecting these young children. As a result, God blessed them and multiplied them even more (Ex 1:20). Deborah's virtue is described in feminine terms, because she "arose as a mother in Israel" (Judg 5:7). Ruth is heroic because she forsook her desire for marriage and motherhood to take care of her mother-in-law. Yet God blessed her with marriage and motherhood anyway, becoming an ancestress to Christ. Hannah was greatly distressed by her inability to conceive a child, and the Lord honored her perseverance by opening her womb. This should not be regarded as merely the story of a barren woman getting pregnant, but a faithful woman's zealous pursuit of her calling to motherhood (1 Sam 1:19).

Similarly, Mary was given the greatest honor a woman could receive when she became the mother of the Lord Jesus. Mary's motherhood came to her in the form of a trial, because she would have faced the shame of being an unwed mother with an unexpected pregnancy. Yet she showed courage by submitting to the Lord's will when she said, "Behold, I am the servant of the Lord; let it be to me according to your word" (Luke 1:38). Mary's feminine virtue was demonstrated in humility when her life was upended by unforeseen motherhood. Feminine virtues are particularly necessary for the building up of a godly household, and members of her household are the main beneficiaries of her service.

In the book of Romans, Paul's concluding greetings include this honorable mention: "Greet Rufus, chosen in the Lord; also his mother, who has been a mother to me as well" (Rom 16:13). This greeting stands out because Rufus' mother had become like a mother to Paul. We know nothing else about her. Paul also greeted other women in Romans 16, but only this woman is singled out for her motherly care for Paul. This is speculative, I will admit, but I can imagine this woman encouraging Paul with kind words, bold faith, prayers, Scripture, and perhaps some home-cooked meals.

Stories Are Archetypes of Virtue

Every culture promotes its values and ideals through stories. Enduring stories are built around familiar character archetypes that reflect universal experiences everyone can relate to. These archetypes are derived from observing human nature, abstracting the most common and powerful elements, refining them into familiar patterns, and repeating them to reinforce or challenge cultural norms. Take, for example, the classic archetype of a daring knight who rescues a woman imprisoned by a dragon. He slays the dragon, rescues the damsel, and she becomes his wife. This archetype conveys a universally relatable message: a dangerous villain, a heroic man, an epic adventure, and the love of a woman. It works because it corresponds with reality; it resonates with the basic desires of men and women. Stories like this are useful in a culture because they reinforce that culture's values and encourage virtuous behavior from its people. They provide guidance. They present a vision of optimal thought and behavior. Through the power of narrative, they embed a deeper moral code into that society's collective consciousness.

Nowadays, it is commonly assumed that stories like this were crafted by wicked men to reinforce cultural norms that give them power to subjugate women.[5] We are told that these stories do *not*

---

5. Kennaquhair, "The Missing Heroic Feminine," https://kennaquhair.substack. com/p/the-missing-heroic-feminine (Accessed May 25, 2022).

reflect universal truths about men and women. They do *not* correspond with reality. They do *not* reflect the universal, deep longings of the heart. Rather, they are sinister impositions upon a gullible populace that hinders progress. If this is the case, then the old archetypal stories must be discarded and replaced with new ones.

And this is exactly what has happened. You may have noticed a growing trend in popular entertainment to invert the "hero's journey" archetype. In modern stories, when the female character is in danger, the men around her often fail to rescue her. Why? Because she's an independent, liberated woman. She doesn't need a man to slay the dragon and rescue her. She's capable of slaying the dragon herself. And she certainly doesn't want to be any man's wife. Marriage is a different kind of prison with a different kind of dragon. She doesn't want any part of that.

Since these are the culture shaping stories forming our thoughts, attitudes, and behaviors, what sort of society will we become? We become less virtuous. Women abandon the glory of a house filled with children and exchange it for the glory of a cubicle and an apartment filled with cats. Men likewise abandon the glory of laying down their lives to raise up a godly seed and exchange it for the glory of a self-indulgent virtual war on a video game console. We need better stories. Stories that reflect the glory of man and woman as God made us. Stories that celebrate and embody true virtue as it is expressed within the contours of God's design, not against it.

Misunderstanding Deborah

Interestingly, if you were to survey Christian women about who is a biblical role model for them, many of them would say Deborah.

Yet Deborah, often wrongly regarded as an Old Testament warrior princess, is not portrayed in Scripture as any kind of role model. Ironically, the opposite is true. The context indicates that her leadership was a rebuke of Israel's men who were weak, passive, and refused to fulfill their duty to lead. They were not strong and not courageous. Thus, God raised up a woman to lead them, which would have been shameful for them. Deborah is not presented as a role model for women to follow, but a rebuke to Israel's passive men. And she knew it, too. As she agreed to go into battle with the men, she said, "the road on which you are going will not lead to your glory, for the Lord will sell Sisera *into the hand of a woman*" (Judg 4:9).

The fact that Deborah is so often taught to Christian women as a sort of a feminine icon is revealing. Deborah may be popular in women's Bible studies, but women are not instructed to follow her as an example. The Holy Spirit did not tell her story to cultivate a "girls can go to war too!" attitude. She does not appear outside of Judges 4-5. Using Deborah's story as an example to follow misses the biblical point of her story. The theme of Judges is a slow descent into chaos through successive, disobedient generations. Yet some read Deborah's rule over Israel as a good thing and thus conclude that Christian women should aspire to be just like her. But in Judges, as in the rest of Scripture, it is considered shameful when men are ruled by women (Isa 3:12). Israel's sin in those days was a desire to be led like the nations around them (Judg 18:1; 19:1; 21:25; 1 Sam 8:4-9). Christians who see Deborah's leadership over Israel as a model for church leadership are doing the same thing: they want a leadership structure that looks like the world.

Since gendered virtue is increasingly denied in the modern world, my aim in this chapter is to recover the principles of gendered virtue while leaving specific applications to the reader.

Before I proceed, I will offer three qualifications. First, gendered virtue does not encompass the totality of Christian obedience. Not all virtue takes an explicitly masculine or feminine form. The goal of this chapter is to simply establish the general fact of gendered virtue and provide guidance about how to pursue it. Second, the subjective elements of gendered virtue need to be applied individually. Many norms and customs of sexuality are culturally bound, which means there's always a degree of subjectivity in applying them. For example, the Bible forbids men and women from dressing like the opposite sex (Deut 22:5), but we aren't given many specifics. There's no fashion catalogue in the Bible, so it must be applied according to reasonable cultural norms. Men and women of good conscience will know what to do. Third, gendered virtue is more a matter of wisdom than precept. My aim is not to prescribe specific rules and behaviors for men and women to follow. Virtue is freely pursued by grace, not prescribed by law. My aim, rather, is to call men and women to use biblical wisdom and freely pursue virtue in Spirit led Christian love.

A Model for Gendered Virtue

The thesis of this chapter is that gendered, Christian virtue is oriented towards fatherhood and motherhood. Tied with this, fatherhood and motherhood are best understood in terms of a biblical household, not the modern nuclear family. To unpack this thesis, let's begin with love. Love is the highest virtue (1 Cor 13:13). It is the animating principle of all Christian obedience. It is the sum of the law and the greatest commandment (Matt 22:37-39) and the initial fruit of the Spirit (Gal 5:22). Love is the word that describes God's very being (1 John 4:7-8). It goes beyond sentimental well wishing. It's not merely a private feeling, but a public good, given for the benefit of others. Naturally, men and women express and receive love differently. A virtuous man loves like a father, and a virtuous woman loves like a mother.

As important as love is, it is often ill-defined. Defined biblically, *love is the sacrificial commitment to the highest good of another.* Love is centered on God, most of all, then on others (Matt 22:37-40). Therefore, with love as the foundation of all Christian virtue, one should be asking, "*who* is this virtue for?" Applied to the sexes, we should ask, who benefits from a man's strength? Who will receive a woman's generosity? Who is protected by a man's courage? Who benefits from a woman's kindness? Who is helped by a man's mercy? Who is healed by a woman's nurturing care? Christian virtue, shaped by Christian love, is ultimately directed outward, towards those in the one's community. Therefore, men and women are naturally equipped to love others in unique ways, with different strengths and priorities. That's a good thing. God designed it that way. We are not merely different *from* each other but *for* each other. Our differences, animated by Christian love, complement and complete what is lacking in others.

For example, my wife's natural inclination to be compassionate draws a measure of compassion out of me, while also summoning my strength and decisiveness to take action to meet needs I might not otherwise have met on my own. A well-ordered household benefits from this dynamic. Masculine weaknesses are compensated by feminine strengths, and feminine weaknesses are compensated by masculine strengths. Such is God's design. My masculine strength and directness meet certain needs in our household, which in turn frees my wife to use her tenderness, warmth, and nurture to meet different needs of the household. Virtue is shaped by the love and service we render to the people God has bound us to.

Gendered virtue is most glorious when it is expressed for the benefit of others, as God designed it in the garden. Adam's task of subduing the earth required his masculine strength to lead, provide, and protect his wife. Eve's task of helping her husband and filling the earth required her tenderness and nurturing help. God designed them both to give and receive according to their distinct bodies and natures. Men and women are at their best when their respective strengths are valued by one another, and who serve one another in love (Gal 5:13). In the Garden, before Eve was created, the only thing that was *not* good was the lack of a woman's potentiality. Creation was incomplete until it received a woman's strength. If creation simply needed more masculine strength, God could have created another man. But that's not what it needed. It needed another being of the same kind but with different potential. Motherhood is the strength of womanhood. It is the potentiality that most uniquely defines her.

Virtue corresponds to design. As J. Budziszewski put it, "Sanity begins with the fact that men are potentially fathers, and women potentially mothers. This is not just a fact about what kind of thing they might or might not do some day, but about what kind of being they are inwardly aimed at becoming."[6] He's right about that. Nature points to something beyond itself. Sexuality has a goal—a purpose, or a *telos*—which, ultimately, is to reproduce. This is why sexual distinctions are more important than other human distinctions. Sexual distinctions were made to accomplish a goal. God does not assign different vocations to tall people or short people, or to people with blue eyes or brown eyes. Those are merely manifestations of God's creativity. But God does assign vocations according to our sex. Masculinity was created for fatherhood, and

---

6. Budziszewski, *On the Meaning of Sex*, 135.

femininity was created for motherhood. The vocations of father and mother do not represent the full range of virtue for men and women, but they do supply the basic contours of each, since they represent the telos of sexuality at its fullest expression.

This is not to imply that biological (or adoptive) fatherhood or motherhood is a prerequisite for virtue. As a model for gendered virtue, I am speaking of fatherhood and motherhood as relational paradigms. A virtuous father is the sort of man that takes sacrificial responsibility for others to lead, provide, and protect them. A virtuous mother is the sort of woman that gives life by nurturing, helping, supporting, and influencing others. These are virtuous relational patterns that can be learned and put into practice. J. Budziszewski writes that the "potentiality for motherhood is not about physical possibility but about design, and that motherhood can be not only bodily and directed toward the marital estate, but also spiritual and directed toward another estate."[7]

I will address singleness more fully in a later chapter, but one comment is in order here. Although marriage and children are not guaranteed for every man or woman, single men and women can grow in virtue by preparing for those vocations anyway. No one waits until their wedding day to start thinking about marriage, and no one waits until they have children to start thinking about parenting. Wise young men and women can approach their single life while keeping these vocations always on the horizon and trusting in God's timing and provision. Yet even if, for a variety of legitimate reasons, a Christian man remains single for the rest of his life, the most virtuous version of himself will nonetheless be fatherly. This was the case with the Apostle Paul, who never married and never had children, yet he was himself a spiritual father to many others (1 Cor 4:15).

---

7. Budziszewski, *On the Meaning of Sex*, 97.

Distortions of God's Design

Just as fatherhood and motherhood can serve as helpful models to pursue gendered virtue, androgyny does the opposite. God is not our "Heavenly Parent," but he is our Heavenly *Father*. God has revealed himself in masculine terms. The modern push towards androgyny does not produce virtue, but is a grotesque, pagan distortion of it. Androgyny diminishes the glory of our differences and compresses them into a bland mold of sameness, all in the name of "equality." At the same time, our differences can be harmfully exaggerated in ways that distort God's design. When sexuality is distorted in these ways, we move against the grain of our design and exchange love for power. The result is less complementarity and more competition between the sexes.

Let me illustrate this with an example. Suppose a family has two vehicles, a Ford pickup truck and a BMW sports car. In many respects, they are the same: both have four wheels that will take you where you want to go. They both have doors that open and close, a sound system, air conditioning, and the ability to drive 65 on the highway. Nevertheless, they were designed for different purposes and have the potential to do different things. It's best when each vehicle is used according to its intended design. For example, if you have a load of lumber to bring back from Home Depot, you'll want to drive the truck. If you're going out for a nice evening on the town, you're going to drive the BMW. In a pinch, you could haul some lumber in the BMW, but it wasn't made for that. And you could go out to a formal evening event in your pickup truck, but it wasn't made for that.

Since men are stronger and more aggressive, they tend to express power more directly. This is not to suggest that women don't have power. They do, but it's a different sort of power. Women tend to express power more indirectly. For example, men can sinfully use their strength to dominate and control women, and women can sinfully use their sexual desirability to manipulate and control men. According to Alistair Roberts, "Women's power is a social and associative power, one resulting from the fact that they have closer and more immediate relationships than men—not just with other women, but with men too. This gives them immense social leverage. Women are the glue of a society, the force that binds societies' members together. Men tend to form larger, shallower, weaker, and looser networks, with more agonistic and combative interactions. Women, by contrast, tend to form stronger, more intimate, more emotional, and deeper bonds. Their relational bonds are far more load-bearing than men's."[8]

Although women form stronger bonds, they also have a great deal of competition among them. The competition amongst women is, Roberts continues, "generally indirect and occurs beneath the radar. The combative form of male competition is overt and on the surface: men are rough with each other and engage in forms of ritual combat, often as a form of bonding. Women's competition, by contrast, is largely carried out by such means as pressure to conform under the threat of social ostracization, leveraging male power to their advantage, recruiting males to attack people they dislike or rally to their aid, forming friendships or relationships with people of power or influence, gossip, cattiness, sassiness, sabotaging other people's reputations, veiled antagonisms in friendships, etc. It is so successfully dissembled that remarkably little is said about the fact, for instance, that the majority of—and much of the most damaging—misogynistic abuse is instigated by women, even in cases where

8. Alastair Roberts, "A Crisis of Discourse—Part 2: A Problem of Gender," https://alastairadversaria.com/2016/11/17/a-crisis-of-discourse-part-2-a-problem-of-gender/ (Accessed July 22, 2022).

men are involved. Within a mixed group, men would rarely be able to bully a woman without permission from or the instigation of other women in the group."[9] In other words, relational differences between men and women can descend into coercive power struggles, manipulation, or even abuse. And yet, these same relational differences can be leveraged in Christian love to virtuous ends.

Exaggerated Masculinity

Masculinity is good and was created to be good by a masculine God. For example, man's natural inclinations to be aggressive is a feature, not a flaw, but it must be controlled and directed towards a noble purpose. "Toxic masculinity" is usually masculine energies that are sinfully exaggerated. Here are some biblical examples of masculine energies being sinfully exaggerated and distorted:

- A man's natural inclination towards aggression and dominance can easily become tyrannical and violent, like Cain who murdered his own brother out of envy, because God accepted Abel's gift (Gen 4).
- A man's competitive energy can lead him to lie, cheat, and steal to get ahead, like Laban did to Jacob (Gen 29:25).
- A man's sexual desire can be out of control, leading him to take a woman by force, as Shechem did to Dinah, Jacob's daughter (Gen 34:2).
- A man's desire for justice may cause him to seek it sinfully, as Jacob's sons did when they turned the sign of God's covenant into an instrument of death when they deceived the

---

9. Alastair Roberts, "A Crisis of Discourse—Part 2."

men of Shechem, convincing them to be circumcised, only to slaughter them during their recovery (Gen 34:13ff).

- A man's greed and lust for power can lead him to force women to murder their own children, as Pharaoh did to the Hebrews in Egypt (Ex 1:15-16).
- A man's hubris and foolishness can lead him into danger, like Nabal, whose disrespect for David nearly got his family killed (1 Sam 25).
- A man's pride can also lead him into sexual conquest, as Absalom did, when he slept with his father's concubines on the palace roof, in the sight of all Israel, spoiling David's dynasty with his own seed (2 Sam 16:22).
- A man's love of pleasure can drive him to overindulgence, causing his heart to be seduced and turned to idols, as Solomon did with his many wives and concubines (1 Kings 11:5-6).
- A man's love of money can cause him to exploit others who are weaker, as Rehoboam exploited those in his charge (1 Kings 12:7-11).
- A man's desire to conquer can lead him to prey on the vulnerability of women to lead them astray, as Paul warned would happen (2 Tim 3:6-7).

Diminished Masculinity

A man may also diminish his masculine tendencies, making him more passive, weak, or "soft." Although men like this may appear harmless, this should not be mistaken for virtue. Masculine virtue is not passive, it takes initiative. Passive men are less prepared to take responsibility for others in a fatherly way. Here are some examples of male passivity:

- Some men are passive like Adam, who failed to teach and enforce God's command with Eve, allowing her to be deceived (Gen 3:6).
- Some men are passive like Lot, who allowed his wife and two daughters to be thoroughly corrupted by the world (Gen 19:26-38).
- Some men passively fail to pass on covenant blessings to their children, as Isaac did when he favored Esau over Jacob (Gen 25:28).
- Some men passively avoid conflict and fail to confront problems head-on, as Jacob did when his own daughter was raped by Shechem (Gen 34:5-7).
- Some men passively fail to protect those in their charge, as Barak did when he refused to go into battle unless Deborah accompanied him (Judg 4:9).
- Some men passively fail to rule by allowing themselves to be manipulated by wicked women, as Ahab did when Jezebel incited him to murder Naboth and steal his land (1 Kings 21:1-16).
- Some men passively "play the woman" in sexual intercourse, as was forbidden in God's law (Lev 18:22; Rom 1:26-27).
- Some men passively fail to lead by allowing themselves to be manipulated by women they wish to please, as Herod did when he executed John the Baptist to save face with his guests and please the daughter of Herodias (Matt 14:6).
- Some men passively fail to financially provide for their families, as Paul warned against (1 Tim 5:8).

- Some men passively fail to recognize the challenges of our day and are weakly disengaged, sitting on the sidelines, as Paul warned (1 Cor 16:13). Men like this are often nice guys, divisive men who use "smooth talk and flattery" to "deceive the hearts of the naive" (Rom 16:18).

The Problem of Effeminacy

The word "effeminate" was once a common way of referring to men who were insufficiently masculine, but the word has fallen into obscurity in modern times. This is not because it isn't helpful but because it isn't comfortable. Effeminate is not the same as feminine, however. Femininity is glorious and beautiful in a woman, which is God's design for her. But men were made for a different, masculine purpose. When men suppress their masculinity and openly embrace feminine characteristics, they sin by pursuing the wrong glory.

Effeminate is a biblical word in the KJV, though modern translations no longer use it. A man of effeminate character avoids taking manly responsibility, and consequently lacks moral weight. One writer said, "In the ancient world, effeminacy entailed a moral frailty (acting cowardly or 'womanish' in battle), inordinate love for luxury (rendering men delicate and tender), and the sexual deviancy of acting like a woman in one's demeanor, speech, and gesture. The Bible addresses each, describing men who 'become women' on the battlefield (Jeremiah 50:37; Nahum 3:13), go 'soft' due to luxury (Matthew 11:7–8), and become sexually deviant (1 Corinthians 6:9). The term effeminacy is not an attack on femininity itself — which is a woman's glory — but rather on femininity when attached to a male."[10] An effeminate man has failed to mature into his masculinity. The most extreme expression of effeminacy is when a man "plays the woman" in sexual intercourse with another man, or even by identifying as a transgender woman.

Exaggerated Femininity

Women possess a natural beauty and attractive power that can be distorted a variety of ways. Further, a woman's natural relational gifts can become twisted and manipulative. Here are examples of such exaggerated femininity:

- A woman may become cruel and manipulative to get her way, as Sarai did was when she required Hagar to act as a surrogate mother for her (Gen 16:1-2).
- A woman may envy the families and children of other women, as Rachel did when Leah conceived four sons for Jacob while she had none (Gen 30:1).
- A woman may descend into a bitter rivalry over the attention of a man, as Rachel and Leah did with Jacob (Gen 30:14-16).
- A woman may use her feminine discretion to deceive, as Rachel did by claiming she could not arise before him because she was menstruating when he inquired about the household gods she had stolen (Gen 31:35).
- A woman may use sex to lure men into an unwanted marriage, as Tamar did when she pretended to be a prostitute and had sex with Judah (Gen 38).

---

10. Greg Morse, "Play the Man You Are: Will Effeminacy Keep Anyone from Heaven?" https://www.desiringgod.org/articles/play-the-man-you-are (Accessed July 22, 2022).

- A woman may play the victim to gain the upper hand, as Potiphar's wife did to Joseph (Gen 39:6-18).
- A woman may overtly seduce or tease a man sexually, as Delilah did to Samson (Judg 16:4-6).
- A woman may seduce a man with flattery, smooth words, and overt propositions, as the father warns his son in Proverbs (Prov 7:4-21).
- A woman may use her feminine influence to draw her husband away from the Lord, as Job's wife did when she told him to "curse God and die" (Job 2:9).
- A mother's grief over the loss of her child could lead her into treacherous sins of bitterness, envy, and deception, as the prostitute in Solomon's court did when she tried to steal another woman's child (1 Kings 3:16-28)
- A woman may draw attention to herself through immodest dress and appearance, as Paul warned (1 Tim 2:9).
- A woman may neglect her household and become a lazy busybody, spreading gossip, as Paul warned (1 Tim 5:13).
- A woman may be weak-willed and led astray by various passions, as Paul warned (2 Tim 3:6).

Diminished Femininity

A woman's feminine tendencies can also be diminished. What is often celebrated as empowerment for women usually requires femininity to be distorted and redefined in masculine terms, which is less virtuous. Her femininity is diminished as she embodies more masculine ways of being:

- Some women overtly grab for power, as Miriam did when she and Aaron conspired against Moses (Num 12).
- Some women take up the masculine vocation of civil protectors, donning battle gear and implements of warfare, as forbidden by Moses (Deut 22:5).
- Some women deny their vocation as life-givers and become life-takers, as Jezebel did when she killed the prophets of the Lord (1 Kings 18:13).
- Some women covertly manipulate men in power, as the prostitute did in Solomon's court when her child died and she tried to steal the child of her fellow mother (1 Kings 3:16-28).
- Some women believe career-building is more valuable than home-building and fail to prioritize their families, against the biblical emphasis on homemaking (Prov 31:11, 15, 23, 28; Titus 2:3-5).
- Some women violently conspire with other women to punish their enemies, as Herodias and her daughter did to have John the Baptist beheaded (Matt 14:8).
- Some women are brash and bossy, like Martha was when she complained to Jesus that her sister Mary wasn't helping out (Luke 10:38-42, Prov 7:11).
- Some women seek their own value by exercising authority over men, violating the created order (1 Tim 2:12-14).
- Some women abandon God's design and seek sexual fulfillment with other women, contrary to nature (Rom 1:26-27).

The Problem of Immodesty

Women are the more beautiful sex. This is a source of great power and great temptation. A woman who is very attractive has power because she will be desired by powerful men, who will compete with one another to win her love. Naturally, men are drawn to feminine beauty. They admire it and desire it. This is not sinful in itself but becomes sinful when that desire turns to lust. Men are responsible for their own lust and must take measures to keep their desires under control.

On the other hand, Scripture warns women to not weaponize their beauty to control or manipulate men. Although men are responsible for keeping their sexual desires under control, women have a responsibility here too. A modest woman honors God with her feminine discretion. She abstains from using her physical beauty for ungodly aims. A modest woman wisely knows what to conceal or reveal. Modesty is *more* than clothing, but not *less*. A modest woman knows that true beauty is expressed through godly character and service. Peter calls this sort of beauty "imperishable." Physical beauty diminishes with age, but spiritual beauty can grow eternally. This is the beauty "of a gentle and quiet spirit, which in God's sight is very precious" (1 Pet 3:4). Until recent times, this was considered a hallmark of feminine virtue. Today? Not so much.

In Proverbs, the young man is warned to avoid immodest women, which is evident in three characteristics. First, her speech is immodest: "The lips of a forbidden woman drip honey, and her speech is smoother than oil, but in the end she is bitter as wormwood, sharp as a two-edged sword" (Prov 5:3-4). Second, her clothing is immodest: "Behold, the woman meets him, dressed as a prostitute, wily of heart" (Prov 7:10). A prostitute wears clothing that advertises her sexual availability. Third, her behavior is immodest: "She is loud and wayward; her feet do not stay at home; now in the street, now in the market, and at every corner she lies in wait. She seizes him and kisses him" (Prov 7:11-13). The young man's parents wisely instruct him to seek out a modest woman, because the immodest woman is ungodly.

Paul said, "women should adorn themselves in respectable apparel, with modesty and self-control, not with braided hair and gold or pearls or costly attire, but with what is proper for women who profess godliness—with good works" (1 Tim 2:9-10). Paul assumes that a woman's natural desire is to be beautiful, but he cautions her to seek the inner adornment of godly character more than outer beauty, especially when God's people are gathered for worship. His immediate concern was to remove the distractions of attention-seeking women in the worship gathering so everyone can focus their attention on God alone. When women show up to worship wearing flashy or revealing clothing, they draw attention to themselves and away from God. When the church gathers for worship, our hearts should be drawn to the beauty of our Lord, not to the beauty of the woman in the pew in front of us. To be clear, a woman's desire for beauty is part of her design. It is not wrong to wear nice clothes, jewelry, or use beauty products. The problem is when these things are pursued for the sake of vanity and entice-ment or in ways that diminish the lasting beauty of godly character.

Some women raise strong objections about modesty, typically claiming that women cannot be held responsible for a man's lust and lack of self-control. They may also object that they are merely dressing comfortably, with no intent to draw inappropriate atten-tion. This may be true. She may not be intentionally enticing men to lust. And yes, men are responsible for their own self-control. But, returning again to our earlier discussion of virtue, what does love require? Suppose a young man is in the fight of his life against lust, and he sees a Christian woman show up to church wearing a lot cut blouse and tight fitting pants that reveal every curve. Is she acting with proper feminine virtue?

J. Budziszewski is helpful on this point—"Even if her intentions are pure, her conduct isn't. Why? Because she has no respect for the efforts of others toward purity. Whether or not she intends to provoke, she provokes; whether or not she intends to arouse, she arouses; whether or not she intends to get attention, she gets it… He wants her to dress modestly because he doesn't want to be a lecher; he is trying his best to keep order among his feelings and desires, and he wishes that someone would have a care. The [immodest] young woman is like someone lighting up a cigarette around gasoline. It doesn't matter that she isn't trying to set the gasoline on fire; she ought to be trying not to… One's most precious treasures, he hides; no one piles his diamonds on the street. Modesty suggests that there is something of great beauty and worth to be concealed; immodesty suggests that it is too plain and cheap to need concealment."[11]

As Budziszewski says, modesty implies something of great value is being guarded. By saying "something of great value," I am not speaking in a crass way of her private parts. I am speaking of the great value of her fertility. Because the "cost" of sex is much greater for women, they have a natural instinct to guard their sexuality until a worthy man comes along who will protect and provide for her and the children of their union. Modesty communicates in a practical way that a woman respects her body and her sexuality is not cheap. It belongs only to the man she selects, and to whom she commits, because he is a worthy man who has likewise committed himself to her.

---

11. Budziszewski, *On the Meaning of Sex*, 122, 124.

Practically speaking, when the Scriptures say that women of feminine virtue should wear "respectable apparel," marked by "modesty and self-control" (1 Tim 2:9), what does that mean? Obviously, this is subjective. Paul did not link to a Pinterest board with examples of acceptable fashion. Cultural expectations of male and female dress can be somewhat malleable because sexual ethics are expressed within a particular context which itself grows and adapts to changing circumstances. Paul assumes that virtuous women will recognize these temptations and respond accordingly. The virtue of feminine modesty will tend towards subtleness and deference which can be displayed outwardly with appropriate clothing and good works.

The tension we have been walking throughout this book is to maintain the goodness of God's design without making prescriptions that lock men and women within a particular cultural expression. Modesty presents a unique challenge in this respect. It involves decisions about how revealing or suggestive a woman's clothing should be. Modesty doesn't mean hiding everything and covering it all up. It's not about being prudish. Women should not make themselves unattractive, nor should they hide their curves or feminine form. She is a woman; she need not hide the fact. But still—even taking cultural variations into account—nearly every culture has *some* standard of feminine modesty. A wise woman will learn to instinctively know when she is dressing in such a way that will draw inappropriate attention to her body. A virtuous woman will dress in such ways that does not flaunt her sexuality. Scripture does not prescribe a "Christian uniform" for women to wear. Modesty or vanity are matters of Spirit-led discernment and wisdom.

Conclusion

As stated already, gendered virtue does not mean masculinity and femininity constitute inflexible boxes that prescribe every specific behavior for individual men and women. Rather, they represent God-honoring ways of being in the world that move with the grain of our created design, and which benefits the communities we belong to. Masculinity and femininity are not merely expressions of individualist sexual identity, but embodied realities that were given for the sake of others. My masculinity is not mine alone, but it belongs to God and others whom God has called me to love and serve with it. My wife's femininity is not hers alone, but it belongs to God and those to whom she is called to love and serve with it.

Therefore, virtuous masculinity and femininity are not pursued by eliminating the distinctions of masculinity and femininity, but by embracing them and living them out fully in ways that correspond to others in Christian love. Eliminating our sexual distinctions might produce a superficial illusion of equality, but that's the sort of equality that distorts our nature, moves against the grain of the created order, and increases strife and competition between the sexes. Gendered virtue calls men and women to work together, in Christian love, to establish and multiply households and churches, and work together to subdue the world for the glory of God. What could be a greater calling that this?

There is a beautiful scene in *The Return of the King*, the final book in J. R. R. Tolkien's Lord of the Rings series, where joy is recovered in the formerly besieged city of Minas Tirith.[12] This return of joy is given a fascinating and compelling shape. Earlier in the story, the women and children of the royal city were sent out for

12. J. R. R. Tolkien, *The Return of the King* (New York, NY: Houghton Mifflin Company, 1994), 944.

safety before the supernatural evil, the dark lord Sauron, arrived to surround and attack the city. During the ensuing siege and battle, life in Minas Tirith is predictably violent, tense, and notably grim. Towards the end of the battle, the men struggled to find any reason for hope. There was no joy. They could not be themselves in a full and healthy way. But after Sauron's defeat, Tolkien, who writes from a traditional Christian worldview, describes what happened when the women and children returned to the city: the men were filled with gladness and hope once again. There is something that filled out the men and their world that only the women could bring. And it's touching how this is pictured and described. In my estimation, it's the little, natural feminine qualities that restore Minas Tirith's full sense of itself as the women carry with them flowers, something I doubt any soldier or servant of the city would have been doing. Just as the children bring their shouts and laughs and games and unpredictable buoyancy and energy to the city and so repair some of its brokenness, the women are what the men cannot be, and the city has missed and needed it.

The world doesn't just need men and women for the purpose of procreation. The world needs masculine and feminine virtue, complementing and completing one another, like a chorus of voices that rise in a harmonious song—bass, tenor, alto, and soprano—singing distinct notes that blend together into a symphony. God's design is pitch perfect and beautiful. And though it is marred by the fall, it is being renewed and redeemed through the church, the household of God. Androgyny turns the music of male and female complementarity into sterile, lifeless "white noise." All the major and minor chords, the melodies and harmonies, the crescendos and diminuendos, get flattened into a single "middle C." The sexual complementarity of men and women contains the life-giving potential to create true beauty. In the church and in the world, masculine and feminine virtue join to create music, art, justice, and wisdom. There is no civilized culture without masculine and feminine virtue. The world needs the life-giving presence women naturally possess. And the world needs the strength and conquering energy men naturally possess. We impoverish ourselves when we expect women to be masculine and men to be feminine. As the music and the dance of sexual polarity is exchanged for lifeless androgyny, the world loses its potential for beauty. It simultaneously becomes uglier and more bizarre. Let us recover God's good design for gendered virtue for his glory and for our good.

CHAPTER 6

The Productive Household

"There is nothing nobler or more admirable than when two people who see eye to eye keep house as man and wife, confounding their enemies and delighting their friends."[1]

HOMER, THE ODYSSEY

"Enjoy life with the wife whom you love, all the days of your vain life that he has given you under the sun, because that is your portion in life and in your toil at which you toil under the sun."

ECCLESIASTES 9:9

Introduction

Planting a church in Cincinnati has been a family project from the beginning. Early in my marriage, my wife, Laura, and I each worked our own jobs, as most people do at this life stage. I worked

---

1. Gerardo Zampaglione, *The Idea of Peace in Antiquity* (United Kingdom: University of Notre Dame Press, 1973), 22.

in computer sales and my wife was an oncology nurse. Then we both joined staff with a collegiate ministry. This season of our lives was formative for me, because for the first time, my wife and I had the same job. We went to staff meetings together, worked on outreaches with our team together, and traveled overseas for mission work together. At every point, we were intimately aware of each other's work and the challenges we each faced. We shared a common purpose and worked together at everything we did.

After doing ministry in this way for a couple of years, I began my seminary education while continuing to work for our college ministry. It was during this time that our first child was born. Even though Laura loved discipling young college women, as a mother her availability was more limited. Fourteen months later, our second child was born, and she decided to devote her full attention to our home and children. About a year later, we moved to Cincinnati to plant a church. Our third child was born two months after we arrived. We spent the next year gathering a core group for our church and launching a public worship gathering. Our fourth child was born shortly thereafter. In five years' time, we added four children to our household, completed a seminary degree, moved to a new city, and planted a new church out of our home. Even though this was an intense time of hard work, we remember this season of life with fondness. We were building something together that, by God's grace, would last beyond our lifetimes. From the beginning, planting our church has been a family project. I've led the effort with my wife working with me at my side. As my children have grown older, they've been part of the effort as well.

When potential church planters are being assessed by sending organizations, one of the most important assessment categories is spousal cooperation. If a church planter meets all the criteria and qualification for planting a church, but his wife is not fully on board with it, it's a deal breaker. Planting a church is a team effort that requires a total commitment from the planting pastor and his family. We know firsthand why this is such an important assessment category for church planters. The church planting family is at the center of a spiritual storm that exacts a heavy emotional toll. You lose friends. You experience betrayal. You endure accusations. The lead pastor's marriage and family must have the strength to withstand these trials.

In 2018, my church gave me my first sabbatical. I took my family on an RV trip through a few national parks in Utah and the surrounding areas. Even though it was technically a sabbatical for me, my family knew it was *our* sabbatical. Even though I am the lead pastor of my church, we are all church planters, because we did it together. My wife and I have pursued a common mission now for over two decades, growing two households together: one at home and one at church. I didn't realize it initially, but one thing has become increasingly clear over the years: sharing a mission together as a family has given us a common purpose that has drawn us closer and held us together. Pursuing this mission with the people I love most has been one of the greatest joys of my life.

The thesis of this chapter is this: *work is a God-given bonding agent that holds the household together.* You may have heard the old saying, "a home that prays together stays together." That's true, but I would also say, "a home that *works* together stays together." Having a productive household isn't impossible in the modern world. It can be done if pursued intentionally. For the remainder of this chapter, I will demonstrate the value of productive households—households that have a common mission they pursue together—and conclude with some practical examples.

Exercising Dominion Through Work

Households were made to be productive. Modern people think of the home as a place of rest and retreat. We leave home to go to work and return home to rest and relax. This was not the case in the ancient world (or even well into the 20th century), where work was regarded as an integral part of household life. Theologically, the doctrine of the household and the doctrine of work go together because God made them to go together. That's what the Creation Mandate is all about. God called the man and woman to establish a household that will accomplish a divine mission.

At first, the scope of the Creation Mandate seems overwhelming. How could it be possible for one human couple to populate the earth while building a global civilization? The simple answer is through a division of labor. Adam and Eve's household would bring many people into the world, with different abilities and personalities, who would have developed different skills to contribute to the household mission. Children would be educated. Skills would be refined. Tools would be created. Civilization would grow. Culture would be made. The one constant in this ever-expanding mission was people: from the beginning, God's mission for humanity was to blanket the earth with people who would build a global civilization for his glory and their good.

Work is good. Work is not part of the fall. God created us for work, and households were created to work *together*. The curse of sin made it more difficult but work itself is what we were made for. It is part of our mission. The call on man and woman to subdue the earth and exercise dominion is a call to work.

Home Economics

When I was in high school, many young women took a class called "home economics," where they learned skills such as cooking and sewing. At the time, I thought the name of the class was strange. I wondered, "why is it called home *economics*? Are they learning how to make a budget?" To my ears, the word "economy" sounded like something that happens "out there," in the marketplace, where goods and services are produced. In modern usage, "the economy" refers to finance and money. This is ironic, given the origins of the word. In the ancient world, economy referred to the way a household was ordered.

The English word economy comes from two Greek words: "*oikos,*" which means house, and "*nomos,*" which means law. Since households can be structured in different ways to meet their needs, every household had its own rules. Originally, economy referred to the way a house is run. Even though different households may have their own unique personality, every faithful household shares the same basic purpose and structure: households are bound together in ties of mutual love, loyalty, and service, and they multiply, support each other, and exercise dominion in the world. There are a variety of ways households can do this, but the basic structure, patterned after God's own household, undergirds the whole enterprise.

So how is it that the word economy has come to refer to the financial sector? Why does the word economy now refer to things like Wall Street, the IRS, and the Federal Reserve? The short answer is that work has moved from the household into the marketplace, where it was commodified and monetized. Rather than growing our own food, we work for money that we use to buy food someone else grew. How did this happen?

How Industrialization Changed Work

Perhaps the most consequential cultural change brought on by the industrial revolution was that it separated work from the household. This fundamentally reoriented the way households functioned. Although the industrial revolution led to incredible innovations and advances in science, technology, and medicine, those great benefits came at a steep price, and the household has been paying the bill.

When industrialization took husbands out of the home and into the factory, women were left to manage their homes by themselves. But industrialization changed their work as well, as sewing, knitting, spinning, baking, and so on were increasingly done somewhere else. Boys no longer worked alongside their fathers. Mothers had fewer skills to teach their daughters. Nancy Pearcy wrote that in this new post-industrial environment, "A mother was called upon to stoke the fires of affection, to minister to her world-weary husband, and to impress moral sentiments onto the hearts of her children."[2] The household was slowly reduced to a place of sentiment, consumption, and entertainment, driving a wedge between public and private life. Important things, like work or civic involvement, happened "out there," in the marketplace. The home became where we spent time with family and watched some TV.

As the world would soon discover, unproductive households are less stable. The work men and women did no longer gave direct benefit to the people they shared life with. And in the workplace, men and women increasingly competed with one another. Technological advances have eliminated many of the sexual differences

---

2. Nancy Pearcey, "Is Love Enough? Recreating the Economic Base of the Family." http://www.arn.org/docs/pearcey/np_familyinamerica.htm (Accessed July 2, 2022).

that are so vital in a healthy household. As a result, the modern workplace treats men and women as interchangeable labor units with dollar values assigned for their efforts.

In the modern world, the father often works to earn a living away from the people he is providing for, spending most of his waking hours on the job. The mother is left to raise her children on her own, without the father's direct influence or support throughout the day, leaving her feeling exhausted and alone. Without the father's influence on his sons during the day, boys often grow up learning about manhood from women, whether mothers or schoolteachers. This leaves boys with an impoverished sense of their own masculine identity. Children no longer begin working because their households need them to, but they work at school, preparing for some future work they'll do somewhere else.

These factors have had a profound effect on how household members relate to one another. When family members spend most of their time in separate spheres, working apart from one another, and developing separate work relationships, they soon find that they don't have a lot to hold them together. They drift apart. According to Pearcey, the home becomes an "empty shell" where "scattered family members come together and somehow relate with each other over nothing at all. We are desperately trying to build families on the fragile base of personal affection and sentiment largely divorced from any material interdependence."[3]

In other words, most modern children grow up without visible role models for work because most work is done *away* from the home. Children do not participate in the work of the household (apart from a few chores, perhaps). The same is true for the husband and wife. When they don't work together, they don't develop

---

3. Pearcey, "Is Love Enough?"

the level of interdependency that sustained marriages of previous generations. The marriage becomes sentimentalized and emotional fulfillment becomes the goal. This isn't healthy or good.

As a result, Pearcey continues, "the family in modern America is more fragile, less stable, and under more vigorous attack than ever. Fathers continue to withdraw from family obligations into their work; mothers are conforming to the same pattern, leaving the home in record numbers for paid employment; divorce continues to rise, tearing apart the emotional fabric of the family; schools and day care are taking over the socialization of ever-younger children. The family doesn't seem to be very good at providing even emotional solace any more. Contrary to the theorists, loss of its erstwhile functions has not made the family any stronger."[4]

Over time, industrialization has pulled the household apart, rafters from beams, little by little, eroding its productive energies until only a thin sediment of its former industry remains. We look outside the home for almost everything of tangible or practical value. We get money from the marketplace. We get education from schools. We have nursing homes to take care of aging parents. We have professionals repair the leaky faucet. The household doesn't *do* much anymore. It can no longer command great allegiance or respect. All the "important" stuff happens somewhere else.

What We Have Lost

Before industrialization, most of the world's population lived in productive households, where men and women labored side by side on farms or household workshops. They were "subsistence

---

4. Pearcey, "Is Love Enough?"

economies," where the household itself produced what it needed to survive.

Nancy Pearcey summarizes the pre-industrial household well: "Prior to the 19th century, the vast majority of people in the world lived on farms or in peasant villages. Productive work was done in the home or its outbuildings, whether for subsistence or for sale. Work was done not by individuals, but by families. Stores, offices, and workshops were located in a front room, with living quarters either upstairs or in the rear. The boundaries of the home were fluid and permeable; the 'world' entered continually in the form of clients, business colleagues, customers, and apprentices."[5] What Pearcey is describing is a productive household. A household where everyone is working together for the sake of everyone else.

How did this affect the household relationships? Pearcey explains, "For husband and wife, it meant they inhabited the same universe, working side by side in a common enterprise (though not necessarily in identical tasks). For the mother, the location of work within the home meant she was able to raise children while still participating in the family sustenance. Marriage in colonial times 'meant to become a co-worker beside a husband, if necessary learning new skills in butchering, silversmith work, printing, or upholstering—whatever special skills the husband's work required.'" These preindustrial wives would be responsible for a wide array of household tasks, such as spinning wool and cotton, weaving it into cloth, sewing clothes for her family, gardening and preserving food, preparing meals without pre-processed ingredients, making soap, candles, and medicines.[6] This is a far cry from the modern housewife, who often works long hours with sleepless nights tending to her children alone, feeling imprisoned

5. Pearcey, "Is Love Enough?"
6. Pearcey, "Is Love Enough?"

in her home while her husband is away at work. If the husband is a hard worker himself, he puts in long hours and only has a couple of hours in the evening to spend with his children before bed.

The father in pre-industrial times would have typically worked from home, integrating work responsibilities with child rearing and household life. Parenting would not have been exclusively the mother's domain, as it is in so many modern homes. As the children grew older, the boys learned their father's trade alongside him and the girls learned to keep house alongside their mothers.

This description is not intended to idealize pre-industrial life, which was often a life of backbreaking labor. But the advantages to household life are obvious. Pre-industrial households benefited from an integration of life and work that is rare in our fragmented age.[7] The benefits of pre-industrial life are now lost. French Novelist Michel Houellebecq put it this way. In the modern world, "I work for someone else, I rent my apartment from someone else, there's nothing for my son to inherit. I have no craft to teach him; I haven't a clue what he might do when he's older. By the time he grows up, the rules I lived by will have no value – he will live in another universe. If a man accepts the fact that everything must change, then he accepts that life is reduced to nothing more than the sum of his own experience; the past and future generations mean nothing to him. That's how we live now. For a man to bring a child into the world now is meaningless."[8]

That may sound bleak, but there's hope. Industrialization is not all bad. I love my modern conveniences as much as anyone. I appreciate the fact that I have half a dozen world-class hospitals within 10 minutes of my house. I thank God that childhood death

7. Pearcey, "Is Love Enough?"
8. Michel Houellebecq, *The Elementary Particles*, trans. Frank Wynne (New York, NY: Vintage, 2001), 140.

is rare, thanks to industrial advances. Yet, we must also conclude that it's a mixed blessing. Many household tasks have been automated by machines, such as doing laundry, washing dishes, raising livestock, growing crops, preparing meals, and sowing clothes. My wife can start a load of laundry, turn on the dishwasher, leave to shop for kids' school clothes, then stop by Kroger on the way home and fill our kitchen cabinets with a week's worth of food in just a few hours. The blessing of having so much household work automated by machines has freed women more than ever to devote their time and talent to other things. I don't hate industrialization, but it has brought about many lamentable problems.

The Vocation of "Homemaking"

Industrialization has also brought some new words into our lexicon. The word "homemaker" emerged in the 1860's to describe women who worked from home while their husbands left home for factory work. Before this, the word wasn't necessary, because most everyone worked from home. But now, a new word was needed to reflect a new reality. Increasingly, homemaking was seen as woman's work, not man's work. But this isn't correct. The Creation Mandate is God's call for both men and women to be homemakers with a division of labor. The word "homemaker" only became necessary when men had to leave home to work elsewhere. Biblically speaking, the husband is also responsible for homemaking, because he is head of house and steward of his household mission. Prov 27:8 says, "Like a bird that strays from its nest is a man who strays from his home." Although it is necessary for most men to leave home to work in the modern world, his absence can be a burden to the household.[9]

Many homemaking mothers dread being asked, "what do you do for a living?" This question can evoke feelings of shame or inadequacy, as though they have forsaken a more meaningful calling out in the marketplace, away from the demands of her children. When she answers, "I'm a stay-at-home mom," it sounds to some women like she's announcing a prison sentence. She is being punished for having children and is missing out on the exciting adventures of corporate life, where she could be spreading her wings and making a real difference. Beneath those feelings of inadequacy are the false assumptions that our jobs are supposed to provide emotional validation and personal fulfillment for us. In a fallen world, almost every kind of work has its perks and headaches. The idea that careers are inherently exciting and fulfilling is a ruse. Most people don't experience it that way. It might be a wonderful adventure for some, but that's not the norm.

Ultimately, in both pre- and post-industrial contexts, husbands and wives serve the same Lord (Eph 6:5-8) and work to receive their commendation from Him (1 Cor 4:5). Both husband and wife are homemakers. Jobs and careers are not where we should pursue emotional validation but should first be regarded as God's appointed means of building up our households. The primary

---

9. Interestingly, the word "husband" itself suggests as much. Rosemary Hopcraft wrote that it is derived from two Old Norse words, "hús" and "bóndi." "Hus" refers to the *house* and "bondi" refers to one who tills the soil. Thus, a husband was one who had a home and could therefore marry and support a family. It reflected the common understanding in the pre-industrial world that a man should not marry until he was able to work and provide. See "The More Things Change: Husband's Income, Wife's Income, and Number of Biological Children in the U.S." Institute for Family Studies. https://ifstudies.org/blog/the-more-things-change-husbands-income-wifes-income-and-number-of-biological-children-in-the-us (Accessed July 7, 2022).

"product" of a household is its people, and it needs fathers and mothers making a home together.

C. S. Lewis once called being a homemaker "the ultimate career." He wrote this in a personal letter to a woman, encouraging her in this vocation. He told her that her work was, in fact, "the most important work in the world." Homemaking is irreplaceable because ships, railways, mines, cars, and government all exist so people may be fed, warmed, and safe in their own homes. He said, "your job is the one for which all others exist."[10]

The Household in the Modern World

Now that much of its productive capacity has been outsourced, the households of today look much different than they did before the Industrial Revolution. Of course, people still go to work, get married, and have children, but we order our lives differently. Pre-modern households were much more self-reliant, providing their own food, childcare, education, security, healthcare, and care for the elderly. Modern households outsource almost all these things. We work jobs to get money. We buy food at the store. We pay the mechanic to fix the car. We buy clothes at a department store or online. We send our kids to school for education. If someone breaks into our house, we call the police. If we get sick, we go to the doctor. When we get old, we move into retirement homes. Children are no longer an essential part of household survival, but more of a lifestyle choice. Almost all production in the modern world happens in manufacturing buildings. We bring these products into our homes, which are places of consumption

---

10. C. S. Lewis, *The Collected Letters of C. S. Lewis, Volume 3: Narnia, Cambridge, and Joy, 1950–1963* (HarperSanFrancisco), Loc. 625.

and entertainment. It seems that only eccentrics and hobbyists do much producing in their own homes.

If most adults were asked the question, "what do you depend on your family for?" what do you think they'd say? Most people would probably focus on love, belonging, or emotional support. But if we changed the question to, "what do you depend on the government for?" it's a different story. People rely more on government entities for tangible needs. This is because government agencies have replaced many things the household was once counted on to provide. If we get fired, we collect unemployment. If we are disabled, we collect disability. When it's time to retire, we collect Social Security.

In 2012, President Obama ran an ad for his reelection campaign called "The Life of Julia."[11] This ad tells the story of a young woman who, from childhood, navigated the various challenges of life with assistance provided by the state. There is no reference to a family. She relied on the government for everything. The ad celebrated this as a good thing, and as a model for how society should be. The government feeds us, clothes us, educates us, provides us with a job, and keeps us healthy. I'm not saying government programs are necessarily sinful or wrong, but they create incentives that weaken the household. As social services multiply, the household becomes more irrelevant to modern life.

Two Errors to Avoid

There are two errors we need to avoid as we relate God's design to the modern, industrialized world. The first is what I call the

---

11. "Obama's 'Life of Julia' Is the Wrong Vision for America," https://www.cnn.com/2012/05/09/opinion/bennett-obama-campaign/index.html (accessed July 22, 2022).

"Amish Error." This is the error of assuming Christians cannot faithfully live in the modern world, so they idealize the past and try to recreate a pre-industrial life for themselves. The Amish community believed that the industrial revolution was a great evil, and they sought to establish an alternate society free of these advancements. Although we may be less extreme, many Christians want to unplug from the modern world and detach from it. Christians who recognize how destructive modern life has been towards the family can idealize an earlier time in history when the household was honored and respected as the norm for society. Certainly, we want to reclaim certain aspects of the past, but we cannot turn back the clock and live in a world that no longer exists. Modern Christians must learn to be faithful to the time, place, and culture in which God has placed us.

Industrialization has brought many benefits into our lives that we should not take for granted. Nor should we ignore the fact that they have come at a steep cost and have created unexpected incentives. But industrialization is not itself the villain to project all our problems onto. Technologies are tools that can be leveraged to enhance household life or diminish it, which is where we need Christian wisdom. Industrialized advances have saved lives, lengthened lives, lifted people out of poverty, reduced hunger, and put men on the moon. The prosperity of modern times surpasses anything known to previous generations. One could argue that industrialization, with all its problems, reflects a significant advance in our calling to subdue the earth. Without a doubt, we are the most materially blessed generation the world has ever known. God be praised for these things, and may we steward these gifts for his glory.

The second error is what I call the "Assimilation Error." This is the error of being so enamored with modern advances that we fail to see the problems it has created. It is arrogant to regard the modern world as more advanced, liberated, and enlightened than previous generations. We should not idealize or romanticize the past, nor should we disregard the past as though we cannot learn from it. To be sure, previous generations had their blind spots, but so do we. The best way to see our modern blind spots is to learn from the "democracy of the dead"[12] and let the saints of the past teach and correct us.

Two Dimensions of a Productive Household

The productive household has two dimensions, as can be seen in the Creation Mandate: internal and external. The first set of commands encompass the internal dimension, which was to "be fruitful and multiply and fill the earth" (Gen 1:28). This is the household at its most basic and familiar: getting married, having children, and bringing them up in the Christian faith. The internal dimension is how the household members are protected and provided for, ensuring everyone is properly fed, clothed, housed, and educated. Beyond this, the internal dimension gives the household a place of fellowship, belonging, purpose, and legacy.

The household set of commands encompass the external dimension, where the household is called to "subdue" the earth and exercise "dominion" over it. The internal dimension will look quite similar from one household to the next, but the external dimension is where great variations will occur as they develop specialties and greater uniqueness. For example, every household needs to eat, make money, buy clothes, and educate their children. But the work they do in the world varies greatly.

---

12. G. K. Chesterton, *Orthodoxy* (Duke Classics, 2012), 63–64.

The external, more public dimension of the household is where they exert influence in the world for the good of others in their communities. This is their work; it's their mission. Like a tree that spreads its branches outward and upward, even providing food and shelter for other creatures, the productive household can also reach outward into the world to participate in civic life and be a blessing in the world. To put it another way, the invitations to follow Christ in the Bible can be obeyed as a household, and not just as individuals (Deut 15:20; Acts 16:31).

For example, one household in my church has devoted themselves to a hospitality ministry of taking in foster care children. The wife is the primary driver of this effort, and she does most of the daily work of caring for these children. But it's a team effort because it is the ministry of their household. The husband is involved in different ways, from communicating with social workers, taking care of paperwork, and managing court hearings. If the wife were to pursue this alone as a solo mission, she would be much less effective and would likely burn out. But as it is, they are more effective because they are pursuing it *together*. Productive households typically begin with a focus on the internal dimension, where its most immediate needs are met, and gradually branch out into the external dimension, where their work benefits others in their scope.

My townhouse overlooks a city park where my kids played when they were little. They befriended a neighborhood boy name Kevin who ended up spending a lot of time with us. He lived close by with his grandmother. We started to detect early on that things were not quite right in his home. His mother had had nine children with several different fathers, most of whom were scattered across different homes around the city. Soon enough it became clear that Kevin came to our house because he could be a normal kid there. Kevin lived with us off and on over the course of several years. He lived with us one entire summer while his mother was in jail. He did family movie nights with us, went to church and small group with us, and went on family vacation with us. One time, he sat next to me during family movie night. Out of the blue, he turned to me and said, "Mr. Michael, you're like a dad to me." He's been calling us "mom" and "dad" ever since. He's been integrated into our household, having his own chores along with my other kids.

As households develop and grow, they can begin to expand their influence and positively impact the lives of others. Some households can grow strong enough to exert great influence in its community as its members focus their collective energies in that direction. Just as the kings of old had their own ruling houses, modern households can similarly rise to prominence to exert great influence in a community. In my city of Cincinnati, Ohio, one of the most prominent Christian families is the Lindner family. The patriarch of the family was Carl Lindner, who was one of the richest men in the world. Lindner grew his family's dairy business into the United Dairy Farmers chain of convenience stores. He expanded into insurance and investments business with his three sons. At one time, he was a controlling owner of the Cincinnati Reds baseball team. As a Cincinnati resident, we know the Lindner family for their philanthropy and civic involvement. They've leveraged their great wealth for civic influence. The Lindners founded the Christian school that my children attend. The Lindner name is enshrined in buildings all around the city. Lindner's grandson founded another professional sports franchise in the city, the FC Cincinnati MLS soccer team.

Of course, their wealth is rare. I mention them because the Lindner name represents a *household*. The various members of the Lindner family are known for the good things they do in our city. Households need not be wealthy to be productive in ways that strengthen the household and benefit their communities. The church I planted was a household endeavor. Although this is becoming less common, many small businesses still have a household structure. Some of them even put it in their name, such as "Smith and Sons Plumbing."

At the national level, some households have risen to political prominence, such as the Kennedy and Bush families. These families produced many talented politicians because their households were internally supported by patriarchs and matriarchs who raised up children, taught them the art of politics, prepared them for public life, and released them into the world to make an impact. Both families exercised dominion, quite literally, through their households.

Headship and Submission in the Modern Household

This brings us to the issue of headship and submission in a marriage, which has caused a lot of controversy in the modern church. We cannot properly understand the scripture's teaching about headship and submission without recognizing the productive nature of the ancient household. Ephesians 5:22-24 says, "Wives, submit to your own husbands, as to the Lord. For the husband is the head of the wife even as Christ is the head of the church, his body, and is himself its Savior. Now as the church submits to Christ, so also wives should submit in everything to their husbands."

We can see what the text says easily enough, but what does it mean? What does it mean that the husband is the head of his wife? What does it mean for the wife to submit to her husband? How do a husband and wife faithfully obey these Scriptures in the modern world? To properly understand this text, we need to account for the ancient context of the household it was written to. In the modern, industrialized world, the husband's headship is seen as irrelevant, arbitrary, and unnecessary. Why does he get to be in charge? Why does she need to submit? Isn't she just as capable and intelligent as he is? What if she is *more* capable and intelligent than him? But in the ancient household, this was not the case. When work is integrated into household life, the need for headship and authority is more apparent. The husband was primarily responsible to provide for his household, and responsibility entails authority.

The text goes on to describe other relationships in the household that came under his headship. He also functioned as a "chief of staff," overseeing the work of the house (Eph 6:5-9). Ancient households needed to be productive to survive and the division of labor was self-evident. Men did the more physically demanding work and women did the more domestic work. It might have taken several men and their sons to till rocky soil, irrigate a farm, raise a barn, fell trees, and saw lumber by hand. Women simply aren't designed for this. But women are designed for childbearing and managing a home. Nobody questioned this in the ancient world. It was accepted as a vocation given by God, evident in their bodies. As modern technology has made the most physically demanding work easier, the lines have blurred between what constitutes man's work and woman's work. As work left the household and relocated into the marketplace, the husband's authority left with it. Authority goes where the work goes.

Headship and submission assume a productive environment because work needs leadership. As industrialization has driven a wedge between home life and work life, the husband's headship has become more abstract and less practical. When the household is little more than a place of recreation and entertainment, there's little use for headship and submission, which is a big part of why so many Christian households have abandoned it. C. R. Wiley said, "The thing about [gender] roles that unbalances people in a world drunk with equality is how roles result in a concentration of authority in the head of the house. Modern people resist this idea in a household, though they accept it with perfect ease when we speak of the workplace. Of course there must be hierarchy at work, that is where we get important things accomplished. The fact that people expect perfect equality in the home is evidence that they really don't think anything productive happens there."[13] That's exactly right. The household is now less productive, smaller, and less central to civic life. When a married couple struggles to apply the principles of headship in their home, the problem is usually not because they don't understand it. The problem is that they need something to do.

Households Without a Mission

A household that lacks a clear sense of mission will inevitably struggle to understand headship and submission. There is no *sub*-mission without a mission. A household without a mission is like a foreman without a factory. The "head" doesn't matter very much if the rest of the body has nothing to do. If the household isn't productive, what exactly is the husband the head of? What exactly does the wife submit to? Does it mean he should make the final decision about paint colors? Or always choose the restaurant? Without a clear sense of purpose for their marriage, sincere

---

13. C. R. Wiley, *Man of the House* (Eugene, OR: Resource Publications, 2017), 16.

Christians who want to sincerely obey Scripture's teaching on this matter find it difficult to apply practically.

Consider this scenario. A Christian husband and wife both work full-time jobs and have three children in school. At home, the wife takes care of things around the house and manages the kids' schedules while the husband handles the yardwork and small repairs as they come up. One Sunday, they hear a sermon at church about the husband's duty to lead his family and the wife's duty to submit to him. He is convicted. He realizes he's been on autopilot for some time and hasn't asserted much leadership in his family. Practically, then, what does repentance look like for him?

Husbands in this scenario commonly assume being head of the household means being more demanding and bossier. He should tell his wife what to cook for dinner. He should manage the budget and make all the financial decisions. He should choose where they go on vacation. He should always get to hold the remote. But if he acts this way, he may soon discover that this is frustrating for his wife, because his exercise of headship ends up taking dominion away from her. She may feel his assertion of headship is at the expense of her own dominion in the home. A woman may resist the idea of submission to her husband out of fear that it will limit her potentiality. Yet God has called them both to exercise dominion, albeit in different areas. The husband has authority over the whole household, but his focus is more external, on providing for and protecting the household. The wife's focus is more internal, on taking care of the people within the household. His headship does not negate or limit her domain. Rather, she is the mistress of the domain, free to manage the interests of the house because he has provided her with what she needs to thrive and keeps them secure.

Men who want to grow in their exercise of headship in their home would do well to lead their families on a productive mission together. The husband is responsible for the overall mission of the household, and the wife is given a sub-mission within it. Her domain exists within his domain. God's design is not to limit her potential, but to unlock it. Her potential is unlocked when he has a clear mission and she combines her potential with his potential to pursue it together.

Households with Conflicting Missions

As discussed previously, households include both its people and its work. In my previous example, the husband and wife both work full-time jobs, which strains the mission of the household. If the wife's boss says she needs to work late one evening, and the husband doesn't want her to, what are her options? She has two heads pulling her in two different directions. If she disobeys her husband, they'll have an argument. But if she disobeys her boss, she could lose her job. Even though her husband is the covenant head over her, her boss at work is the functional head over her in that situation. Her work has become a wedge in her marriage, yet she must submit to her boss to keep her job.

Every full-time job is a mission and every full-time worker reports to the "boss," who is the "head" of that mission. The husband and wife in our example have at least three conflicting missions: (1) the mission of his job, (2) the mission of her job, and (3) the mission of their household. A household with three missions is less stable, because there are multiple "heads" competing for that household's limited resources. The husband's and wife's separate careers become independent missions that pull them in different directions. Schools have their own mission too. As children go through school, they develop their own independent missions that revolve around friends and school activities, which take precedence over household priorities. Eventually, the household slowly scatters, with everyone pursuing their separate missions. Home is a pit stop to grab something from the fridge between work and soccer practice.

Work binds people together in a household. It is natural for people to develop friendships when they serve a common purpose together. Interestingly, many modern workplaces recognize this and are starting to act more and more like families. Proctor and Gamble, for example, has its own daycare center at its headquarters in Cincinnati. Parents who work for P&G can bring their kids to work with them, drop them off at daycare, visit them on their lunch break, and bring them home after work. Other companies try to curate a sense of belonging at the workplace by offering recreational events, classes, fitness programs, addiction treatment, and so on. Since many people are delaying marriage or choosing to not get married at all, the workplace is increasingly becoming the focal point of one's personal and social life as well.

In this sort of environment, how does the Christian teaching about headship and submission apply? How does a husband meaningfully lead his wife, when she must also report to her boss at work? How does a wife meaningfully submit to her husband, when most of her time and productive energy is given to a boss at work? For most Christians, their only option is to yield to all the demands of their employers and apply Scripture to the few areas that remain.

Developing Your Own Household Mission

In a fallen world, husbands and wives will have less than ideal circumstances and limited time and resources. Thus, they will need to economize and prioritize to maximize their efforts. There is no one-size-fits-all solution. God has given us his Word and Spirit to lead us in the way of wisdom, and we respond by taking steps of obedience to move in that direction. The biblical vision for the household is a unified mission, led by the husband, and all the household members pursue it together. Here are some practical examples I have personally witnessed.

When my wife was young, her parents owned a convenience store in Cleveland, Ohio. My wife's father was the owner of the store. He managed the inventory, placed orders with vendors, hired and fired employees, and was responsible for the overall success of the business. My wife's mother worked part time running the cash register, handling customer service, and keeping the place clean when she wasn't managing things at home. My wife even worked there too when she was a teenager, spending her summer months making some extra money helping around with various tasks as needed. At the store, my father in law was head of household because there was work that needed to be done and people who needed direction.

A man in my church was once laid off from his job, so his wife got her real estate license and began selling houses. After some time, he ended up returning to his old job in a role that required a lot of travel. This frustrated him because he didn't like having to be away from his family like that. As a result, he ended up getting his own real estate license and going into business with his wife. Now, they sell houses together as a team. This arrangement enables them to make the money they need with minimal interference with family life. Working together, they are able to share a more unified mission. He can tell his wife, "You head on home and get dinner started while I stay late and do the showing at 6 PM. I'll be home around 7 PM and we'll have dinner together."

Eric is a fellow pastor in my church who runs a few businesses out of his home. He built a recording studio in his garage, which enables him to be more present at home while working at the same time. He's recorded several well-known bands whose music has been featured on the radio and TV shows. He also uses his construction skills to flip houses with his wife. They have a couple of houses that they use as short-term rentals on Airbnb. It's a family project; they manage these rentals as a household. His wife decorates them and makes them hospitable. They prepare the listings on Airbnb together. His wife cleans one of the houses between guests to earn some extra money for herself. He has hired his oldest son to handle some guest relations, making sure their check-in process is smooth and they have everything they need. The income from the rentals pays the mortgage on those houses and generates extra income on the side. This is not the only way, but it does help bring a measure of productivity back to the household.

Of course, the mission of every Christian household should prioritize a commitment to following Jesus wholeheartedly and raising up a godly legacy. It's not going to look the same for every household practically, but these bedrock principles from Deuteronomy 6:4-7 should be part of every household mission: "Hear, O Israel: The Lord our God, the Lord is one. You shall love the Lord your God with all your heart and with all your soul and with all your might. And these words that I command you today shall be on your heart. You shall teach them diligently to your children, and shall talk of them when you sit in your house, and when you walk by the way, and when you lie down, and when you rise."

Establishing a productive, Christian household is an act of spiritual warfare. Men and women who fill their households with children who bear his image and are equipped to exercise dominion are pushing back against the darkness of the world with the light of Christ. Households that are laser focused on these priorities can be formidable. They are doing something good. They are producing something eternal. To be sure, there are unique challenges in the modern world, but it's not impossible. When husband and wife are committed to this calling and are willing to do what it takes to see it through, they will gladly orient their lives around it because they are making an eternal difference.

The Proverbs 31 Household

One of the most powerful portraits of the productive household in Scripture is Proverbs 31. Proverbs 31 famously praises the woman who fears the Lord, but she is praised for how she builds up her household. She is praised because she expresses her virtue as a wife and mother. She is industrious and hardworking, which brings incredible value to her household. This text is often cited as a biblical example of an entrepreneurial career woman managing a small business, but this interpretation misses the mark. She is not a career woman but a mother exercising dominion in a godly way in and for her home.

The context of Proverbs 31 is King Lemuel passing on his mother's advice (v. 1) to his own son. She said, "do not give your strength to women, your ways to those who destroy kings" (v. 3). In other words, his mother advised King Lemuel to not seek the kind of wife who would tear his house down, but the kind of wife who would build his house up with him. She would be the kind of woman who would not take away his virtue and strength, but a woman who has virtues and strengths of her own that would join his to create something beautiful and powerful.

King Lemuel's mother describes her as an excellent wife (v. 10). She is the queen of her domain, the internal dimension of the household, earning the trust of her husband (v. 11), clothing her family (v. 12), feeding them (vv. 14-15), expanding her household's influence (vv. 16-18), leveraging the strength of her household to feed the poor and needy (v. 20), anticipating and preparing for hard times (v. 21), transforming her home into a place of beauty and rest (v. 22), and educating her children with kindness and wisdom (v. 26). Notably, her husband is "known in the gates when he sits among the elders of the land" (v. 23). Important business and legal matters were often handled at the city gates. Her husband was able to be exert influence in the community because he trusted that she had things well managed at home. This chapter concludes with the praise and blessing she receives from her household: "her children rise up and call her blessed; her husband also, and he praises her… let her works praise her in the gates" (v. 28, 31b). Clearly, this woman has made her most significant and lasting contributions through her household as a wife and mother. She is not leaving her most meaningful marks on the world by closing major deals as Vice President of Sales for a pharmaceutical company.

In other words, the Proverbs 31 woman is praised because she excels at her mission. She oversees the workers in their household and manages the affairs of the household with excellence. She supports her husband. She works with him, not against him. She's giving him her strength, not draining his. She does not seek a mission of her own, apart from his, but she joins his mission and works hard to help him accomplish it. This is the calling that animates her whole life. She is compelling because her mundane tasks are orchestrated by a grand purpose. She prepares meals, sews clothes, decorates her house as a woman on a mission. Her husband and the people under her care know they could never have gotten where they are without her. She builds them up. She nurtures and amplifies their gifts. They flourish under the canopy of blessing she has created, which is large and strong enough to welcome in the poor. She is a multiplier.[14] She is praised not merely because she works hard, but because she serves her people with her work, and she trusts in God in her work. "A woman who fears the LORD is to be praised" (v. 30).

---

14. Rebekah Merkle, *Eve in Exile and the Restoration of Femininity* (Canon Press, 2016), 25–26.

CHAPTER 7

How Boys Become Fathers

"By the time a man realizes that maybe his father was right, he usually has a son who thinks he's wrong."

CHARLES WADSWORTH[1]

"I write to you, young men, because you are strong, and the word of God abides in you, and you have overcome the evil one."

1 JOHN 2:14

Introduction

Alta was a poor, young woman who worked at a shoe factory in Huntington, West Virginia in the winter of 1946. That's when she met Ron. Ron lived with his wife and children in Kentucky, a few hours away, but was traveling through Huntington on business. Being poor and naive, Alta didn't have a lot going for her, but she was young and pretty enough to attract Ron's attention.

---

1. A cultural proverb attributed to Charles Wadsworth. Precise citation unknown.

Ron smooth talked his way into her arms, and they spent a night together. They never spoke again.

Ron never knew the consequences of that night. He lived the rest of his life in middle class comfort with his intact family until he died in 2010. For him, it was an easily forgotten, one-night stand with a girl that meant nothing to him. For Alta, her life was changed forever. Later that year, she gave birth to a little boy. That little boy grew up to become my father.

My dad never met his own father. He grew up not knowing his name, occupation, or anything about him. Ron was a phantom—the missing father of my dad's childhood. There were uncles, however, that stepped in to fill the void. Dad always speaks highly of these men who loved a fatherless boy. They were like fathers to him.

My dad enjoys doing family research in his spare time, tracking down distant family members using an online database. That's how he eventually learned his father's identity. As a man in his 70's, using DNA technology, he was able to finally answer the question that had haunted him his whole life. Through this process, he was also able to meet one of his half-sisters, developed a relationship with her, learned more of his father's backstory, and even got to see photos of his father for the first time. His father served in the Navy, just as he did. It is remarkable to look at photos taken of them both in uniform when they enlisted. This stranger, my grandfather, looked just like my dad.

Fathers matter. Way more than we realize. These days, however, it seems as though fatherhood is optional. According to some estimates, roughly 40% of children grow up without a father in the home. Compare this to the roughly 10% of fatherless homes in 1960.[2] The social and psychological consequences of this fact cannot be understated. It's a disaster.

Of all the various factors that contribute to a child's future success, such as income potential, personal stability, and emotional health, nothing remotely compares to being raised in a two-parent home with mom and dad. According to Edward Davies, citing research from the parliamentary education committee in the UK, a 40-year trend of declining marriage rates maps almost perfectly onto declining achievement rates in children. A father's presence in the home matters more than race, poverty, or any other factor. Looking at the data for white families, Davies writes, "In the wealthiest fifth of white families by income, 84 per cent are married and reaping the benefits of that stability, with a further 12 per cent co-habiting. In the poorest fifth just 19 per cent are married with a further 9 per cent co-habiting — there is a pretty straight line through the income groups in between. It means if you are born into a wealthier family, you have a 96 per cent chance of having two parents. In our poorest communities, your chances are just 28 per cent and falling. In real and stark terms it means this: if you're white and rich you get a dad, and if you're white and poor you probably don't. Teachers, mentors, youth clubs, and investment are all great, but the ultimate privilege in life is now a present father." Considering the data for all ethnic groups, Davies says, "the marriage rates of each ethnic group map almost perfectly onto the school achievements of their children." He concludes, "There is no other form of relationship that offers anywhere near

---

2. Kate McKay, "The Importance of Fathers (According to Science)," https://www. artofmanliness.com/people/fatherhood/the-importance-of-fathers-according-to-science/ (Accessed July 22, 2022).

the same level of stability in any thriving culture in the whole of human history."[3]

Let that data sink in. *The single biggest indicator of adult success is growing up with an intact family.* That means the presence of a father. Countless empirical studies have shown that children who grow up with fathers at home are less likely to end up in poverty, do better in school, far less likely to end up in prison, less likely to abuse drugs or alcohol, less likely to be promiscuous as teenagers, less likely to be obese, have stronger vocabularies, take healthier risks, and generally enjoy happier lives.[4] Former President Barak Obama once said, "We know the statistics — that children who grow up without a father are five times more likely to live in poverty and commit crime; nine times more likely to drop out of schools and 20 times more likely to end up in prison. They are more likely to have behavioral problems, or run away from home or become teenage parents themselves. And the foundations of our community are weaker because of it."[5]

Patriarchy Is Good

If you go to Google and type "masculinity is…" in the search field, you'll see "toxic" as one of the top auto-responses. That's because our culture has come to regard masculinity as poisonous. This makes it difficult to have a productive discussion of patriarchy. If

---

3. Edward Davies, "Forget Race or Class, Marriage Is the Big Social Divide," https://www.spectator.co.uk/article/forget-race-or-class-marriage-is-the-big-social-divide (Accessed July 22, 2022).

4. Kate McKay, "The Importance of Fathers (According to Science)," https://www.artofmanliness.com/people/fatherhood/the-importance-of-fathers-according-to-science/ (Accessed July 22, 2022).

5. "Text of Obama's Fatherhood Speech," https://www.politico.com/story/2008/06/text-of-obamas-fatherhood-speech-011094 (Accessed, July 7, 2022).

masculinity is toxic, then "the patriarchy" is the poisonous blanket suffocating our society. In our society, the word patriarchy is a junk-drawer word for oppression and cruelty. Without question, some masculinity is truly toxic. Satan is a father of sorts, because Jesus tells his opponents, "you are of your father the devil" and calls Satan the "Father of Lies" (John 8:44). This is wicked patriarchy.

But there is another kind of patriarchy that's good. The heart of patriarchy, in the biblical sense, is the godly exercise of headship. When men of God submit to his design, patriarchy is glorious and good, because thriving societies are built on the shoulders of fatherhood. God is the eternal father who delights to make boys into men and make men into fathers. To put it another way, God is a Patriarch (Eph 3:14-15). Not only that, but heaven is a patriarchy because heaven is the realm of God's perfect, fatherly rule. Further, God's design for society, from the beginning, is patriarchal. Although men and women are called to accomplish the Creation Mandate together, men must actively take the lead. To subdue the world, men need to master skills, learn competencies, and develop specialties to be productive. Men will invent new technologies and develop new tools of proficiency to maximize their output.

The Vocation of Fatherhood

Growing up without knowing his father, my dad eventually found fathers in the workplace. He's a union man, an electrician by trade. After completing his service in the Navy, he became an electrical apprentice, learning the trade from more experienced electricians. "Apprentice" is the first step of certification, followed by "Journeyman" and "Master." He belongs to the International Brotherhood of Electrical Workers, I.B.E.W. for short. As a child, I remember going to the union meetings at local #317 in Huntington, W. Va. After conducting their annual business, they held a raffle with lots of fun prizes. Kids got tickets too. I got so excited listening to each number get called, hoping to hear mine.

My dad's union is called a "brotherhood" of electrical workers, but it's actually more of a patriarchy. A brotherhood is egalitarian because everyone is the same. A patriarchy is hierarchical because there are ranks and authority. That's how healthy societies are built. Passing on skills is fatherly. Those with more skill and experience outrank those with less skill and are granted authority to train them. My dad was a son in the trade to the men who taught him. Later, he became a father in the trade to other men. I knew some of these men. They developed close relationships with my dad as they worked together. As men accumulate years of electrical expertise, they pass down their skill through the generations, like fathers training their sons. It's a legacy.

Fatherhood is a built-in feature of the Creation Mandate. Adam would fulfill it by becoming a father. Fatherhood is the work of begetting, reproducing one's life in another. A healthy, patriarchal society harnesses the strength of men and directs it towards constructive, noble goals. Masculine energy was designed to subdue, cultivate, put things in order, and build. Of course, masculine energy can be twisted sinfully into a domineering and conquering spirit, but it can also be channeled constructively for the good of humanity and the glory of God.

As discussed previously, fatherhood is the shape of masculine virtue. Men are sanctified through the vocation of fatherhood, in both the biological and spiritual sense. The world is starving for fathers, which is what Christian men aspire to be. Fatherhood is more than a biological fact. It is a vocation. A man may biologically father a child without embracing the vocation of fatherhood.

This is why so many children grow up with single mothers. Their fathers have left the scene. Fathering a child biologically is hardly the full expression of masculinity. Conversely, a man may embrace the vocation of fatherhood without ever fathering a child biologically. This is what the Apostle Paul did. He was not a biological father, yet he was a father to the church (1 Cor 4:15).

Biological fatherhood is easy. Men play a brief and minor role in the process of reproduction. Vocational fatherhood, however, is a commitment of a lifetime. Embracing the vocation of fatherhood is what separates boys from men. Just as the physical teleology of maleness is fatherhood, the spiritual teleology of masculinity is the vocation of fatherhood, where men gladly take up great responsibilities and lay down their own lives for the sake of others. The masculine design is honored when a man begets another life—building his life into someone else—not merely as a sperm donor, but as a disciple maker. This is why the Apostle Paul could rightly regard himself as a father not only to his disciples Timothy, Titus, Barnabas, and Silas, but also to entire churches. The church needs fathers (and mothers!) because the Great Commission is itself an enterprise in building a spiritual household (Matt 28:18-20).

The Father's Mission

Fatherhood is also about rule. God made Adam rule as a priest-king over a garden-temple. His ruling duty was to subdue the uncharted wild beyond the borders of Eden, tame it, civilize it, and fill it with people, all for the glory of God. Men thrive when they are driven by a clear sense of mission. Men aspire to greatness because they are naturally attuned to build things and accomplish goals. When a man knows that his vocation is to take a wife and establish a multiplying household with her, he can order his life and priorities around that mission. A man who lacks this sense of mission for his life will either devote his life to something else, or wander aimlessly through life, not knowing exactly why God put him on this earth. Although exceptions do exist, most men need to recognize their basic mission includes marriage, children, and his work to provide for them.

In practical terms, these concepts can be distilled into three "M's"—master, mission, and mate. The top priority in any man's life is surrendering himself to Jesus Christ as Lord, or in this case, master. The second priority for any man is to understand his mission. Broadly speaking, a father's mission is to establish a productive household that can exercise godly dominion in the world. As discussed in chapter 6, the man's work is part of the household building project, for this is how he provides for his family. Any man's mission will include both his family and his work. Therefore, a wise man will weigh the cost any career field will have on his future household. For example, a man may think twice before entering a career field that pays well but requires overly long hours or demanding travel schedule. Third, to accomplish his mission, a man needs a godly mate who wants to join him and help him fulfill his mission.

Wise fathers develop some kind of a "spiritual vision" for their households, which helps everyone know where they are going and the part they play in it. When a household has a clear sense of mission, it summons an unyielding, transcendent, moral obligation from its members, because God has called them to a purpose beyond anything they can accomplish apart from him.[6] A household with a clear sense of mission can also clarify responsibilities and roles.

---

6. Pearcey, "Is Love Enough?"

A wife is more likely to respect a man who knows *where* he wants to lead her, not simply *that* he wants to lead her (1 Tim 6:11-12). After all, doesn't a wife's submission imply a prior mission?

The Father's Emotional Presence

A wise father can bring an emotional balance and relational stability to the household. He can balance out the mother's virtue with his own corresponding virtue. When they are functioning together in a healthy way, they have emotional range. A mother's strength at nurturing bonds of love and fellowship may lead her to strive for peace at all costs in order to maintain a pleasant and comfortable household. But this virtue can become a vulnerability, for example, if she has a young son who threatens to upend the peace of the family by throwing tantrums if he doesn't get his way. This boy needs firm correction, but a peace-loving mother may acquiesce to his demand, just to get him to calm down. She may be able to maintain a veneer of external pleasantness in the home, but this is achieved by appeasing a two-year old tyrant. She needs the balance of a loving father's firm discipline.

A single woman in my church had a sister with three children move in with her. She needed help with the kids and her sister was happy to help. When I asked her how things were going at home, she said having another adult manage the kids was helpful, but they still needed a man in the home to maintain order. This was an insightful statement. She was acknowledging that the household needed complementary balance, not merely a second adult. Children innately recognize and respond differently to masculine and feminine authority. Both are needed. Scripture recognizes this as well. In the Bible, the discipline of the home is typically the father's domain. The household needs the father to provide the household with justice through wise and appropriate discipline.

From the above example, the mother is terrorized by a young son who doesn't respect her authority. He exploits the vulnerabilities of her feminine nature and drives her to exasperation. This child needs a father's authority to back the mother's authority. His authority is different from hers, and children innately recognize the difference. She needs him to reinforce her authority with his authority. His discipline may cause discomfort for the child, but this discomfort is for the good of the child and the rest of the family. A child's tears may tug at the mother's sympathies until she relents, as would be expected from a mother. The strength of a father is the capacity for emotional distance, making him well suited to be impartial. A wise father can separate himself from the emotional field around him to settle disputes, discipline wrongdoing, and bring order and justice within his household. This isn't easy. It takes a degree of emotional detachment to bring the pain of discipline. Men can excel at this, provided they keep their strength under control. Certainly, fathers have their own vulnerabilities too. Scripture warns fathers to not be domineering, lest they exasperate others (Eph 6:4).

This same principle applies at the societal level also. Societies benefit when motherly virtues are balanced with fatherly virtues. For example, a society that lacks fatherly virtues can become "over-mothered." Over-mothered societies favor compassion at the expense of justice. The motherly virtues that make a society more compassionate and hospitable need to be balanced with the fatherly virtues that make a society more just.

Women Are. Men Become.

The journey of fatherhood begins in childhood and grows as boys reach puberty. As their bodies physically mature, the hearts and minds of boys need to mature along the same trajectory. They are becoming men, which means they are becoming potential fathers. Adam was not a father at first, but God created him with this potentiality. God prepared him for it by giving him a garden to tend (Gen 2:15), a command to obey (Gen 2:16-17), animals to name (Gen 2:19-20), and a wife to lead (Gen 2:21-25). Adam's preparation was a sort of masculine journey whereby he developed the skills he'd need to fulfill his vocation. Under the Lord's tutelage, Adam matured until he was ready to take on the massive responsibilities the Lord had in store for him.

In his book, *The Church Impotent*, Catholic scholar Leon Podles wrote about a "masculine journey" that all boys go through to become men. His theory of masculinity includes a relational pattern with femininity which moves from union, separation, and reunion with the feminine. Here's how it works. All children have a natural attachment to their mothers, but boys need to differentiate themselves from their mothers to become masculine. As their masculine identity develops, boys need masculine role models in their lives to teach them masculine virtue. Without a fatherly, masculine presence in a boys' life to shape his masculine identity, boys often look to other boys to define masculinity in competition with each other, or to their mothers who cannot properly teach manhood to them. A father's presence in a boy's life can show a maturing boy the proper way for a man to relate to a woman and lead his son to develop a healthy male-female relationship with his mother. Although this developmental process is not always obvious or linear, it is nonetheless an important aspect of becoming a man.

Podles explains it this way: "A boy is born of a woman and has an intense and close relationship with a woman for the first years of his life. At first the child is not even aware of his mother as a separate being. He gradually realizes that his mother is a separate being, a separate person. He then starts realizing that his mother differs from him in an extremely important respect: she is what he cannot and should not become—a woman. The boy must break this intense, close relationship with his mother to establish his separate identity… The boy cannot become masculine by imitating his mother; he must turn from her to other models, usually his father."[7]

It's not the same with girls, however. Girls do not need to differentiate themselves from their mothers. Pastor Bill Smith said, "transitioning into womanhood is effortless and clearly defined; womanhood is granted. When a female begins her menstrual cycle, she is considered to be a woman. Womanhood is defined by her natural biological progression. This is not to say that women have no responsibility at all to cultivate their womanhood. Women have the responsibility to add character to their physical attractiveness so that their beauty is more than skin deep (1 Pt 3.3-4). It is this character that will cause her husband to cherish her even when her physical attractiveness fades (Prov 31.30; 'beauty is vapor' not 'vain;' it appears for a time and vanishes away; see Jms 4.14; this is the 'everything is vapor' theme that Solomon picks up in Ecclesiastes). Womanhood is given, but it must be cultivated, developed, and maintained… Women don't have to achieve anything in the beginning to be attractive to a man or even to be a woman. They just pass right into it naturally, and everyone acknowledges it."

---

7. Leon Podles, "Missing Fathers of the Church," https://www.touchstonemag.com/archives/article.php?id=14-01-026-f&readtherest=true (Accessed July 22, 2022).

Pastor Smith summarizes this dynamic with this simple phrase: "*Women are. Men become.*"[8]

Boys do not become men by simply going through puberty. Manhood is not merely the result of the biological processes of maturation. It is cultivated through intentional action that is oriented towards the virtues of fatherhood. Historically, various cultures around the world bestowed manhood upon younger men by older men. This developmental process has been observed by both anthropologists and developmental psychologists who have studied masculinity. Typically, cultures pressure boys to mature into men by developing the strengths and skills they and their society needs them to have.

Podles explains, "[A boy] learns that at all costs he must become a man. A man has other responsibilities in life; he takes up the dangerous work of a society. He may work himself to death as a lawyer, or get shot in war, or anything in between. Even in the United States, men hold almost all the dangerous positions in our society, as measured by the chance of death or serious injury. Only after he earns his spurs as a man can the male reconnect to the world of women by marrying and becoming the father of a family. As a boy the male is protected and provided for; as a man he must protect and provide for others, even at the cost of his own life... This pattern is almost universal. Societies in general have... an ideology of masculinity. Boys all over the world are subject to initiations and trials to break their relationship with their mothers. Boys must learn to endure pain and suffer deprivation, so that they will undertake the dangerous... work that all societies have."[9]

---

8. Bill Smith, "Letters to Young Men: The Burden of Performance," https://kuyperian.com/letters-to-young-men-the-burden-of-performance/ (Accessed July 22, 2022).

9. Podles, "Missing Fathers."

The qualities boys need to become men will not develop naturally on their own. Rather, they must be instilled in them by an attentive father. In their early years, boys cling to their mothers who take care of them, provide for them, and give them loving support. But boys must learn to recognize that being over-mothered may threaten their own agency and limit the self-development they need to take care of others. Good fathers know that boys need to "toughen up" to take on grown man responsibilities. A boy's masculinity develops by differentiating himself, becoming more independent, and resisting his mother's nurturing impulse to keep him dependent on her. This differentiation is necessary for him to take on responsibilities for a future wife and children. In a way, his mother's nurturing virtues can be a hindrance to his masculine development. These motherly instincts are good in themselves but need to be counterbalanced by fatherly instincts that challenge him towards greater independence.

Although this process begins when boys are young, the need for them to resist the mothering instincts of women and of society must continue for the rest of his life. Virtuous men act like fathers. They do not look to others to provide for them, but they look to themselves to provide for others. Of course, there are exceptions. A disabled man is not a lesser man due to his disability, since the disability is beyond his control. I'm not talking about the various misfortunes that may cause men to become dependent on others for legitimate reasons. Besides, every man becomes more dependent as he grows older and physically weaker. What I am saying is that the virtue of masculine strength is oriented towards taking responsibility for others, which is something he must cultivate within himself.

Some societies have developed specific rituals to cultivate masculine strength and initiate boys into manhood. In these rituals, boys are only welcomed into the fellowship of men once they have proven themselves able and willing to confront the dangers of life. When societies lack these explicit rituals, such as modern western society, boys are left to determine for themselves whether or not they have yet passed the test and proven themselves men. In such cases, fathers are all the more important to confer upon boys a mature masculine identity.

Podles explains, "a boy must complete his masculine identity by identifying with a male, especially his father, whom he sees is loved by his mother. He must give up his desire to be his mother, and learn to love her, or at least to love another woman. But to love any woman as an adult the boy must first reject... being mothered - because her femininity is a trap that will lure him back into an infantile narcissism... Likewise, he must give up a desire to love the male erotically, as his mother does, and instead learn to be a full male, that is, a father."[10] Podles concludes, "A man must give up the state of boyhood, in which he is protected by women, fed by women, and cared for by women, so that he may become a protector and provider for women and children. In other words, he must give up being mothered before he can become a father. He must reject the feminine in himself, cultivating a distance from the world of women, so that he can one day return to it, not as a recipient, but a giver."[11]

In short, godly masculinity doesn't happen on its own. It needs to be cultivated in boys so they can learn the necessary skills to take on manly responsibilities. As indicated in the Creation Mandate, God created men to exercise dominion, and men do well to prepare themselves for it.

---

10. Leon J. Podles, *The Church Impotent: The Feminization of Christianity* (Dallas, TX: Spence Publishing Company, 2005), 43.

11. Podles, *The Church Impotent*, 41.

Simple Steps of Preparation

I've never been a great athlete. I played baseball and basketball as a kid, but I was only about average. Maybe that's too generous. I wasn't very good at all. I never stood out as an athlete. So, as I grew into adulthood, I didn't do much to exercise or stay physically fit. That all changed when my family doctor told me I was at a high risk for diabetes. That scared me, because I have several diabetic family members and I've seen how disruptive it was for them. I remember watching with strange fascination as my grandfather gave himself insulin shots in his stomach. He loved sugary food, but my grandmother wouldn't let him eat it. She always made him special food to manage his diabetes. But sometimes, he would sneak and eat a whole box of donuts. He died at age 64.

My doctor told me this news in 2013, when I was 39 years old. I had never exercised regularly before that, but this was a wakeup call for me. She told me the best thing to do in my situation was to change my diet, lose some weight, and get regular exercise. I was motivated, but not educated, so I took the nutrition class she recommended. There I learned healthier eating habits and made changes to my diet. I used an app to track my caloric intake. The hardest part, however, was exercise. My wife and I started waking up early six days per week to do 25 minute exercise DVDs together. Even in beginner mode, it was miserable. I hated every bit of it. I hated the aching of my joints and the soreness of my muscles. Many times, I found myself thinking, "I'm just not an 'exercise guy.' Why am I doing this? I can't keep going." But I found the motivation to keep pressing on until I saw results. I was losing weight, feeling better, and more energetic. By the time my 40th birthday rolled around, I had lost 40 pounds and was literally in the best physical condition of my life. Even better, my blood sugar returned to normal range. It worked. In the years since then, my wife and I have moved on from beginner DVDs and added weight training. I've been able to maintain a high level of fitness ever since.

Men at any stage of life can cultivate masculine strength, whether it be physical, emotional, mental, or spiritual. Suppose a young, single man is captivated by the high calling of the Creation Mandate, and the Lord burdens him to pursue it with a whole heart. Further, he makes it more specific. Ambitiously, he envisions his life 50 years into the future. He imagines a wife, children, and grandchildren who are committed Christian disciples. He even writes it down in his journal as a personal mission statement: "I hereby commit my life to build a Christ-like legacy for the glory of God." He begins praying for it. It's a wonderful aspiration, but it isn't quite actionable just yet because it lacks specificity. So, he begins to think of specific goals. He begins to prayerfully trust God for a larger family with four children or more. He begins to think about their children and their legacy. If each of his children were to have three children, he would have twelve grandchildren. He dreams about the godly impact that he, his wife, his four children, their spouses, and their twelve grandchildren could make. He commits all these things to prayer, asking God for a godly wife, many children, their future spouses, and their future grandchildren.

Certainly, he can't control all these things, but that's okay. A mission is something that inspires action in us and it will include things beyond our control. And yet, part of what it means to subdue the earth is to bring it under our control in a godly way. So as this young man dreams and prays about his mission, he can also take steps to orient his life towards fulfilling it while trusting God to bring it about. So, how might he order his life around this goal? What are the "costs" he should count in preparation for it (Luke 14:28-30)?

First, he can prepare himself by developing the character traits needed to lead a household on mission, such as strength, decisiveness, courage, skill, and wisdom. He needs to work towards becoming the sort of man that would be more worthy of his future wife's affection and submission. He can do this by committing himself to his local church, taking personal sanctification and growth in Christ seriously, repenting of sin, walking in spiritual disciplines, and developing his own convictions. A man who has developed these sorts of skills and knows what he wants to do with his life will more likely attract a woman who will join him and help him. Alistair Roberts wrote, "A man who can act with mastery, competence, assertion, confidence, honor, courage, strength, nerve, and the like—especially if he acts as a skilled possessor of a behavioral repertoire, which he can deploy with discrimination, discernment, and self-mastery—compels respect as a man. Such traits, well-exercised, are manifestly attractive to women."[12]

Second, he will need to marry a godly woman who will help him accomplish his mission. In other words, he needs not just a Christian woman, but one who is compatible and supportive of his goals. Third, he will need to earn a sufficient income to support a large family, but not one that not overly interferes with his other goals. For example, if possible, he would avoid careers than demand long hours and heavy travel schedules. Fourth, he and his wife will need to have children, train them in the Christian faith, and instill in them the value of leading productive households themselves. Perhaps they too will be inspired by their father's vision, continue his legacy, and pursue it in their own households. As an older man,

---

12. Alistair Roberts, "The Virtues of Dominion," https://theopolisinstitute.com/conversations/the-virtues-of-dominion/ (Accessed July 7, 2022).

he and his wife could make themselves available to their children and grandchildren to help raise the next generation in the Christian faith. Of course, good goals are attainable yet uncertain. Much of the uncertainty is overcome through a persistent ethic of hard work. Finally, he will need to instill in his household a sense of multigenerational legacy and identity. Even though the particulars will vary from one household to the next, this is the basic shape of God's design revealed in the Creation Mandate.

When I was a young boy, I was dissatisfied with how much playing time I was getting in little league baseball, so I wanted to quit. When I told my dad about this, he said something that I'll never forget. He said, "Clary's don't quit." The way he said it sounded like this was some ancient Clary tradition stretching back centuries. But it wasn't. It was simply something he valued that he wanted to instill in me. And that was all I needed. He gave meaning to my name. He told me that being a Clary meant more than getting called early when the teacher took the roll. Being a Clary was a tradition I inherited from him, part of a larger story that summoned particular virtues I would need to succeed in life. "I am a Clary, and Clarys don't quit."

As I have reflected on this over the years, something else dawned on me. My dad grew up without a father. He grew up in poverty with his mother and grandmother, getting some occasional fatherly instruction from a few uncles. Once his mother married and changed her name, he was the only one with the name "Clary." Like a weight suspended in mid-air, the name was not attached to any particular legacy. It was up to him to define it for his progeny. As his only son, it passed to me. Among other things, I learned to associate my name with perseverance because of an offhand remark dad once made to me. It isn't written in Latin on a family crest somewhere, I learned it in a teachable moment when I was discouraged. I have since told this story to my own sons, as I hope they will instill it in theirs. Clarys don't quit. A multigenerational legacy was born because a kid wanted to quit baseball. That's what fathers do. They give their sons a vision of a world that is bigger than them and call them to embody the virtues needed to meet the challenges they will face.

The Father's Leadership

Great leaders are like fathers to those they lead because great leadership is fatherly. Likewise, Christian leadership is a service, first to God, then to those being led. In the household, God delegates authority to the husband. His authority is not absolute, as it is derived. The husband is under God's authority, his wife is under his authority, and his children are under their authority. God holds the husband/father responsible for his household and God gives him the requisite authority to lead it properly. The leadership he provides is for their benefit. It's a service to them. He serves them by leading them. He may not abuse his authority by mistreating his wife or children. Rather, he must use his authority to build them up in love (Col 3:18-21).

In Ephesians 5, Paul likens a marriage to a body. The husband is the head of his wife. In verse 23 he adds, "the husband is the head of the wife even as Christ is the head of the church, his body, and is himself its Savior." The husband acts in a Christ-like way towards his wife, taking care of her the way he takes care of his own body. "Husbands should love their wives as their own bodies. He who loves his wife loves himself" (v. 28). It would be absurd for him to abuse his wife because, in a very real way, he would be abusing himself. "For no one ever hated his own flesh, but nourishes and cherishes it, just as Christ does the church, because we are members of his body" (vv. 29-30). The head and the body work together for mutual benefit, joined together by covenant, mutually supporting each other. The head directs the body, and the body supports the head. They need each other.

In 1 Peter 3, Peter tells wives to "be subject to your own husbands" (v. 1). He mentions Sarah's example, noting that she "obeyed Abraham, calling him lord. And you are her children, if you do good and do not fear anything that is frightening" (v. 6). Peter recognizes that it can be frightening for a wife to submit to her husband because he is a sinful man and she is a weaker vessel. This is why the next verse exhorts him to "live with your wives in an understanding way, showing honor to the woman as the weaker vessel" (v. 7). The husband should lead her in a way that demonstrates understanding of her desires, needs, and concerns, and in a way that honors and elevates her as an equal. A husband may abuse his God-given authority by not understanding his wife or showing her honor. Naturally, this possibility can cause her to "fear anything that is frightening." In other words, she is doubly vulnerable. She is a weaker vessel and she is under his authority. Therefore, he is responsible for creating a household environment that gives her the security she needs to thrive. Further, his headship implies a body that supports the head. He isn't a head in a jar. He is the head of a body, and he takes care of his body as if it were his own. That's how he treats his wife. A husband who doesn't lead with understanding or show proper honor can be frightening for a wife who is covenantally obligated to submit to him. Her duty is to trust God with her fears as Sarah did and submit to her husband, while his duty is to take his responsibility seriously and earnestly seek to honor God in his headship.

In the household, the husband serves his family by leading them. His leadership is first a service to God and then a service to his wife and children. He takes responsibility for their household priorities. He sets a direction and leads them on a mission. He makes decisions for God's glory and their good. He does not lead them in a domineering or controlling way because, like Christ, he is among them as one who serves. A godly husband doesn't lord his authority from on high, as though he is superior to everyone else. He may not be the smartest or even the godliest person in the household. His wife may exceed him in knowledge and holiness. That's common. He isn't called to be smarter or godlier than her. He is called to love her and *lead* her. Also, he listens to her. After all, God gave her to him to help him. What kind of leader would he be if he did not listen to his closest and most trusted advisor? He would be a fool to not listen to his wife or consider her desires and insights. Oftentimes, he will do what she says because she is a godly woman with wisdom to offer. But he is ultimately account-able to God for his leadership. He is a man under God's authority, and he will give an account to God. Leadership is his burden, no one else's, and he must carry it. She may help him carry it, but she cannot do it for him.

The Father's Strength

I once had a conversation with a pastor friend of mine about one of my church members who was neglecting his family. As I described the situation to my friend, he said this man was being effeminate. Surprised to hear this, I corrected him. I said, "He's not effeminate; he's an accomplished body builder!" In my mind, physical strength was masculine strength. But I was wrong. My pastor friend helped me see that body sculpting in a weight room does not make one masculine. In fact, in some cases, it may be the opposite. Some men, in pursuit of vanity, lift weights not for the sake of health, or for strength, but to make themselves attractive. This is not the same thing as masculine strength. Men make themselves strong so they can use their strength for the benefit of others.

Once I recognized this, I was able to see something I had missed. My bodybuilding friend had been deeply wounded by the fact that his alcoholic father abandoned him as a child. Lacking a good father's love, discipline, affection, and approval, his anger drove him to bodybuilding as a form of self-improvement, thinking this was what would make him a real man. But he was failing as a man to lead his home. The other pastor was right. Even though this man outwardly exhibited the strength of a man, he was weak in true masculine virtue.

Another man I knew was similar. He spent many hours each week in the weight room but otherwise had little ambition for his life. When a family from church was moving and needed help unloading their truck, I asked him to come help out, but he wouldn't do it. Easily, this man would have been stronger than anyone else who would have been there, but he was unwilling to use that strength for the benefit of others. Even though he was physically strong, he was a weak man. This became even more clear as it was later revealed that he was deep in the throes of a pornography addiction.

The world is an evil place, and God calls men to be strong in the power of the Spirit so they can subdue evil and overcome it with good (Rom 12:21). A man cannot conquer the evil in the world until he has conquered the evil in his own life. The name for conquering evil in one's own life is self-control. A man who lacks self-control can be his own greatest enemy because he has not yet exercised dominion over himself. He can be a champion in the weight room and still be a weak man. A weak man is his own greatest enemy. He will be of little value to the kingdom unless he slays his inner dragon. Psychologist Jordan Peterson once said, "It is more difficult to rule yourself than to rule a city."[13] Peterson is not a Christian, but this insight certainly is. Proverbs 25:28 says, "A man without self-control is like a city broken into and left without walls." Without self-control, a man's masculine strength will likely be directed towards wicked pursuits. This sort of masculinity is truly toxic. A man who wants to control everything and everyone around him but cannot control himself is a dangerous man. His strength is not constrained by virtue. He can't be virtuous because he cannot control himself. Strength unrestrained is weakness.

Self-control is a fruit of the Spirit (Gal 5:22) and is freely available to every Christian man who pursues it. It begins with an honest self-assessment of one's own life and need for growth. Romans 12:3 says, "For by the grace given to me I say to everyone among you not to think of himself more highly than he ought to think, but to think with sober judgment, each according to the measure of faith that God has assigned." Many young men, who have strong desires and physical strength, will find that their greatest challenge in life will be subduing their own bodies and wills so they can become instruments of righteousness. They must view this work of self-mastery as becoming a "living sacrifice" to the Lord (Rom 12:1). They must humbly surrender themselves to God in order to take on the challenges of their masculine duty.

The source of masculine strength is the Spirit, not the flesh. In 2 Corinthians 12:9-10, Paul records the words Jesus spoke to him

---

13. Jordan Peterson, 2017, "It's More Difficult to Rule Yourself than to Rule A City," YouTube, October 11, 2017, (Accessed February 13, 2023), https://www.youtube.com/watch?v=vyeik_iBKf4.

in a vision, where he said, "My grace is sufficient for you, for my power is made perfect in weakness." Paul goes on to say, "Therefore I will boast all the more gladly of my weaknesses, so that the power of Christ may rest upon me. For the sake of Christ, then, I am content with weaknesses, insults, hardships, persecutions, and calamities. For when I am weak, then I am strong." Men grow in Christian strength as they rely more fully on the Spirit, whose power in them grows with an increased recognition of their own innate weakness, frailty, and failure. Masculine strength is born out of the humble recognition that all men are weak apart from the strength of Christ. Though our masculinity is often marred by failure and disappointment, the Holy Spirit can strengthen men to succeed where Adam failed.

When Paul gives his exhortation to "act like men; be strong" (1 Cor 16:13), he grounds that masculine strength in Christian love. "Let everything you do be done in love" (1 Cor 16:14). A man loves differently than a woman. Women love primarily with their hearts. It's a more emotional kind of love. Masculine love is strong, full of conviction and resolve. Men love primarily with their strength. They do things for others. A man's love is most potent when he is relying on the strength of God working through him. "Be strong in the Lord and in the strength of his might" (Eph 6:10). Men are called to be "steadfast, immovable, always abounding in the work of the Lord, knowing that in the Lord your labor is not in vain" (1 Cor 15:58). This is how men love.

The Father's Gravity

A man who leads his household with clarity and strength develops a kind of gravity around him that pulls others into his orbit.

The ancient Romans spoke of a certain characteristic some men possess that encapsulated much of what masculinity was all about and what all men should acquire. They called it "gravitas," which is related to the word "gravity." Gravity is an invisible power that draws you in and holds you in its orbit.

Imagine a trampoline with a bowling ball in the middle. It weighs the trampoline down. If you add some marbles to the trampoline, they will roll towards the bowling ball. The heavier the ball, the lower it sinks, and the greater the pull. A man with gravitas draws attention because his presence has weight, like a natural authority that commands respect. Pastor C. R. Wiley said, "We've all known people that just can't be taken lightly. When one of these people enters a room you feel his presence, your eyes lower and so does your voice... Gravitas is for serious people. Serious people take things seriously and they expect you to too... [S]ome men have weight—and they naturally make others feel it... Gravitas starts with, 'who needs you?' And unless you can say it and really mean it, you have no gravitas."[14] A man with gravitas need not be morose or somber. He can give a hearty laugh or tell a good joke. A man who takes himself too seriously may not be taken seriously by others, because it is obvious that his self-seriousness is just his own insecurity.

The opposite of gravitas is levity. A man who lacks gravitas will not be taken as seriously. A marble by itself on the trampoline has no gravitas because it doesn't weigh very much. It does not draw other objects to itself. This is what it's like for a man who lacks gravitas. He has no weight. He lacks presence. Wiley continues, "Levity is humor; it lightens things up: it seems to make things levitate... But sometimes things get too light. Our time is

---

14. Wiley, *Man of the House*, 81.

characterized by a retreat into irony. Everyone wants to remain aloof, to float away from entangling commitments."[15]

In the household, a father's gravitas can hold his people together, like the earth holds the moon in orbit. Just as the earth orbits the sun, a man's own sense of purpose and direction is not his own, he is a man under the authority of Christ. He is an enlisted man, called into the service of his king, and he fulfills his duty. This sort of man can be counted on and the people in his life know it. The gravity of the sun holds him in place, and his own gravity holds them in place.

At the end of the Sermon on the Mount, Matthew records how the crowds responded to Jesus. It says, "when Jesus finished these sayings, the crowds were astonished at his teaching, for he was teaching them as one who had authority, and not as their scribes (Matt 7:28-29)." To put it another way, Jesus had *gravitas*, which astonished the crowds because they'd never seen anything like it before. At the same time, Jesus exposed his opponents as unserious men. They were lightweights. They had no gravitas. They had no authority. The world needs more men like Christ. Men who can be taken seriously. Men who carry themselves with weight and authority. Men who are fathers.

---

15. Wiley, *Man of the House*, 78.

CHAPTER 8

Blessed Motherhood

"Being a Mom is just as important as any career."[1]

ELON MUSK

"As you do not know the way the spirit comes to the bones in the womb of a woman with child, so you do not know the work of God who makes everything."

ECCLESIASTES 11:5

Introduction

On a recent plane ride from Orlando to Cincinnati, I had just enough time to rewatch "Saving Private Ryan" for what must have been the 10th time. "Saving Private Ryan" tells the story of a young man whose three brothers were killed in combat in WWII. Private Ryan was the only brother to survive D Day. When military

---

1. Elon Musk, "Being a Mom Is Just as Important as Any Career," Twitter, August 17, 2022, https://twitter.com/elonmusk/status/1559823434028400640.

officials realized this, they dispatched a special regiment of eight soldiers to track him down, somewhere in France, to retrieve him and bring him home.

Saving Private Ryan is a masculine movie. It's all about brotherhood, war, duty, honor. When I watched the movie this time, however, I noticed something I hadn't noticed before—*mothers*. Many of these young men, who were fighting for their lives on another continent, were thinking about their mothers back home. In a particularly disturbing scene, a soldier lies on a beach in Normandy, clutching his bloody stomach that had been blown open, crying out "mama!" while he died. The mission to save Private Ryan was deemed urgent because the military command wanted to spare his mother the overwhelming grief of losing her last remaining son. One scene depicts the awful moment just before she learned the news that she'd lost her other three sons. She is standing at the kitchen sink washing dishes as she notices a military vehicle approach. A man dressed in a military uniform exits the front passenger side of the vehicle, turns toward the back door of the car and opens it. A chaplain steps out. She knew immediately. She falls to her knees in grief, knowing that she'd lost one of her sons. Surely her mind is racing with questions. "Which son? How did he die?" But the audience knows the situation is much worse. She'd lost *three* of her sons in one day, and the fourth was still missing.

In another scene, one of the soldiers who was sent to find Private Ryan shares a childhood memory of his mother. She had come home late from work one evening after he'd gone to bed. She came into his room to say hello and kiss him goodnight, but he pretended to be asleep and didn't feel like talking at that moment. This decision haunted him. Knowing the reality of war, he realized she may never see him again, and he wished he could go back and give her that simple moment. With his eyes filled with tears as he told the story, he said, "I don't know why I did that." In the next scene, he gets shot by a German soldier. He lies on the ground, bleeding out and dying. As his friends desperately try to save his life, he says repeatedly, "I wanna go home! I want my mama! Mama!" And then he's gone.

These scenes in Saving Private Ryan show the power of motherhood. When strong, young men in war are in the throes of death, their hearts are naturally drawn to the safety, comfort, and love of home. They long for the woman who gave them life. Mothers embody everything they hope for in dangerous times. War is death. Motherhood is life.

The World's View of Motherhood

Many young women feel the need to suppress their maternal instincts because they've been culturally conditioned to devalue motherhood. They've grown up watching shows and hearing stories celebrating how girls can do anything boys can do. A friend once noticed a poster in a school highlighting girl's potential in a series of pictures associated with different careers. One was a doctor, another was a business executive, a third was an astronaut. Of all these images inspiring young girls about what they could become in life, none of them depicted mothers.

During a small group discussion with people from my church, one young woman sheepishly admitted that what she most wanted out of life was to be a wife and a mother. She was hesitant to acknowledge this, because she felt that this was somehow aiming below her potential, wasting her gifts, and settling for second best. All her life, she'd heard about how exciting a career can be, but she'd heard relatively little celebrating the fact that she can create and nurture new life. In pop culture, a girl getting pregnant is often seen as a problem. Pregnancy is depicted as a hurdle to overcome. But the testimony of scripture is that children are a blessing and motherhood is a glorious vocation (Ps 127:3-5). This is not to say that women should not get an education or have a job. This question will be addressed at the end of this chapter. For our purposes here, it's a matter of priority. Motherhood is highly valued in Scripture but devalued in modern culture. That's what this chapter is all about—the value of motherhood.

Motherhood has never been an easy calling ever since it came under the curse of sin (Gen 3:16). Nevertheless, throughout history, societies have always valued motherhood as a social good to preserve and nurture civilization. As the industrial revolution radically changed the household, some feminist thinkers began arguing that the traditional household was outdated, oppressive to women, and needed to be changed. It was holding women back, enslaving them to their husbands and children. But women could be liberated from this bondage by seeking careers outside the home the way men did. They assumed that women could be more free, more fulfilled, and more valued in the marketplace than in the home.

Carl Trueman noted that one of the original goals of feminism was to abolish motherhood as a vocation. For example, feminist thinker Friedrich Engels argued that the traditional family structure turned women into chattels, like pieces of property, and the only way to free them from this enslavement was to find employment away from the home. Other writers went even further than this, arguing that the family itself needed to be dismantled for the good of society. They asserted that the key to overturning the oppressive family structure was to dismantle marriage, separate sex from procreation, and promote sex as recreation. Feminist thinker Shulamith Firestone said, "the end goal of the feminist revolution must be, unlike that of the first feminist movement, not just the elimination of male privilege but of the sex distinction itself: genital differences between human beings would no longer matter culturally… The tyranny of the biological family would be broken."[2] Trueman concludes his survey of feminist literature in this way: "the sexual revolution ultimately has one great goal, the destruction of the family."[3] The feminist project has been largely successful, as is plain to see in modern society. It is now obvious that the family, and motherhood in particular, were major casualties of feminist thinking.

Even though most Christian women would quickly recognize the error of this thinking when expressed so vividly, the basic assumptions and desires of feminism can nevertheless seep into our unconscious minds, training us to devalue the vocation of motherhood. Women are being subtly conditioned to believe that the marketplace is immanently desirable—where they can find true happiness. Motherhood is a secondary endeavor if a woman chooses to succumb to her own biology. Homemaking should rarely be the top vocational choice, but perhaps it can be a respectable option in extreme cases. This thinking is ungodly. Nevertheless, the feminine nature has a way of asserting itself. It cannot be so easily denied. Women are naturally inclined to make homes. It is instinctive.

Spiritual Motherhood

As we have acknowledged already, women can embrace the vocation of motherhood with or without biological children of their own. The Lord does not guarantee that every woman will be blessed

---

2. Trueman, *Rise and Triumph*, 261.
3. Trueman, *Rise and Triumph*, 261.

with children. This can be a great trial for these women, as Scripture consistently attests. Nevertheless, every Christian woman can pursue the vocation of motherhood because women have a life-giving nature that transcends biological motherhood. Motherhood is at the core of her identity as a woman, and it develops into a maternal, Christian maturity that will be a blessing to others (Titus 2:3-5).

As an example, Amy is an unmarried woman in my church who has served faithfully through outreach, prayer, and children's ministry. Her sweet, feminine spirit has been a life-giving presence to me, as I've watched her take great steps of faith over the years. When her mother was dying of an illness, Amy became a mother to her, bringing her into her home and taking care of her all the way to the end. During our church's weekly video prayer calls, Amy is always there, praying for unbelieving family members. Amy is introverted and quiet, but I've seen her faith grow as she has boldly shared the gospel with them. Although Amy isn't married with children of her own, her motherly presence is a delight to all who know her.

I know of an older, single woman who works for a college ministry near Cincinnati. She is legendary for how she became a spiritual mother to hundreds of women. She has led countless people to Christ and discipled them during her many decades of ministry. Her spiritual family tree includes several branches of leaders and thousands of disciples. She is a spiritual matriarch who has impacted a generation of Christian women and men.

Mandy is a married mother of three in my church who has become a mother to some other boys in her neighborhood who do not have a mother present in their lives. Consequently, these boys have not learned how to relate to a woman properly. These boys have had behavior problems in school and seem to be headed for bigger problems later in life. Mandy saw their need for a mother, so she has welcomed them into her home, fed them meals, talked with them about Jesus, and given them an example of a healthy Christian home. The women in all these examples have demonstrated their maturity in Christ by becoming mothers to others. Their presence is life-giving, which is the heart of the feminine nature.

The Feminine Design

I have pastored many women through infertility struggles and have personally seen how devastating this trial can be. For these women, their missing motherhood can feel like a personal failure. One woman in my church suffered several consecutive miscarriages before eventually giving birth to four children. Marcus and Danielle came to me for counsel because they were told she could not conceive children. They were devastated and began to pursue adoption. But after beginning the process of adoption, God opened her womb (Gen 29:31; 30:22; Ps 127:3) and she conceived and gave birth. She went on to have two more children of her own.

Why is missing motherhood such an emotional weight for so many women? Because it's their design. Motherhood is the goal (or *telos*) of the feminine design. Women are physiologically oriented towards it. A woman's menstrual cycle is a monthly reminder that her womb was designed to bear life, and her breasts were designed to feed and nurture life. This astoundingly powerful ability to create life should be affirmed and celebrated, not minimized or dismissed.

The Scriptures present motherhood as one of the greatest blessings a woman could receive. Similarly, a barren womb was one of the greatest trials she could endure. Womanhood cannot be properly understood apart her potential for motherhood. It is the unique design of her body. When God created Eve, he was not merely solving a loneliness problem. God created Eve to be a "helper fit for him" (Gen 2:18). She alone was the answer to man's inability to fill the earth on his own. This is why Adam named her "Eve, because she was the mother of all living" (Gen 3:20). God gave him much more than a wife. He gave him a potential mother.

A common word Scripture uses to describe motherhood is "fruitfulness" (Gen 1:28). This word appears in the Bible over 200 times, covering a range of interrelated meanings from gardening to sexuality. Fruitfulness is multiplication. Just as the Garden of Eden was meant to grow, expand, and multiply to cover the earth, Eve was meant to be fruitful and grow, like a garden. Women are uniquely equipped to multiply and amplify things. A woman's body can take a single sperm from a man and knit together a new human being from it. Just as her name suggests, Eve truly did become the mother of all living, giving birth to the whole human race. This feminine ability goes beyond physical childbearing. Femininity represents the ability to expand what is received. As author Rebekah Merkle put it, "When God gave Eve to Adam, he was handing Adam an amplifier... Adam is the single acorn sitting on the driveway which, no matter how hard he tries, remains an acorn. Eve is the fertile soil which takes all the potential that resides in that acorn and turns it into a tree, which produces millions more acorns and millions more trees."[4]

In addition, women can function as mothers within society, who create culture by domesticating and beautifying things. Werner Neuer said, "The woman is the preserver and keeper of

---

4. Rebekah Merkle, *Eve in Exile and the Restoration of Femininity* (Canon Press, 2016), 25–26.

intellectual values, whereas she sees the man as the creator of culture who needs woman to receive his work…"[5] In other words, culture is a precious thing. Culture needs fathers to build it, and mothers to carry, protect, and nurture it. At the broadest level, culture itself is comprised of the individuals within it, and women can act as mothers within culture—protecting its people, nurturing its virtues, and promoting goodness and peace within it.

A few blocks away from my church's building is an old Roman Catholic church named after a thoroughly feminine saint from over 1,500 years ago. We don't have any direct written words or speeches from her. There are no recorded feats of physical strength or governmental accomplishments. What we do have is the testimony of lifelong, ceaseless prayers, pleadings with God for the souls of her son and her husband. They were recorded by the man who was made a Christian through those prayers and who became the most widely revered church father in Christian history. Monica, mother of Augustine, is considered a saint in highest regard by all Christian traditions because of what she accomplished as a Christian wife and a mother of unshakeable faith. Her sainthood is her motherly faith, and thus it is a most feminine and most glorious sainthood.

Throughout Augustine's young life, Monica prayed for the salvation of her son. After his conversion, Augustine reflected upon his mother's unceasing petitions for him. She persevered in prayer because she believed God would use her prayers for her boy's eternal good. She was strengthened in hope that "the child of those tears shall never perish." She died in peace and joy, enjoying the

---

5. Neuer, *Man and Woman*, 45.

fruit of her feminine faith. Monica blessed the world through her motherly faith.[6]

The Vocation of Motherhood

As we have already acknowledged, women are natural homemakers. Marriage is all about making a home, and wives will naturally devote themselves to it. The question is not whether she'll do it, but how much it will be her main priority. Every household will need its cabinets stocked with groceries, meals prepared, and laundry washed. Beyond this, the children will need to be fed, nurtured, clothed, disciplined, and educated. Typically, the mother is the one who takes care of these chores. She may do them all herself, or she may outsource some or all of them to others. For example, a well-trained and qualified nanny can be hired to come into the home and perform all these tasks. She may be a better cook, better housekeeper, and better teacher of the kids. This being the case, why not hire nannies to do as much as possible? Some families see this as the wisest option, since, after all, the nanny is the professional. She's the expert at managing a home. But homes need more than expertise; they need a mother's presence.

Nancy Pearcey observed a trend that began to emerge around childcare literature around the 1870's. She noticed that most of it was written by child study "experts" who were trained in psychology. This led to a professionalization of motherhood, which left ordinary mothers feeling ill-equipped to raise their own children because they lacked the sophisticated training of the experts. "Of course," Pearcey writes, "to treat mothering as a profession is

6. Augustine, *Confessions*, trans. R. S. Pine-Coffin (New York: Penguin Books, 1961), Book 9, Chapter 10.

eventually to invite the conclusion, let professionals do it. With the growth of early childhood education and the childcare industry in our own day, increasing numbers of parents seem to be reaching precisely that conclusion."[7] Motherhood cannot be professionalized. No matter how well trained someone is in early childhood psychology, there is no substitute for a mother's attention and love.

The temptation in the modern world is to separate biological motherhood from the vocation of homemaking. In other words, motherhood is simply the biological fact of bearing and nurturing a child, whereas homemaking is a list of disembodied chores that can be outsourced with little consequence. But since motherhood encompasses the whole domestic realm, motherhood cannot be so easily abstracted from homemaking. A homemaker doesn't merely do the domestic chores, she creates a loving environment for her people, serving her husband and the children that came from her body. This is not to say that the mother must do all the work, because that's not how households operate. It is good that modern tools have made household work easier. But at the same time, much of what makes a house a home is the fact that a mother is personally invested in the particulars. She's there. She's invested. She's making decisions.

My great grandmother taught my mother to sew when she was a little girl. It's a skill that she has been able to use her whole life. She'd go to the fabric store and choose fabrics, colors, and patterns she wanted, with matching thread, and bring them home to make clothes. When I was about four years old, she made my dad and me matching suits. I still have the suit. When my firstborn son was about the same age, he wore it too. My mom could have saved a lot of time and energy by just going to the store and picking out

---

7. Pearcey, "Is Love Enough?"

two suits for my dad and me to wear, but it wouldn't have meant anything to us. It would just be clothes. But my mother *made* these suits, and in so doing, she created something that has lasted in my memory for decades. I don't remember any other stitch of clothing from my childhood, but I remember that suit.

As my mom has gotten older, she stopped making clothes, but she kept her skills sharp with quilting. One year for Christmas, she gave each of her three children a quilt that she had made. I wasn't expecting that. She had spent several months working on them, practically night and day. They were intricately detailed, stitched by hand, and incredibly beautiful. She later shared with me a picture of her sitting on a couch between her mother and grandmother. Three generations of mothers, sitting together, each with a quilt on their laps and a needle and thread in their hands. The quilt my mother gave me was not just a fancy blanket. It was a treasure because it was a labor of love. I wouldn't trade that quilt for anything.

I've eaten lots of Thanksgiving meals with my family, but one year stands out from the rest. The family gathered at my younger sister's little farmhouse. It was practically falling apart. It was small, old, and poorly built. My sister and her husband were learning to raise crops and farm animals, so they wanted to slaughter and prepare the turkey at home that year. They did, and it was terrible. We all thought so. The meat was dry, gamey, and tasted horrible. The grownups didn't say anything out of respect for their work, but children lack such tact. My kids openly complained while my wife and I tried to keep them quiet. I've eaten Thanksgiving turkey every year of my life and don't remember much about any of them. But I do remember this one. This was easily the worst Thanksgiving turkey I'd ever had. And it was also my favorite because my sister made it, and I adore her. Homes don't need expertise. They need presence. Even the imperfections are *her* imperfections. (For the record, my sister is a wonderful cook!)

While much work of the home can be outsourced, or simplified by modern technologies, the mother's presence is the one thing that can never be outsourced or replaced. She is the home. A woman is replaceable in any other area of life, but she is irreplaceable in her home. It's her domain. She animates it with her presence. A home bereft of a mother's presence can quickly become merely a house people live in.

The vocation of motherhood is an embodied reality. It cannot be reduced to a set of household chores. It is a way of being that most fully represents her life-giving feminine nature. Further, the homeward orientation of women is not an imposition of a patriarchal society, but rather a design feature of her own body. For example, when a woman conceives a child, her own body immediately becomes a home. During gestation, the child cannot survive apart from the sustenance of her body. He and his mother are one. At this stage, "mother" and "home" are the same thing. When he is born into the world, "home" is wherever mother is. He is comforted in her arms and nourished at her breast. A baby in the earliest developmental stages cannot distinguish himself from her. The recognition that he is a distinct person apart from his mother is a process that develops slowly over time.

A house is not the same thing as a home. Your address is where your house is, but your home is where your people are. You may live in many houses during your lifetime, but it's the people living with you that make them homes. For most people as they grow up and move away, "home" is uniquely associated with mother. Just as God originally designed her body to be a home to create and nourish new life, she continues to embody the meaning of home.

Home is not a place where everything is perfect, it's simply where mother is. My own parents divorced when I was seven years old, and my mother married a man who became cruel and abusive. Even though my father lived just a few miles down the road, I didn't live with him. My friends at school would ask me, "why don't you just go live with your dad?" The answer was simple: I want to be with my mom. Home is where mom is. I wanted to be home with her, even if a cruel stepfather came with the deal.

As a wife becomes a mother, she is like a human tree of life, bearing fruit within her own body and bringing life into the world. Giving life is her defining function, not only in bearing children, but in her life-giving presence wherever she goes. For these reasons, the home is the mother's primary domain. She is the life-giving heart of the household. This is why most people love a "home cooked" meal. A home cooked meal is special not only because of the people it is enjoyed with, but often because it was prepared by a loving mother.

Of course, a mother cannot do everything, nor should she work alone. Homemaking is a cooperative project pursued by the husband and wife together. A well-managed household will maximize the mother's presence with her people. For example, machines that streamline household chores such as dishes and laundry are truly blessed gifts to enjoy because they can help maximize her presence with her people. She is involved. She knows what's going on with her children. She knows their friends and their interests. Even though the father is head over his household, the home is the mother's domain more than anywhere else. In many domestic issues, it is good for a husband to defer to his wife because she is living out her God-given duty to rule as queen over her domain. A mother's presence is at its life-giving peak when she is fully available to her people, especially her children. A mother's absence from the home carries a great cost.

Mommy Economics

In modern society, Christians need to reclaim a Christian vision of the household. Few would challenge the idea that men should work to provide for their households. The more pressing question is about the value of a mother's work. This is a unique challenge in the modern world because we have grown accustomed to assigning value in terms of dollars. Alistair Roberts writes, "Many of the 'sacrifices' of motherhood appear more like costs unjustly imposed, costs that enable their husbands and children to achieve their full potential in the market, but which hold mothers back from achieving their own."[8] In other words, a mother's labor defies measurement. It can't be quantified in terms of dollars and cents. Modern society often tries to quantify the value of the mother's work in monetary terms, which obscures the eternal value of her work. The value of her work is incalculable.

For example, consider a restaurant that pays an employee minimum wage to prepare food. Thus, it is assumed, preparing meals is low-value work. What then could be said of a mother who prepares a meal for her family? Would we say that she is doing "low-value" work? Of course not. But if we try to measure the value of the mother's work by the income earned from similar work in the marketplace, she will be grossly undervalued. Her work may seem like an unfair imposition upon her, burdening her, holding her down, squandering her talents, and preventing her from fulfilling

---

8. Alastair Roberts, "The Revolutionary Work of Motherhood," https://alastairad-versaria.com/2017/05/15/the-revolutionary-work-of-motherhood/ (Accessed July 22, 2022).

her potential. The mother's work cannot be separated from her presence. She is not merely "making sandwiches," which is a task someone of lesser skill and competence could do for her just as easily. She is personally invested in the health and nourishment of her children. She is amplifying her world, subduing her domain by creating something unique that is hers for the people she loves. She is driven by a maternal impulse to love those she is covenantally bound to.

A mother cannot fully outsource her responsibilities. Just as her body was the site where her motherhood began, the home around her is an extension of her presence, where she expresses her womanly agency and power according to her skills, preferences, and desires. Motherhood "resists the logic of abstraction and alienation."[9] It cannot be reduced to a list of domestic chores and outsourced to "the experts." In the marketplace, all work correlates to some financial value. Motherhood, however, cannot be depersonalized and commodified in such a way. The labor is love, valued with eternal treasure. The work of motherhood might seem mundane at times, but her work need not be exciting to be glorious (1 Cor 10:31). God is glorified as her faith transforms her effort into something eternal. Not only this, but her children benefit from her attention and presence more than anyone else. In the biblical vision, the mother is a bonding agent that pulls people together. A mother's transformative presence in her home is unparalleled.

Working Mothers

Let's face it. Managing a household with children is a full-time job, especially when they're young. It also isn't cheap. It takes

---

9. Roberts, "The Revolutionary Work of Motherhood."

money and time, which are limited and valuable resources, to raise a family. Lower income mothers need to balance the competing desires of doing what's best for their children and having enough money to survive. For a single, Christian mom, her income is all she and her children have to live on. Since the Scriptures also teach the homeward priority of mothers, these mothers may feel torn between competing priorities. She may strongly wish to be at home with her children, but she has no alternative but to go to work. This burdens her with "mommy guilt" because she can't be in two places at once.

The Scriptures assume all Christian men and women are called to work (2 Thess 3:6-12) within their own respective domains. Obviously, motherhood is physically and emotionally demanding. In a perfect world, her husband will earn enough income to provide for the whole household, freeing the mother to focus on her work at home. But we do not live in a perfect world. Nor do we live in a preindustrial world. This complicates matters.

In the ancient world, almost every woman was expected to marry and bear children. Ancient women did not usually have "careers" as they do today. In the modern world, however, women have pretty much the same career options as men. Additionally, many families simply cannot survive on the father's income alone, so they have no other option but for the mother to go to work.

Nevertheless, some Christians argue that God requires every mother to be a stay-at-home mother, usually citing Paul's teaching that women should be "working at home" (Titus 2:5). But this does not sufficiently account for the contextual differences between the ancient world and modern world. When Paul says in Titus 2:5 that older women should train the younger women to be "working at home," he is prohibiting laziness by promoting industriousness. There is no command prohibiting a mother from working outside the home, though home should nonetheless be her first priority.

The label "stay-at-home mom" is a relatively new designation, popularized during the industrial revolution, to describe an emerging class of women who chose to forego the career opportunities many other mothers were pursuing.[10] Before the industrial revolution, nearly every mother worked from home. After the industrial revolution, some women pursued careers while others were "stay-at-home moms." Regardless, whether a mother works a job outside the home or not, *the home is still her primary domain*. It is the God-appointed place of her dominion, alongside her husband.

In my view, the husband is responsible to free his wife to prioritize her home. This involves two significant commitments. First, he does everything in his power to earn enough money to provide for his household. Second, he and his wife work together to build a lifestyle around his income rather than dual incomes. In other words, they strive to maximize his income potential while minimizing household expenses. Someone might raise an objection and say that this is a middle-class luxury that many families cannot afford. I acknowledge that this may indeed be the case with some poorer families, not to mention single mothers who need to be breadwinners. Nevertheless, it is also possible that we've grown too accustomed to the comforts and conveniences of a dual-income lifestyle. The modern economy favors two income households, so a typical household living on a single income will require some sacrifices. But when a husband and wife are on the same page, they can agree to forego the advantages of a dual-income lifestyle for the sake of the household they are building together.

---

10. Katy Steinmetz, "'Stay-At-Home Mothers:' Why We Still Use This Clunky, Outdated Term," *Time* (April 11, 2014), https://time.com/59807/stay-at-home-mothers/.

Ultimately, however, whether or not a mother works outside the home is a matter of conscience (Rom 14:1-5). Some mothers have no choice but to work outside the home to make ends meet. Many Christian mothers would love to be full-time homemakers but it's not a realistic option for them financially. This is delicate tightrope to walk. The benefits of stay-at-home motherhood are easy to demonstrate, yet I cannot deny that this ideal is out of reach for many faithful, Christian mothers. As a pastor, I offer this simple counsel: households should prioritize the mother staying home with her children as much as possible, especially when they are very young. But if this is not possible, it is not a sin. It is a sin, however, for a mother to neglect her household because she's pursuing personal fulfillment in a career or working to have a more lavish lifestyle.

Households should consider what's best for them with prayer, the wisdom of Scripture, and the guidance of the Holy Spirit. When praying about whether a mother should work outside the home, there are two key factors to consider. First, consider the timing and the impact on the children. Full-time employment is now the norm for mothers in the United States, with about 75% returning to work within the first year of a child's life. Since the typical maternity leave is about four to six weeks, many of these mothers return to work while the child is still an infant, leaving the child in daycare centers, with nannies, or with family members.[11] According to several studies, the child's cognitive and behavioral functions were negatively impacted when the mother returned to full-time employment during the first year of the child's life. The most noticeable impact on childhood development became

---

11. David Pelcovitz, "The Impact of Working Mothers on Child Development," OU Life (January 3, 2013), https://www.ou.org/life/parenting/impact-working-mothers-child-development-empirical-research-david-pelcovitz/.

evident as the child reached the first grade. The first year of a child's life is particularly significant for his or her development, and the long term value of the mother's constant presence and loving interaction with the child is incalculable. Working mothers who participated in these studies acknowledged that they were often too tired to interact with their children or help them with activities after working all day.[12] Therefore, since the earliest years of a child's life are so formative, mothers should try to delay returning to work as long as possible.

The second factor to consider is the ratio of the mother's income potential to childcare expenses. In other words, a working mother's income would need to substantially exceed the costs of childcare to offset the costs of returning to work. Part-time work may be a good option for a mother to supplement her husband's income without overly depriving her children of her presence. In some cases, an employer may offer a remote work option that could enable a mother to be present at home with her children. Practically, I recommend this as a rule of thumb for families with young children: *mothers should work outside the home only as much as her income is needed for the family to be financially secure.* The more a mother can be present with her children, particularly in the early years, the better their overall development.

Preparing for Motherhood

With the modern world's devaluing of motherhood, it falls to the church to continue upholding the priority of motherhood for Christian women. Our society celebrates what women accomplish

---

12. Tracey Reynolds, Claire Callender, and Rosalind Edwards, *Caring and Counting: The Impact of Mothers' Employment on Family Relationships* (Bristol, England: Policy Press, 2003).

in their careers more than what they accomplish as mothers. Pop culture promotes the idea that society is better off when mothers have careers and leave the childrearing up to "the experts." These cultural messages shape our social imagination more powerfully than we realize. Through TV shows, books, movies, commercials, social media, and just about any other kind of media we can imagine, the world shapes how young women perceive their purpose in life and their value as women. From their youth, girls are conditioned to find their value in the marketplace, though she has to deny her maternal instincts in the process. They learn to seek affirmation in just about anything *except* motherhood. Motherhood is regarded as an incidental feature of womanhood, perhaps an optional add-on to a life where fulfillment is found elsewhere. In such an environment, a career feels more important than changing diapers and singing nursery rhymes. The sacrifices of motherhood cannot compete with the perceived fulfillment of an exciting career. All this stands against the eternal testimony of Scripture, which regards motherhood as a higher, more noble, and more glorious calling.

I recently attended a high school ceremony recognizing inductees to the National Honor Society. As each student crossed the stage, the announcer mentioned the student's name, expected destination for college, and career aspirations. Most of these students were girls, and nearly all of them were planning to enter demanding fields that will require long hours to succeed. Motherhood was not mentioned. None of these young women saw it as a worthy place to utilize their gifts. But why would they unless the culture-shaping institutions that form their hearts uphold it? Most likely, few of them have given much thought to motherhood at all. Motherhood is an abstraction, something that may or may not happen one day in a future she cannot entirely control.

Her preparation for the future is almost entirely oriented around a future career, not her future children. For many of them, they will spend their twenties preparing for and entering a career that will demand the best of their thirties.

The church is the best place to tell women a different story. Melissa is a young, married woman in my church who manages a multi-million-dollar budget for a prominent company in Cincinnati. She is a high-achieving woman with extraordinary talent and intellect. She was quickly climbing the corporate ladder, fast tracking her way to an executive suite. But everything changed when Melissa became a mother. She was surprised by how much holding an infant in her arms changed her. Her maternal instincts activated. Her priorities realigned. At this point, all she wanted was to take care of her daughter. She told me that once she became a mother, all she could think about was singing songs to her and being with her. Shortly thereafter, when her second child was born, she could no longer resist the impulse to stay home with her children. Against her employer's pleas for her to stay, she walked away from it all to focus her energies on her home where she was irreplaceable.

One of the best things pastors and churches can do is to help young women prepare for motherhood before they become mothers. This is what happened with Drew and Ellen, a couple in my church that came to me for premarital counseling. In one of our sessions, we talked about their future and how they would prepare themselves. Ellen, being very successful in her field, was making far more money than Drew was. She was obviously very confident and capable. She had the characteristics any employer would want. So I asked her what she wanted. What did she hope for in marriage? In life? Given the successful career she'd built for herself, I was surprised by her answer.

Some years prior, her parents had been profiled in the *New York Times* Weekend Edition. Her dad and mom represented "the changing landscape of America's workforce." Her father had lost his job when his company downsized just about the same time her mother's career was beginning to blossom. She became the breadwinner, and her father struggled to adjust. After telling me this story of her parents, Ellen said, "I don't want that to be my life." "Well, what do you want?," I asked her. She said what she most wanted was to be a wife and mother. I caught Drew's eye at that moment. It seemed he was surprised by her answer as well. She was somewhat hesitant, perhaps even embarrassed, to admit that this was her true ambition. Drew was delighted, because her desire summoned in him a sense of his duty as her future husband. If this is what she wanted, he would do everything within his power to give it to her. Within a few months, he'd found a different job with higher pay, and they committed to build their lifestyle around his income. It doesn't always work out this way, but I'm glad it did in this case. They now have two children that she happily raises from her home.

When we began having children, my wife and I decided that she would work from home to raise them. She's given birth to a total of four children, and we haven't regretted our decision for a moment. When our youngest child approached school age, we began to explore options for her to find part-time work. As a registered nurse, she has a marketable skill that is always in demand. Since we'd built a lifestyle around my income, we were able to turn down job opportunities that would have negatively impacted our home. Eventually, however, a great opportunity came up that suited us perfectly. Our church supports a Christian pregnancy resource center a half-mile from our house, and they were looking for a ministry minded nurse that could perform ultrasounds on pregnant mothers. She was a great fit for the job. We arranged her schedule to work two days a week, only during school hours. This was right in the sweet spot for us. Ever since then, she's been able to use her gifts of mercy to serve people in need while generating extra income for our family. And she's done all of this without overly depriving our household of her presence.

Conclusion

As I said before, we do not live in a perfect world. Every household will make decisions based on their life circumstances, and Christians should avoid being overly prescriptive about these matters. God is honored when Christians prayerfully consider how to best pursue their God given priorities. Even though motherhood is diminished in the world, the church can uphold its glory and dignity. In Titus 2, Paul calls on the older women of the church to be the champions of motherhood and homemaking for the younger women—"Older women likewise are to be reverent in behavior, not slanderers or slaves to much wine. They are to teach what is good, and so train the young women to love their husbands and children, to be self-controlled, pure, working at home, kind, and submissive to their own husbands, that the word of God may not be reviled" (Titus 2:3-5). Don't miss that last line, "that the word of God may not be reviled." Women who highly esteem motherhood and homemaking are upholding the Word of God. With their lives, they are proclaiming a countercultural message that says, "God's word is true. Motherhood is glorious."

CHAPTER 9

Singleness in the Modern World

"Let no man rashly despise marriage as a thing useless or superfluous to him; let no man long for celibacy unless he is able to dispense with the married state." [1]

JOHN CALVIN

"Only let each person lead the life that the Lord has assigned to him, and to which God has called him."

1 CORINTHIANS 7:17

Introduction

Societies that hold marriage in high regard are more likely to flourish than those that don't. Marriage binds people together. Why else would we call it "tying the knot?" Further, having children anchors

---

1. John Calvin, *Institutes of the Christian Religion* (Bellingham, WA: Logos Bible Software, 1997), Vol II, viii, 43.

people to a community that can support raising them. Marriage is a gift of God's common grace. Nearly every culture from the dawn of man has valued, protected, and promoted it as a social good. The stability of marriage lies in its permanence, as God joins man and woman together in what was originally designed to be an unbreakable covenant union (Matt 19:6). A stable marriage is the optimal environment for raising healthy children. This is where children can observe living examples of manhood, womanhood, and how the sexes relate. It is perilous to deprive our society of this fundamental good. And yet, that is what is happening.

In our day, marriage has a public relations problem. Certainly, in a fallen world, the intimacy and privacy of marriage is often exploited to enable some of the vilest evil humans are capable of. As people hear stories of abuse, infidelity, cruelty, and divorce, one could easily conclude that marriage itself is the problem. Instead of regarding marriage as a good gift to be pursued by most people, it is regarded as a high-risk, high-reward scenario. Only a lucky few will find themselves happily married. Everyone else is consigned to marital misery. As a result, marriage has been devalued in our society and fewer people are choosing it.

The CDC reports that in the year 2000 the marriage rate was 8.2 marriages per 1000 people. That number decreased steadily over the next 20 years to 5.1 by the year 2020.[2] Unmarried cohabitations increased during that time, but cohabitations are less stable than marriages because there is no covenant that binds them together. The rise of easy divorce doesn't help either. The divorce industry is booming. The report continues, "the probability of a first marriage ending in separation or divorce within 5 years is 20

---

2. "Provisional Number of Marriages and Marriage Rate: United States, 2000-2020 Year Marriages Population Rate per 1,000 Total Population," https://www.cdc.gov/nchs/data/dvs/national-marriage-divorce-rates-00-20.pdf (Accessed July 7, 2022).

percent, but the probability of a premarital cohabitation breaking up within 5 years is 49 percent. After 10 years, the probability of a first marriage ending is 33 percent, compared with 62 percent for cohabitations."[3] In 2020, the total number of marriages recorded was the lowest it had been since 1963.[4]

The two most prominent factors indicating successful marriages were spouses that came from intact homes and religious involvement. Without a doubt, the Supreme Court's 2015 *Obergefell* decision legalizing gay marriage undermined it by redefining it entirely. With marriage devalued, weakened, and redefined, it's not surprising that many people have decided that long-term singleness is the way to go, a choice aided by a promiscuous hookup culture.

The Christian Messaging of Marriage and Singleness

These trends have made their way into the church. There has been an increase in Christian articles, blogs, podcasts, and books addressing singleness. From a business standpoint, it's a growing market. At the same time, there's also a bizarre trend of speaking of marriage and motherhood as "idols."[5] While it is certainly possible for Christians to idolize family life, it could hardly be said that this is a significant problem in the modern church. In a post-familial age of declining marriage rates, plummeting birth rates, rising median marriage rates, it's astonishingly tone deaf that Christian

---

3. "NCHS Pressroom - 2002 News Release - Trends in Marriage and Divorce," https://www.cdc.gov/nchs/pressroom/02news/div_mar_cohab.htm (Accessed July 22, 2022).

4. "States Where Marriage Rates Plummeted During the Pandemic," https://www.usnews.com/news/best-states/articles/2022-05-18/states-with-the-biggest-drop-in-marriage-rates-in-2020 (Accessed July 8, 2022).

5. Jen Oshman, "When Marriage and Motherhood Become Idols," Crossway, August 1, 2022, https://www.crossway.org/articles/when-marriage-and-motherhood-become-idols/. This article is merely one example among many that use the language of "idolatry" to refer to family life.

media outlets would warn against the potential idols of the family in order to affirm singleness. I suspect this is because singleness is a touchy subject, and publishers do not want to alienate this growing demographic. As a pastor, I, too feel the discomfort of bringing up the subject. I do not wish to communicate to the single members of my church that they are "lesser than" or undesirable because they're single. And yet, it's a necessary subject to address because I'm unwilling to mortgage the potential blessing of family life for my people in the future to avoid an unpleasant topic in the present.

The simple fact is this: Christians are delaying marriage later and later into adulthood, while many others have made the intentional choice to remain single indefinitely. This shift has fueled the need to speak directly to singles as a growing demographic within the church. Single Christians often feel alienated in their churches, especially as they get older, as their friends get married and start families. Beyond this, finding a suitable Christian spouse can be a great challenge, filled with potential rejection and pain. This experience can be heightened if one comes from a broken or abusive home. Marriage can seem like taking a great risk. Other Christian singles may struggle with homosexual desires and conclude that marriage is not a viable option for them.

Some churches needlessly obscure the real challenges of marriage, leaving newly married couples unprepared for the sanctifying difficulties they will face. Other churches have the opposite tendency. The painful difficulties of marriage steal all the headlines, and the beauty, glory, and joy of marriage is obscured. These churches do not present a positive vision of married life that would make it appear desirable enough to aspire to it. In these cases, singleness is often promoted as superior to marriage. One writer observed that some American pastors paint a bleak, "anti-marriage" picture of marriage.[6] He cites several examples of well-known pastors and authors telling marital horror stories that make people think twice before considering marriage. In response to this, one man commented, "I have personally never heard a positive, public exhortation to the young to pursue marriage, in any church or college ministry, ever."[7]

Overall, Scripture celebrates marriage as a great gift and blessing that pictures the gospel. And it's important for churches to give a balanced message, acknowledging the pain and challenges of marriage that accompany the blessings. But with all the negative messaging surrounding marriage, some have concluded that singleness is just as good. Maybe even better. If singleness isn't a sin, then why get married?

The logic of this thinking goes like this: First, there is no biblical command to get married. Marriage is a gift for those who receive it. Second, getting married involves factors beyond one's control. It doesn't "just happen" to people, but one must be open and willing to pursue or be pursued by a potential spouse. Third, Scripture acknowledges that marriage can be a potential distraction from the things of God. Paul said, "the married man is anxious about worldly things, how to please his wife, and his interests are divided. And the unmarried or betrothed woman is anxious about the things of the Lord, how to be holy in body and spirit. But the married woman is anxious about worldly things, how to please her husband" (1 Cor 7:33-34). Based on this text, some have suggested that being single is the spiritually superior choice. Besides,

---

6. Aaron M. Renn, "Newsletter #28: The Anti-Marriage Message of American Pastors," December 12, 2018. https://aaronrenn.substack.com/p/newsletter-28-the-anti-marriage-message?s=w.

7. Monte Fischer, "I Have Personally Never Heard a Positive, Public Exhortation to the Young to Pursue Marriage, in Any Church or College Ministry, Ever," https://twitter.com/themontefischer/status/1535676825241722881 (Accessed June 11, 2022).

the Apostle Paul was unmarried. He devoted his life to service in the kingdom of God. He said, "he who marries his betrothed does well, and he who refrains from marriage will do even better" (1 Cor 7:38). Jesus himself was not married in the earthly sense, though Christ does have a bride, the church. Fourth, marriage can be risky. Some marriages are simply so horrible that both spouses wish they had never gotten married.

In most cases, those who uphold singleness as a blessing that is equal to marriage do a disservice to singles. They often have an overly idealistic view of the church as a suitable replacement for the natural family. But it's not. The church cannot replace the natural family. It wasn't meant to. The church can relieve the sense of loneliness for singles, but not the same way a natural family can.

I have personally encountered several instances of "communal living," where a small group of Christians try to live life together the way a family would. Some of these groups have even tried sharing a common purse, citing Acts 2:42-47 as their model. These communities are often unhealthy, dysfunctional, highly controlling, and rely on heavy handed leadership. The individual relationships in these communities do not have a natural glue that holds them together the way families do. These communities do not hold together very well, because there is no divine order or particular logic to them. Households, on the other hand, are internally ordered towards a divine purpose. God ordered the natural family with father, mother, brothers, and sisters—blood relations—living and working together. The natural family also has a built-in authority structure that gives it cohesion. All family members have a shared ancestry that binds them together with cords not easily broken. This underlying structure holds people in its grips much more powerfully than voluntary church commitments. The structure, when working properly, is designed to promote health and flourishing amongst all its members. Communal living arrangements, on the other hand, lack a cohesive structure. As a result, they are less stable. For better or worse, natural families are more invested in one another because they share a common history and common blood. Christian communal arrangements have no such cohesion. You can always find another church down the street.

Historically speaking, singleness, as it is experienced in the modern world, is a novelty. I moved out of my parent's house when I was 18 years old and lived the next several years as a single man until I got married. This is the expectation in the modern world: men and women leave their parents' house and go live on their own somewhere when they reach adulthood. This was unheard of in the ancient world, where the household was the context of one's entire life. You were born into a household, you lived your life in a household, you married into a household, or you were given in marriage to another household (Gen 2:24). The household was where everyone derived their deepest sense of belonging. But there would never have been a time when someone was disconnected from household life. If they were, it was a crisis, because people without households were extremely vulnerable. The potential loneliness of modern singleness cannot be fully removed by church life.

A church is a meta-household, built upon the strength of the individual households that comprise it. Most churches have a number of prominent families whose commitment sustains and stabilizes the whole church. Singles participate in church life by working alongside existing households, but a church comprised entirely of singles in inherently less stable. Households are a stabilizing force that anchors people in a community, and the church is built upon the natural strength of believing households. Churches would do well to not only provide pathways for single Christians to belong to the church itself, but also for singles to more fully integrate into healthy and strong households within the church.

Being an urban church close to a major university, my church has always had a number of singles. Over the years, I've seen first-hand the many challenges they face as Christian men and women who truly want to honor God with their lives. Most of them want to be married and establish households of their own, but they need to find a suitable partner first. Changes in our culture have affected the landscape of dating and marriage for Christians, making it complicated. In some ways, internet-based dating services can help Christians meet one another. This is becoming more and more common, if not the most common way Christians meet dating partners in my context. But it's still a challenge. Although many of them meet the right person and get married, some of them may not, which is a great trial for them.

Compassionately Upholding Family Life

For the remainder of this chapter, I want to make the simple case that the majority of Christians should reasonably pursue marriage and avoid prolonged singleness. Further, for those who desire marriage, have reasonably pursued it, but remain single, their singleness should not be considered a special calling from God, but a trial to faithfully endure. Before I proceed, I want to make one thing especially clear. Some people who sincerely desire marriage and family experience their singleness as some sort of personal failure. I am not saying that singleness is wrong or sinful. Everyone is born single. It's a life stage that everyone experiences, and one cannot fully control his or her marital options. From my experience, most single Christians very much want to be married but circumstances have prevented them from doing so. Their hearts are obedient, but they have not found the right mate yet. As time goes on, the pain grows, along with the fear of never getting married. They may perhaps feel shame that is only exacerbated by well-meaning friends and family who play matchmaker without permission. Single men and women in the church need the continual reassurance of God's love and grace, to know that they are wanted and valued, and to feel that they belong and have a meaningful place in the body of Christ.

In addition, the church would do well to uphold the value of marriage and family in a culture that no longer does. Marriage, with all its challenges, is upheld in Scripture as the norm for believers. Proverbs 18:22 says, "He who finds a wife finds a good thing and obtains favor from the Lord." In Scripture, God's people are continually pointed to the value of marriage, children, and household life.

What About Paul's Singleness?

With the ascendency of prolonged singleness in our modern culture, it is unsurprising that modern Christians regard Paul's unmarried state with a kind of mystical fascination, as though desiring marriage is driven by little more than a carnal desire for sex. But Paul's view is not so simple. His most extended teaching on the matter is found in 1 Corinthians 7. In verses 6-9, he says this: "Now as a concession, not a command, I say this. I wish that all were as I myself am. But each has his own gift from God, one of one kind and one of another. To the unmarried and the widows I say that it is good for them to remain single, as I am. But if they cannot exercise self-control, they should marry. For it is better to marry than to burn with passion."

On the surface, one might think Paul is arguing that singleness is the preferred state for Christians. But this cannot be the case for at least three reasons. First, it would contradict other Scriptures upholding the goodness of marriage. Marriage is not merely an outlet for sexual pleasure, but it is the fundamental institution upon which society is built. God did not create Eve merely for Adam's sexual pleasure, but he created her as a co-worker in the Creation Mandate. Paul assumes marriage and children in his list of qualifications for eldership (1 Tim 3:4; Titus 1:6). The New Covenant blessing of the gospel does not replace God's prior blessings of marriage but adds to and expands them. Second, it would not make logical or practical sense for singleness to be the norm for Christians. If singleness were widely adopted in this way, the church would be robbed of her children, which are her most fertile and receptive mission field. Third, the context of Paul's comments in 1 Corinthians 7 include some unknown, extenuating circumstance that made the prospect of marriage more complicated and difficult at that time.

In other words, Paul is offering practical, pastoral wisdom for people who were facing unusual challenges, which is indicated later in the passage. Verses 26-28 say, "I think that in view of the present distress it is good for a person to remain as he is. Are you bound to a wife? Do not seek to be free. Are you free from a wife? Do not seek a wife. But if you do marry, you have not sinned, and if a betrothed woman marries, she has not sinned. Yet those who marry will have worldly troubles, and I would spare you that." We do not know what the exact nature of "present distress" was. Some have speculated a severe famine, outbreak of persecution, or similar trial. Whatever it was, Paul thought it important enough to consider whether or not to get married. In short, singleness should not be considered a spiritually superior state, though unusual circumstances may prompt one to delay marriage for a time.

Here's an example. Suppose a couple is engaged to get married during the time of World War II. Shortly before their wedding day, the man is notified that he will be required to report for active duty shortly after their scheduled wedding day. Once he departs, he may be gone for a year or more with a strong possibility he could be killed in action. The prospect of making a widow of his betrothed weighs on him so greatly that he considers whether he should delay their marriage. He might read 1 Corinthians 7 and conclude that, in view of his distress, it would be better for him to postpone their marriage plans. But if his sexual desire for his finance is too great to resist, he is not in sin if he proceeds with the marriage.

God's design is for marriage and children. Hebrews 13:4 says, "let marriage be held in honor among all." Paul does not overturn the normative vocation of marriage and household life, but he does acknowledge the need to consider the various practical and extenuating circumstances. Modern Christians should resist the world's impulse to devalue marriage and promote singleness because singleness is the exception, not the rule. Singleness in the modern world is fraught with temptations to sexual immorality, and God gave marriage as the remedy.

Suppose a young woman has grown up in an abusive, broken home without a healthy male-female relationship being modeled for her. Further, all her life she's been exposed to cultural messaging that trains her to think healthy marriage and fulfilling motherhood is the rare exception. Thus, she decides that marriage is probably not for her. In her church, she hears more stories about how painful and difficult marriage can be, and she personally knows a few couples who have gotten divorced after brief marriages. She thinks to herself, "marriage isn't worth the trouble. Who wants that kind of heartache?" She dives into her career and becomes quite successful. As years go by, she dates a few Christian guys and falls into sexual sin with two of them, but nothing more serious develops. Fast forward 20 years. She's now in her 40s, and she faces the prospect of growing old alone. Although she has seen some heartbreaking marriage situations, she also notices that many of these rocky marriages ended up smoothing out as the couples grew in Christ, had children, and learned how to thrive in marriage. Although her heart has changed regarding marriage, and she finds herself desiring it strongly, she recognizes that her options are more limited now. Singleness might seem more appealing for young people, who lack the foresight to envision growing old and frail and having no children to look after them. Sadly, for those who remain single, the second half of life is filled with more deaths than births. The single life loses its luster when it's Christmas morning and you're in your late fifties with no children or grandchildren to visit you. I suspect most people in this situation would love to travel back in time and tell their 20-year-old selves to prioritize finding a spouse and having children.

This scenario is becoming increasingly common in churches that end up affirming singleness in ways that discourage Christian men and women from pursuing marriage when they're younger. Acknowledging the difficulties of marriage should not lead people to conclude that marriage isn't worth it. Pursuing marriage is an act of faith and requires trusting God for the future in the unknown things that are beyond our control. But nothing is beyond God's control. That's the faith part. The possibility that God may not provide a spouse for someone should not lead them to abandon the pursuit.

The Singleness of Men

Since God made men and women differently, men and women will experience singleness differently. For example, God designed men with greater strength and a greater inclination towards independence. There's a reason for this. God made man first, and he was alone. Adam survived alone and went about his work alone, but that wasn't ideal. He was capable of being alone, but it was not good for him to be alone. His strength and independence were given so he could take responsibility for others who would rely on him. God gave him a woman who would benefit from his strength.

Glenn Stanton wrote, "Anthropologists have long recognized that the most fundamental social problem every community must solve is the unattached male. If his sexual, physical, and emotional energies are not governed and directed in a pro-social, domesticated manner, he will become the village's most malignant cancer."[8] A man with nothing to do, no one to live for, and no sense of purpose is a man in danger and a dangerous man. Men thrive when they are throwing themselves at a cause they believe in that is bigger than themselves. That's precisely what marriage is. As marriage binds a man to a woman in a covenant relationship, his most powerful, masculine energies are directed towards a good and glorious purpose. Only marriage can sufficiently direct his masculine drive in a positive direction. As one man noted, "men settle down when they get married; if they fail to marry, they fail to settle down."[9] Marriage drives a man to take on new identities that forces him to change his behavior, almost always for the better. Men are prone to certain vices that are curbed by social relations with women. This is not to say that women are inherently more virtuous than men,

---

8. Stanton, "Why Man and Woman."
9. Stanton, "Why Man and Woman." Stanton was quoting Nobel Prize winning economist George Akerlof.

but that men and women are virtuous in different ways. In short, "the flourishing of male virtue is catalysed and encouraged by the presence and the activity of women."[10] Women have the power to help men become the best version of themselves.

Everyone who's paying attention already knows this. Men tend to change when a woman enters the room. Her presence affects them, though they may not realize it consciously. Groups of men tend to create power, but the presence of women alters the trajectory of male power. Women have a different power than men. A woman's presence can catalyze male virtue and direct his masculine strength towards her desires. Put simply, masculine virtue can flourish under feminine influence because masculine strength was given for the protection and provision of a woman. Men tend to be at their best when their masculine energy, strength, and independence is channeled for the benefit of the women (and children) who are depending on them.

The results of this fact are undeniable. Stanton wrote, "Husbands and fathers become better, safer, more responsible and productive citizens, unrivaled by their peers in any other relational status. Husbands become better mates, treating their wives better by every important measure—physical and emotional safety, financial and material provision, personal respect, fidelity, general self-sacrifice, etc.—compared to boyfriends, whether dating or cohabiting. Husbands and fathers enjoy significantly lower health, life, and auto insurance premiums than do their single peers, for a strictly pragmatic reason. Insurance companies are not sentimental about husbands. Husbands get lower premiums because they are different creatures in terms of habits, values, behavior, and general

---

10. Alistair Roberts, "Natural Complementarians: Men, Women, and the Way Things Are," https://calvinistinternational.com/2016/09/13/natural-complementarians-men-women/ (Accessed July 7, 2022).

health."[11] Therefore, Stanton concludes, "Woman is the most powerful living force on the globe. She creates, shapes, and sustains human civilization."[12] It isn't good for a man to be single unless he is specifically called by God to be celibate so he can direct his masculine energy for the kingdom of God.

The Singleness of Women

Women are designed to be more relational than men. Since the female body is oriented towards motherhood, and since women have a limited window of fertility, singleness is arguably an even greater difficulty for them. Historically, many societies have taken care to protect women by using special language to communicate their relational status. For example, societies have historically recognized unmarried women as "maidens" or "virgins." Men, on the other hand, are just men.

Herman Bavinck wrote, "the manner in which the woman received her existence served to place her in the kind of relationship to the man such that she is inseparably bound to him, and thereby the unity of the human race is completely preserved. The woman was created not to be self-sufficient, nor to be independent of the man, nor apart from his mediation; she is not a unique principal and head of the human race, but she herself was formed out of the man, out of his flesh and blood. The human race is one entity, a body with one head, a building with one cornerstone."[13]

The words used above to describe a woman's marital status assume that women are always connected to a household (whether her father's or her husband's). In modern society, we have simplified

---

11. Stanton, "Why Man and Woman."
12. Stanton, "Why Man and Woman."
13. Bavinck, *The Christian Family*, 4.

this to "Ms." or "Mrs." If she is unmarried, she is connected to her father's household, so she would be called "Miss" or "Ms." But when she gets married, she joins her husband and becomes a "Mrs." If her husband dies, she is called a "widow." This is an important designation because she has presumably lost her provider. A widow was a crisis in the community because one of their members was financially vulnerable. This is why the Scriptures consistently call upon God's people to care for "widows and orphans" (James 1:27).[14] If she remarries, she is no longer a widow, but she becomes a "Mrs." again and her husband is responsible for her.

In traditional wedding ceremonies, the bride is given away, but not the groom. Why? Because men were made to be more independent. A woman was either attached to a husband in marriage or attached to her father as a virgin. A virgin would remain in her father's house and under his protection until her wedding day, at which time the duty of protecting and providing for her was ceremonially transferred to her new husband. In the modern world, women are certainly capable of earning an income and providing for themselves, but this was not the case in the ancient world. In the ancient world, women would rarely have been independent the way they are today. Of course, these traditional customs are not universally recognized any longer, but they are informative for our discussion here.

The Example of Ruth

Consider the story of Ruth. When the story opens, Ruth had a husband. She had a life and a future with him. But when he died,

---

14. A man who has lost his wife is called a "widower," but this word is not as socially significant as widow. A man who has lost his wife is grieving, but it would not be assumed that she was providing for him.

she lost everything. She had no hope or future. Ruth's mother-in-law, Naomi, had lost her own husband and her two sons. She was independent; her hope of a future died with them. In a moving part of her story, she clung to Naomi, her mother-in-law and fellow widow, and the two of them looked out for each other. An ancient reader would have immediately recognized the tragedy of their situation. Ruth refused to abandon Naomi because she would have been left all alone with no means of survival. She would have been completely independent, which would have been a death sentence. Ruth, being a younger woman of marriageable age, chose to stay with her, essentially taking her on as a dependent. This would have limited potential marriage suitors for Ruth, because marrying Ruth would have meant providing for two women, not just one. These two women were in dire circumstances, but God saw them.

The story ends with God restoring to Ruth a life and a future by giving her a new husband, Boaz, who was her "kinsman redeemer." Boaz married Ruth, taking her and her mother-in-law into his home. The beauty of the story is not only that God gave her a husband, but also gave her a hopeful future. This hope was powerfully demonstrated at the end of the story, where it is revealed that Ruth was the great grandmother of Jesse, the father of David. From a New Testament perspective, we can see something even greater. Ruth was a great-great-great (plus many more "greats"!) grandmother to Jesus Christ, the Messiah. Not only did God give Ruth a husband and child, but he blessed Naomi as well. When her husband and two sons died, Naomi never would have dreamed of holding her own grandchild in her arms, but this is exactly what God gave her. The book of Ruth is a story about real life in a world that is hard for women. But God is a God who sees their need and provides for them.

So what if, at the end of the story, Ruth remained single? Biblically speaking, it would have been a tragedy. This is because the story is about a woman in need of the protection and provision only a household could provide. But she and Naomi didn't have that. They were alone. Vulnerable. God gave Ruth a husband to provide all these needs for her and Naomi. God saw two vulnerable, widowed women, and brought a kinsman redeemer into their lives to protect and provide for them.

In modern times, and in modern stories, women are celebrated for being independent. The most prominent cultural narratives of the modern world tell women they don't need a man and they can take care of themselves. Women aren't supposed to *need* a man. That's a sign of weakness. Women are taught that they should take care of themselves, be independent, and not rely on a man to take care of them. These narratives seem empowering to women, but ultimately, they lead women away from the uniquely feminine glory of marriage and motherhood.

A woman's unique strength, her potential to bear and nurture life, entails a natural vulnerability. Women are certainly capable of taking care of themselves, as Ruth and Naomi did, but that isn't ideal. If Ruth had remained single, she and Naomi would likely have struggled for the rest of their lives. Ruth's marriage to Boaz meant provision for them both and freed them both to embrace feminine vocations within Boaz's household. Ruth became a mother and Naomi a grandmother.

In the Garden, the man's curse was the toil of provision, and the woman's curse was the toil of childbearing. Women who choose to be single are exchanging the typical curse of women for the typical curse of men. They are foregoing marriage and motherhood and choosing to be their own providers and protectors. This might seem empowering, but only because she is exchanging a feminine vocation for a masculine vocation. To embrace the ideals of the modern woman, women must suppress their own nature as the more relational sex and reject their biology as potential mothers. For men, the choice to be single is different. Men do not exchange a masculine vocation for a feminine vocation to be single. Single men retain their masculine vocation without having others to provide for and protect.

God's design joins the unique strengths of men and women in ways that are mutually beneficial. The man's capacity for independence needs to be joined with a woman's capacity for relationship. These strengths were principally designed to be expressed in the covenant of marriage. Even though marriage has its own challenges, choosing singleness over marriage is not a better alternative.

God's design is for people to be connected to households. Scripture assumes that marriage and household life are necessary for survival. But since this isn't as true in the modern world as it was the ancient world, marriage doesn't seem as necessary anymore. Instead, modern marriage has become more about companionship and emotional fulfillment. When so many people experience unhappy marriages, abusive spouses, and divorce, some conclude that the potential benefits aren't worth the risk. In short, singleness is increasingly seen as the superior option.

Perhaps the single greatest pathogen to godly marriage today is the viewing of marriage as something that is primarily for personal fulfillment and emotional satisfaction instead of something that is constructive for society and the kingdom of God. Marriage is a divine gift for the purpose of exercising dominion over the earth. Adam certainly enjoyed the beauty of his wife and doubtless they satisfied each other intellectually, emotionally, and sexually, but personal gratification was not the end of their God-authored marriage. Their purpose was to work together to establish a household and subdue the earth.

Singleness vs. Celibacy

God may, in rare cases, call someone to a life of celibacy to free him for particularly demanding service in his Kingdom. Jesus said, "For there are eunuchs who have been so from birth, and there are eunuchs who have been made eunuchs by men, and there are eunuchs who have made themselves eunuchs for the sake of the kingdom of heaven. Let the one who is able to receive this receive it" (Matt 19:11-12). In other words, Jesus acknowledges that some will choose singleness (i.e., "make themselves eunuchs") in order to serve the kingdom of God in an unusual way. In the ancient world, a eunuch was a man whose genitals were intentionally damaged or removed so he could serve in a king's harem without being tempted by his concubines. Eunuchs surrender the possibility of procreation by making a total, irreversible commitment. They forsake their sexual desires for the sake of their service to the king. In other words, the calling to Christian celibacy is the calling to serving as, metaphorically speaking, a eunuch for the kingdom.

Celibacy is not the same thing as singleness. Celibacy is a divine calling into an unusually demanding service for God's kingdom. Singleness is simply a fact, a stage of life. It isn't a spiritual gift, and it has no particular meaning. It should be regarded as a temporary life stage before one gets married. The rare calling to celibacy entails the self-control necessary to fulfill it. All those called to celibacy will be single, but not all single people are called to lifelong celibacy. It is unwise to confuse the two categories. If a man or woman is single, that should not be regarded as a divine calling any more than unemployment is a calling. God did not make singleness the norm because otherwise the human race would die out.

I make this distinction because of the rising popularity amongst many Christians of referring to singleness as a gift. In an effort to dignify single Christians, singleness is over spiritualized and confused with celibacy. To put it plainly, a single Christian man who looks at pornography is most likely not called to celibacy because he lacks the self-control necessary for it. He's not a "eunuch for the kingdom of God." He's just single. He should repent of his porn use and pursue a wife.

God declared it from the beginning: it is not good for man to be alone. That is, it is not good for man to be *single*. That doesn't mean singleness is sinful, just as Adam wasn't in sin before God created Eve. But even though Adam's singleness wasn't sinful, it wasn't good either. God remedied Adam's singleness by giving him a wife. Likewise, the Apostle Paul exhorted younger widows to remarry (1 Tim 5:14).

In the church, rather than letting the aches for intimate fellowship drive single Christians to pursue the gifts of marriage and childbearing, churches too often try to keep them busy with activities and affirmations to assuage their fears of growing old alone. But the Apostle Paul didn't do that. He advised younger widows to marry for a reason: marriage is good and should be pursued with the same degree of focus, effort, and intentionality as any other significant life commitment.[15] No network of church friends, no club or program, however spiritually rich and rewarding, can effectively supplant the family's central place in the human life.

---

15. Aaron M. Renn, "Newsletter #73: Ten Theses on Marriage and Family," February 13, 2023, https://aaronrenn.substack.com/p/newsletter-73-ten-theses-on-marriage. This is one of Renn's ten theses from this newsletter.

Heather is a young woman in my church who has expressed the increasingly common perspective about marriage that I hear from young singles. Heather says she is open to marriage, but quickly adds that she is content to remain single. When I challenged her with a few probing questions, the deeper truth came out. She wants to be married very badly but she's also afraid of it. She's afraid that no man would find her attractive enough to marry her. I reassured her that this was a lie. There were some deeper heart issues and fears that were plaguing her that were exposed through gentle pastoral care. But she'd been handed a roadmap for singleness by Christian blogs and articles that had convinced her that she should "just be content" with singleness and see that as godlier. Her desire for marriage and motherhood might even be an idol, she's been told. I challenged her to trust the generosity of God to provide a man for her who will love her in a Christlike way. It's not a worldly desire; the desire is good and godly.

Don't Waste Your Singleness

Singleness, as long as it lasts, is an opportunity for greater Christian service. How you live as a single man or woman will show if Christ is your highest treasure. Some fill their single years with travel, career advancement, and other hobbies. Others, however, use their singleness to serve the kingdom of God in greater ways. Singles have more time, more money, and more emotional and mental capacity to devote to the kingdom. Singleness can be more than a season of career building and leisure, as it can be a time of potent impact for Christ. So then, what are some practical ways singles can do this? I'll suggest three simple ways.

Unceasing Prayer

A single Christian can devote more of his prayers to specific members of his church, revival in his city and region, and godly governance from his political leaders than a Christian who has a spouse and multiple children. One Christian man I know prays daily for the salvation of his six children and for the upcoming adoption of a seventh. Those prayers are perhaps the most important part of his day, but they are also minutes and energy he cannot simultaneously expend on prayers for the woman who sits near him at church with a broken foot, for the salvation of the tens of thousands of unbelievers who live near him, or for wise and prudent leadership from the governor of Ohio and the president of the United States. We are finite creatures. We have only one mouth, one mind, and one pair of knees from which to lift up our prayers. While he is certainly called to pray for people outside his home, the fact is that his single brother or sister in Christ can devote more time and effort to prayers for God's work in our wider world than he can. How many godly revivals have been ushered in by the prayers of single Christians who have devoted themselves to the toil of prayers to Almighty God? How many evil institutions have been brought to the ground by the prayers of single saints like Amy Carmichael, John Stott, or Augustine? I suspect more than we will know this side of glory.

Work and Good Works

Single men and women can devote themselves to good works building up God's household with the time and energy they otherwise would have spent building up their own households. When Paul addressed whether to enroll widows in the financial assistance programs of the early church, he said they should only be enrolled if they have "a reputation for good works," which includes having faithfully raised her own children (if any), shown hospitality, washed the feet of the saints, cared for the afflicted, and "devoted herself to every good work" (1 Tim 5:10).

There are so many things I would enjoy doing for the church that, in God's providence, I am simply not able to do. The lion's share of my finite time and physical energy must be given to God through my work for the church and for my wife and children. My evenings and weekends are mostly spent with them. There is less time and physical and emotional energy to give to my neighbors than if I were single. But to my brothers and sisters who are single, there is more freedom to serve the saints during the week.

Generous Giving

Each person in a state of singleness will live under different circumstances. This is how God made the world. It is a world of variety and differences, of times and seasons and a wide array of giftings, afflictions, abilities, desires, and temperaments. A single Christian woman caring for an aging mother while working as middle manager in Omaha, Nebraska will have financial giving to the kingdom that looks very different from a healthy 35-year-old single Christian man working as an executive at Boeing in Seattle. But within that wide array, there is a truth that applies almost universally: you will have money to give to your local church and to mission work that you would not have to give them if you had a spouse and children. This is a tremendous blessing to the single Christian's church and to the missionaries or other Christian ministers he can support. The single Christian can make a greater financial impact for Christ's kingdom than he could if he were married with a family. That giving brings great glory to God and is a lasting testimony to his church and neighbors.

Am I a lesser Christian if marriage, for one legitimate reason or another, seems to not be available to me? Absolutely not. The normative calling to human beings is to marry rather than be single, but to receive the alternative calling doesn't impact one's worth in the slightest. The price of a single Christian's body and soul has been set at the same level as the married Christian's: the unimaginable worth of the blood of God's Son. He has redeemed the Christian single person, called him into his church, desires to bless him with spiritual gifts, and hears his every last prayer. A single Christian has no less intrinsic worth or purpose in the kingdom of God.

The Apostle Paul did not take a wife, and by God's grace he put his greater availability as a single man to powerful use in his mission to make much of Christ throughout the Roman Empire. Paul's missionary travels took him from place to place across the known world, and his particular assignment from the Lord as a single man doubtless made those labors easier than they would have been if he were married. While Peter the Apostle had a wife and family, and while Phillip the deacon had four grown daughters who lived under his roof, the Apostle Paul was more free to rigorously devote his time and energy to the ministry of the gospel. There is much a single Christian can do that a married Christian simply cannot, and there is an unusual fervor and intensity that a single Christian's service to the church can take. If God has called you to be single and celibate for life, like the Apostle Paul, then he has called you to a life that can do wondrous things for your church, for the lost in your community, and for the Kingdom of God.

Conclusion

I conclude this chapter with a few words of pastoral counsel for my single brothers and sisters in Christ. First, make the most of your singleness. There are real advantages to being single and you can make the most of them while trusting God for a spouse. Second, have faith that God is a good father who gives good gifts to his children. In other words, trust God to give you a godly spouse. Reject the lie that being single is just as good as being married. It isn't. Getting married doesn't solve all your problems and often creates even more problems, but this is the typical path of sanctification for God's people. Single men need to walk by faith and pursue a woman. Single women need to trust God and make themselves available for pursuit. Pursue the gendered virtues of fatherhood and motherhood that would make you a godly husband or wife and trust God with the outcome.

I have a further word of practical counsel for how men and women can approach singleness differently, given the different natures of men and women and what marriage means for us. For men, the pursuit of marriage includes a readiness to provide. Therefore, a single man would be wise to build a modest lifestyle where he can easily provide for a wife and himself on his income. This will look different for different men, but this is a good general principle. For women, the pursuit of marriage includes the potential for motherhood and the priority of the home. Therefore, a single woman would be wise to pursue education and work opportunities that give her the most flexibility to prioritize her home after getting married. For example, if a single woman accumulates a lot of school debt that will require her to work full time for many years to pay off, she has limited her ability to prioritize her home even before she gets married. This may seem like a gamble since she would be choosing to impose limits on her future earning potential. But she's doing so trusting God that he will give her a husband that will provide for her and her future children. This decision will require her to trust God, face her fears, and walk by faith. Her future household will be all the better for it.

CHAPTER 10

Sexual Dynamics in the Church

"Men who are led in the Church by women are less than men. Women who lead men in the Church are less than women." [1]

WILLIAM AND BARBARA MOUSER

"This mystery is profound, and I am saying that it refers to Christ and the church."

EPHESIANS 5:32

Introduction

If you've hung with the argument of the book so far, you know that the whole cosmos is God's household, and God's household is built into the created order. Likewise, ancient societies were also ordered around a household structure, where the king or ruler was seen as a father to the people. Unsurprisingly, therefore, we find that the

---

1. William E. Mouser and Barbara Mouser, *The Story of Sex in Scripture* (Waxahachie, TX: International Council on Gender Studies, 2006), 113.

church is a household too. The structure of the church is patterned after the household, where the responsibilities and duties of the elders mirror those of fathers in the home (1 Tim 3:15). This is why the Apostle Paul can draw instruction for the church from the biblical story of Eden. Eden was the first church. Adam was the first elder, responsible for teaching the commandments of God to his congregation, which was his wife. To demonstrate this properly, we need to look at Genesis 1–3 again.

The creation stories of Genesis can be summarized in this way: in the beginning, the earth was formless and void (1:2), untamed and wild, but Eden was created as a place for God to dwell with his human family (2:8). It was a temple; a place of worship, prayer, and fellowship, under the rule of God, all ordered according to his design. In this natural sanctuary, God met with his people and walked with them in the cool of the day (3:8). God blessed them (1:28). He fed them with food that sprouted from the ground (1:29), but they were not permitted to eat God's holy food in the center of the garden (2:17). Within this context, God gave them the work of making disciples of their children (1:28). Thus, in God's original design, the household and the church were one and the same.

The author of Hebrews put it this way: "Now Moses was faithful in all God's house as a servant, to testify to the things that were to be spoken later, but Christ is faithful over God's house as a son. And we are his house, if indeed we hold fast our confidence and our boasting in our hope" (Heb 3:5-6). In other words, the people of God are constituted as God's household. Moses was a prominent servant in God's house under the Old Covenant, and the New Covenant was ushered in by Christ, a faithful son over God's house. Then he says, "we are his house," meaning the church. The church maintains the basic household structure.

In short, the church is a household, just like the family, only bigger. The essential patterns for each are basically the same. The natural family produces biological children, the church produces spiritual children. The members of each household relate to one another as fathers, mothers, husbands, wives, brothers, and sisters (Matt 12:47-50). The father is the head of the household in the natural family, elders are the spiritual fathers of the church (1 Cor 4:15), and they are responsible for leading the church. The function of the natural family is taught principally in the Creation Mandate (Gen 1:28-29), the function of the church is taught principally in the Great Commission (Matt 28:18-20).

The church is founded upon the structure of the natural family, and the structure of the church reflects this reality.[2] Since the people of God are a household, the essential household structure remains the same. Just like the natural family, the church has spiritual fathers (1 Cor 4:15) and mothers (Rom 16:13), every Christian is a "son of God" through faith (Gal 3:26-28), and all Christians are united as brothers and sisters as legitimate heirs (v. 29). The church's relationship to Christ follows a marriage pattern. Christ is the bridegroom (Eph 5:23), the church is the bride (Rev 21:2). As a bride, the church submits to the Lordship of Christ in everything (Eph 5:24). Unsurprisingly, this bride becomes a mother (Gal 4:26). The union of Christ and his bride bears fruit— the spiritual children born through evangelism and discipleship (Gal 4:27-31). The common New Testament word to describe these children is "brother," which includes both men and women. In the natural family, brothers and sisters are those who come from the same womb. In the church family, the womb they share is the empty tomb, where Christ lay dead and was brought back to life,

---

2. Andreas J. and Margaret Elizabeth Kostenberger, *God's Design for Man and Woman: A Biblical-Theological Survey* (Wheaton, IL: Crossway Books, 2014), 268–69.

from whom proceeded the Holy Spirit, who blows into the hearts of men and women to bring them to faith (John 1:12-13). Since the elders of the church are spiritual fathers to God's people, they need to demonstrate the ability to manage a household well (1 Tim 3:4). As Paul says, "if someone does not know how to manage his own household, how will he care for God's church?" (1 Tim 3:5).

The relational patterns of the natural family are expanded and mapped onto the church (Rom 16:1-16, Eph 5:22-33, Titus 2:2-6). The callings and boundaries that exist in the natural family are mirrored in the callings and boundaries in the church. Since some members of one's natural family may not be believers, the church needs to be distinct, even though they share the same basic structure. Jesus said, "For I have come to set a man against his father, and a daughter against her mother, and a daughter-in-law against her mother-in-law. And a person's enemies will be those of his own household" (Matt 10:35-36). Even still, conversion of entire households isn't uncommon in the NT (Acts 11:14) and should even be expected (Acts 2:39).

Therefore, the sexual dynamics between men and women matter in the church just as they do in the home. In particular, the principle of male eldership in the church is an extension of the fatherly leadership pattern of Genesis 1. God appointed man to be the head of his household with his wife and children following his lead. There is an accountability that comes with this responsibility. Just as God held the man accountable for his leadership in the garden (Gen 3:9), God holds the elders accountable for their leadership in the church (Heb 13:17). This responsibility is given to the man because God designed him to bear this weight and will hold him accountable for it. It is the God given nature of man to accept responsibility and exercise authority. Since the Garden of Eden was a sanctuary temple, Adam played a dual role of both priest and king. The liturgical setting of Eden is important because both the garden and the church are "sacred spaces," designated for worship. This is why Paul used the creation order from Genesis to ground his instructions about the church in 1 Timothy 2. The church's gathering for worship should follow the pattern established in the Garden of Eden, because Eden was a place of worship too. Eldership is the NT counterpart to this role, which is why the office and function of elders is restricted to biblically qualified men.

The Liturgical Garden

The clearest example of this is 1 Timothy 2, where Paul addressed how men and women should conduct themselves when they are gathered for worship. This text merits careful examination because Paul's argument is grounded in the created order. There are six observations I'd like to make from this text.

First, Paul's concern in this text is with how men and women conduct themselves when the church is gathered for worship. He says in 1 Timothy 2:8-10, "I desire then that in every place the men should pray, lifting holy hands without anger or quarreling; likewise also that women should adorn themselves in respectable apparel, with modesty and self-control, not with braided hair and gold or pearls or costly attire, but with what is proper for women who profess godliness—with good works." The church gathering is where God's people assemble to worship God, pray, receive communion, and hear instruction. Men are called to be humble and prayerful, resisting the vices of anger and arguing. Women are called to modesty and good works, resisting the vices of attention seeking dress or demeanor.

Second, Paul ensures that both men and women are given full access to learn Christian theology. Second Timothy 2:11 says, "Let a woman learn quietly with all submissiveness." The words "quiet" and "submissive" grab a lot of attention, which overshadows the fact that this is an invitation for the women to learn Scripture and theology. This is important. Paul did not want women kept in the dark about what the Scriptures teach, but to learn Scripture in order to fully participate in the household life of the church. Paul wanted the women of the church, no less than the men, to be good theologians. This indicates an equality of status and intellect for women in the church that would have been unexpected in the ancient world. Nevertheless, Paul calls women to learn differently than men; women are instructed to learn with a quiet and submissive demeanor. These commands for women mirror the role of Eve in the garden. Although Eve was equal to her husband, she was nevertheless submissive to him. Adam was her teacher.

Third, Paul prohibits women from teaching or exercising authority over men. Second Timothy 2:12 says, "I do not permit a woman to teach or to exercise authority over a man; rather, she is to remain quiet." These words may unsettle or even shock modern ears, but Paul is promoting something good which corresponds to the creation order in the garden. Notice how verses 11 and 12 mirror each other by teaching parallel commands. It is good for a woman to *learn* the church's theology and *submit* to the church's authority; it is not good for a woman to *teach* the church's theology or *exercise* the church's authority. This is not because women are incapable of teaching or are intellectually inferior. It has nothing to do with her ability and everything to do with her design. God did not design women to carry this responsibility. Not even Eve, a perfect woman, was expected to do it. Just as she was not called to be head over her natural family, Christian women are not called to lead men in the church. Eve would certainly have been a woman of extraordinary capability, in her unfallen state. Nevertheless, God's design for her was to follow the lead of her husband.

Fourth, Paul grounds his instruction in 1 Timothy 2 explicitly in the creation order. These were not cultural accommodations to a patriarchal society, but a universal teaching about God's design. Verse 13 says, "For Adam was formed first, then Eve; and Adam was not deceived, but the woman was deceived and became a transgressor." The context of Genesis is crucial. Paul's commands are not arbitrary or based on human custom but are more deeply rooted in God's ordering of creation: "Adam was formed first, then Eve." The sequence of events in the Genesis 2 story is key. In verses 7-17, God commanded Adam to not eat of the forbidden tree *before* Eve was created. After Eve was created (vv. 18-23), she entered into the stewardship previously established between God and Adam. She was not given a separate command. She received and inherited the command given to Adam and she becomes an essential part of fulfilling the command as Adam's bride, helper, and queen. Eve is equal to Adam in dignity yet under him in authority. Since God commanded Adam to not eat the fruit of the tree before Eve was created, it was his responsibility to teach her the command and ensure that she obeyed it. Adam's authority to rule in the garden entailed a specific responsibility, under God's authority, to teach the command God had given him. Thus, even though both sinned, God held Adam, not Eve, directly responsible (Rom 5:12). Adam failed in his masculine duty to safeguard the word he received from God. Paul instructs the church to not repeat his mistake.

Fifth, authority in the church is directly linked to the responsibility to safeguard the truth of God's word. Later, Paul closes his letter to Timothy with a final reminder to "guard the deposit entrusted to you" (1 Tim 6:20). The same exhortation could have been given to Adam in the garden because he carried the same responsibility. First Timothy 2:14 says, "Adam was not deceived, but the woman was deceived and became a transgressor." What does this mean? It might seem at first glance that Paul was insulting Eve for being gullible, but this is not the case. To understand this properly, we need to examine the text closely. Paul does not praise Adam for avoiding deception. After all, he ate the forbidden fruit just as she did. Rather, Paul is criticizing Adam for failing to protect Eve from deception. How? Because Adam alone heard God's command firsthand. Eve was not there to receive the command, because she had not been created yet. Since Adam heard God's command directly, it was not possible for him to be deceived. Satan deceived Eve, who wasn't there, and her deception was enabled by Adam's silence. Eve had only heard the command of Adam second-hand, which is a fact that Satan exploited. When Adam, "who was with her (Gen 3:6)," failed to correct Satan's teaching, however, she believed the serpent and was deceived. Satan deceived her because Adam failed to teach her. They both sinned, but they sinned in different ways. Eve was deceived; Adam rebelled. Eve would not have been deceived if Adam had taught her properly.

Sixth, Paul's teaching prohibits women from doing two things: (1) holding the office of elder and (2) performing the authoritative function of elders. Adam's authority and responsibility in the garden correspond to the authority and responsibility of elders. An elder's authority is indicated by the office he occupies. An elder's responsibility entails the range of duties that he must perform, and for which he will give account to God (Heb 13:17). Although the authority of a church's elders will be exercised in different ways in different churches, their authority is most explicitly expressed in its teaching and preaching ministry. Thus, both the official and unofficial authority of the church is to be carried out by biblically qualified men. Eve was certainly Adam's equal, but she was not Adam's leader, either in title or in function. She was called to work alongside Adam, following his lead and helping him, but not exercising authority over him. Paul is saying that the order of the church should mirror the order of the garden because that's where God's uncorrupted design can be seen.

At the fall, the order of the garden was inverted and over-thrown. The serpent ruled Eve through deception, Eve ruled Adam through influence, and Adam rebelled against God's rule. Adam failed to rebuke the serpent and teach his wife. The serpent exploited Adam's passivity and Eve's vulnerability. Yet her vulnerability was no excuse. Having heard one version of God's command from Adam and an alternate version from the serpent, she chose to listen to the voice of the serpent, not her husband. She broke rank and followed the serpent's lead. Nevertheless, Adam was responsible for her, and God held him accountable for this failure. Therefore, Adam and Eve sinned differently at the fall. No one is innocent—all are guilty and condemned (Rom 3:23). Both failed, but they failed in different ways.

God's original design for men and women, rejected in the garden, was redeemed at the cross and renewed in the structure and practice of the church. Qualified men are called upon to succeed where Adam failed—to teach God's word and humbly enforce it with the authority of the church. This is what elders do. Likewise, the women of the church are called upon to succeed where Eve failed—to learn and submit to the commands of God while trusting God to work through the flawed yet qualified men who are charged with leading them.

Therefore, Paul's argument in 1 Timothy 2 is that women should not hold the office of an elder nor perform the teaching duties of an elder, not because she is incapable, but because that's not what she was made for. When Adam passively failed to lead Eve, he acted like less of a man. When Eve led Adam to eat, she acted like less of a woman. When a woman teaches or exercises authority over men in the church, she's repeating the sin of Eve. When a man passively fails to lead his home, or when a church elder fails to guard the authoritative teaching functions of the church, he's repeating the sin of Adam.

Objection: Doesn't This Lead to Spiritual Abuse?

There are plenty of examples of church leaders who have abused their authority, most heinously to sexually exploit vulnerable members of their congregations. This is an inexcusable and unspeakably wicked evil, and these men will give account to God for these actions. These stories grab headlines and create the perception that all men abuse power, and these problems can be minimized by creating a more egalitarian leadership structure that ensures more women occupy positions of power. This doesn't solve the problem, however. The system does not create the sin; sinners exploit the system. Abusive pastors exist in every leadership structure and in every denomination. Men who lust for power can bully their way through any leadership structure. In a fallen world, there is no leadership structure that can prevent abuses from happening. The existence of abuse does not determine the rightness or wrongness of a particular structure, and appointing women to leadership positions often puts them more directly in an abuser's path. The solution is not fewer men in leadership, but better men. Men of holiness and godly character, the kind of men Paul describes in 1 Timothy 3 when he listed the qualifications for eldership.

Eldership is a masculine calling, because elders function as the spiritual fathers of the church.[3] Men of holiness and proven character are called to do this work. It is unsurprising that Paul follows his teaching about male authority in the church (1 Tim 2:12) with a detailed list of character qualifications for elders (1 Tim 3:1-7). Further, the Scriptures describe the work of elders with words that correspond to more masculine callings. The following is a sample of texts that directly or indirectly describe the work of elders. They are either taken from the pastoral epistles (which largely give instructions about church leadership) or are Scriptures that directly address the duties of elders:

- Maintain the church's discipline by delivering unrepentant Christians "to Satan for the destruction of the flesh, so that [their] spirit[s] may be saved in the day of the Lord" (1 Cor 5:5).
- "Wage the good warfare" (1 Tim 1:18).
- An elder must "manage his own household well, with all dignity keeping his children submissive" (1 Tim 3:4).
- "Command and teach these things" (1 Tim 4:11).
- "Devote yourself to the public reading of Scripture, to exhortation, to teaching" (1 Tim 4:13).
- "Keep a close watch on yourself and on the teaching. Persist in this, for by so doing you will save both yourself and your hearers" (1 Tim 4:16).
- "Command these things as well, so that they may be without reproach" (1 Tim 5:7).
- "Let the elders who rule well be considered worthy of

---

3. This is evident in the fact that Catholic and Orthodox traditions still call their leaders "father."

double honor, especially those who labor in preaching and teaching" (1 Tim 5:17).

- "Teach and urge these things," referring to various instructions pertaining to different people in the church (1 Tim 6:2).
- "Fight the good faith of the faith" (1 Tim 6:12).
- "I charge you in the presence of God... to keep the commandment unstained and free from reproach until the appearing of our Lord Jesus Christ" (1 Tim 6:13-14).
- "Guard the good deposit" of the gospel (1 Tim 6:20, 2 Tim 1:14).
- "No soldier gets entangled in civilian pursuits, since his aim is to please the one who enlisted him" (2 Tim 2:4).
- "Preach the word; be ready in season and out of season; reprove, rebuke, and exhort, with complete patience and teaching" (2 Tim 4:2).
- "I have fought the good fight, I have finished the race, I have kept the faith. Henceforth there is laid up for me the crown of righteousness" (2 Tim 4:7-8).
- An elder "must hold firm to the trustworthy word as taught, so that he may be able to give instruction in sound doctrine and also to rebuke those who contradict it" (Titus 1:9).
- "For there are many who are insubordinate, empty talkers and deceivers, especially those of the circumcision party. They must be silenced, since they are upsetting whole families by teaching for shameful gain what they ought not to teach" (Titus 1:10-11).
- "Therefore rebuke them sharply, that they may be sound in the faith, not devoting themselves to Jewish myths and

the commands of people who turn away from the truth" (Titus 1:13-14).

- "But as for you, teach what accords with sound doctrine" (Titus 2:1).
- "Declare these things; exhort and rebuke with all authority. Let no one disregard you" (Titus 2:15).
- "Shepherd the flock of God" by "exercising oversight" (1 Peter 5:2).
- Elders must "keep watch" over the souls of the church, knowing they will have to "give an account" (Heb 13:17).

This sampling of texts describes the range of work elders do and the character of the men who are called to do it. The church needs to be protected from wolves, false teachers, predators, and all other kinds of threats. Shepherding a church includes a great amount of conflict, including low-grade conflict such as correcting, warning, and rebuking others. Of course, women do this work, too, which is a good thing. But it is not good to require them to do it by making them elders. Besides, who is more likely to confront a false teacher in the church? Both men and women can do it, but men are more likely to do it. And it is the elder's formal duty to do it. The Scriptures do not shy away from the language of warfare and combat to describe pastoral ministry. Teaching and preaching in the church are not merely conveying information but are spiritual warfare. Gospel ministers are called to proclaim the light of God's truth into the darkness. I heard one pastor say that "the reason God calls men to preach is the same reason God calls men to go to war."[4]

Without a doubt, women are also called to participate in the spiritual battle as well, but in ways appropriate to the feminine

---

4. Toby Sumpter, "Immortal Combat: A Word for Pastors," https://www.tobyjsumpter.com/immortal-combat-a-word-for-pastors/ (Accessed May 9, 2022).

nature. The women of the church follow Eve's design, while the men follow Adam's. Adam was the field general who failed in his deployment. His failure led to hers. Eve was responsible for her own actions, not Adam's, because God did not put her in charge of the garden. When men fail to teach and exercise authority over the church, both men and women suffer for it. Women are called to demonstrate strength in their own ways, with courage, to fight sin, to defend the truth, and to be mighty in prayer.

Going back to the idea of the church as a household, there are fathers and mothers who produce spiritual children in the faith. The order of the church is like the skeletal structure that holds the organic parts together. Men are naturally oriented towards hierarchy and authority; women are naturally oriented towards equality and inclusion. Men are made to be fathers, and the fatherly duties in the church are more oriented to leading and protecting. Women are made to be mothers, and the motherly duties in the church are more oriented to helping, caring for, and influencing others. When the strengths and contributions of both are recognized and valued, a church can more readily accomplish its God honoring purpose.

Domestic Ministries

A common objection is that restricting the office of elder to biblically qualified men needlessly devalues the feminine contributions of women. Some think Paul is teaching that the men are to go out there and do "real ministry" while all the women stay in the kitchen baking cookies. This way of thinking is wrongheaded. Women should not be restricted in the church beyond the Scripture's teaching.

Some Christians speak as though domestic ministries are somehow beneath the dignity of women. Domestic ministry can include all things related to hospitality, such as organizing potlucks, decorating the church building, or taking meals to new mothers and their families. Domestic ministry is closely related to homemaking, so women will more likely be drawn to it than men. Domestic ministry is real ministry needed by the church. To devalue domestic ministry and those who are gifted in these ways dishonors the body of Christ. First Corinthians 12 says, "The eye cannot say to the hand, 'I have no need of you,' nor again the head to the feet, 'I have no need of you.' On the contrary, the parts of the body that seem to be weaker are indispensable, and on those parts of the body that we think less honorable we bestow the greater honor, and our unpresentable parts are treated with greater modesty, which our more presentable parts do not require. But God has so composed the body, giving greater honor to the part that lacked it, that there may be no division in the body, but that the members may have the same care for one another" (vv. 21-25).

Take church potlucks, for example. These kinds of events facilitate deeper relationships and springboard into future ministry opportunities. If a church wants to have a potluck, it will likely be organized by the women, or it won't happen at all. Women naturally transform their environments into homes, and homes are a great place for ministry. For example, difficult, interpersonal discipleship doesn't usually happen in sterile classrooms with fluorescent lights. It often happens in a home, or perhaps in a counseling office that feels like a home, with warm décor, comfortable seating, and something to drink. It isn't beneath the dignity of women to create these environments. My wife and I like to do counseling ministry together when appropriate. Her warm, friendly presence puts people at ease and helps them feel safe. She's better at the sort of small talk that helps people get comfortable before I take over and get to the business at hand. She helps create an environment that is more conducive to having difficult conversations. In short, she makes my pastoral ministry better. We work as a team, like a father and mother, doing ministry together in our church.

Formal and Informal Authority

Although women are more likely to do domestic ministries, the Scriptures do not teach that women are restricted to them. Discipleship ministry takes many forms, and it belongs to the whole church, both men and women. Take Aquila and Priscilla, for example. They appear together in the book of Acts, Romans, 1 Corinthians, and 2 Timothy. They're always mentioned together. They clearly had a significant ministry as husband and wife, laboring side by side for the gospel. Paul lived with them for a brief period, joined them in the tentmaking trade (Acts 18:1-33), and discipled them in the faith. When Luke introduces them in the book of Acts, he follows custom and introduces the husband first. When he mentions them again later in the chapter, he twice mentions his wife's name first (18:18, 26). When Paul addresses them in his letters, on two occasions, he does the same (Rom 16:3; 2 Tim 4:19; compare 1 Cor 16:19). Why? Most likely, Priscilla was more prominent and well known in the early church. She was a talented and respected woman. Paul valued them so much that he took them both with him for a part of his missionary journey.

Their experience in Ephesus is instructive: "Now a Jew named Apollos, a native of Alexandria, came to Ephesus. He was an eloquent man, competent in the Scriptures. He had been instructed in the way of the Lord. And being fervent in spirit, he spoke and taught accurately the things concerning Jesus, though he knew only the baptism of John. He began to speak boldly in the synagogue, but when Priscilla and Aquila heard him, they took him aside and explained to him the way of God more accurately" (Acts 18:24-26). The fact that Priscilla is mentioned first in Luke's narrative clearly signals her leading role explaining the Scriptures to Apollos. But she was not teaching in a formal church gathering, as it says, "they took him aside" (v. 26). The NIV translates that same phrase "they invited him to their home."

Priscilla explaining the way of God to Apollos was appropriate because she was not acting on behalf of the church in an official capacity. To state it differently, she was not exercising authority in a way Paul prohibits in 1 Timothy 2:12 because she did not occupy the office of elder, and she did not perform the function of an elder by authoritatively teaching in a worship gathering. Certainly, her teaching was authoritative in the sense that a man of Apollos' stature was persuaded by it, but it was not a formal authority. Teaching has formal authority when it is done on behalf of the church, which is most often done when the church is gathered for worship. Paul restricts this teaching with authority to biblically qualified men. Teaching without authority happens all the time as believers open the Scriptures and challenge each other. This is what Priscilla did. She and her husband took Apollos aside and corrected his theology privately, in their home.

Therefore, teaching with the formal authority of the church belongs to the elders, and they will give account for their leadership (Heb 13:17). The teaching of the church's elders is based on the authority of Scripture and the authority of the office. This does not mean he is infallible; he will uniquely give account for his teaching because the church looks to him to represent the whole. James 3:1 says, "Not many of you should become teachers, my brothers, for you know that we who teach will be judged with greater strictness." This combination of biblical and church authority is clearest when the church is gathered for worship.

There is another kind of teaching that belongs to the whole church. Colossians 3:16 says, "Let the word of Christ dwell in you richly, teaching and admonishing one another in all wisdom, singing psalms and hymns and spiritual songs, with thankfulness in your hearts to God." The "teaching and admonishing" in view here is not exercised in a church office, but on the authority of the Scriptures alone. This kind of teaching is not restricted to the elders, but belongs to the whole church, both men and women. What I have in mind here are informal conversations, between individuals or groups of friends, where Christians are discussing Scripture. If women were prohibited from sharing their insights in this kind of environment, they might as well be prohibited from having conversations at all.

When Women Rule Over Men

No one likes being under leadership they don't respect. This is especially true of men. When someone has a formal position of authority, but are not able to command respect, it causes frustration or even resentment. This is why character qualifications for eldership are so important. The men leading the church need to be the sort of men others can respect because they have exemplary character.

Since many Christian women have exemplary character, some argue, why wouldn't God allow them to be elders? We've already covered some of the reasons, but I'll add one more here. Men don't respond to women the same way they respond to men. Someone might object that that's his problem; men should be willing to follow good female leadership. If he's unwilling to do so, there must be something wrong with him. But the opposite is true. God made man to lead from the beginning. That's not a flaw, it's his design.

Men are built for strength. They desire it and follow it. Men follow strength by nature, so it is natural when a man of strength is in authority over other men. Women have their own kind of strength as well, but feminine strength is something men want to pursue, not follow. Feminine strength is beautiful, which elicits desire in men. It doesn't command respect in them the way masculine strength does. Men desire beauty. They pursue it; they don't follow it. Men follow strength. When a woman is placed in authority over a man, he has to adapt to a mode of leadership that doesn't come naturally to him: he has to follow something he was designed to pursue and lead.

This isn't the result of social conditioning, as some might suggest. Werner Neuer, citing a significant and thorough anthropological study, wrote, "throughout the world, past and present, there has never existed a society in which the overwhelming majority of key positions in state, industry and society were not occupied by men. In other words, and contrary to the opinion of many feminists, there is nowhere evidence of a matriarchal society (that is a society led by women)."[5] The reason for this is plain: this is God's design, and it is good. It is more in man's nature to lead and more in woman's nature to follow. Men and women have different bodies, brains, and temperaments that consistently demonstrate these basic innate tendencies that persist across time, place, and culture.

In the church, it is sometimes assumed that the best way to truly value women is to make them elders. This sends a subtle

---

5. Neuer, *Man and Woman*, 55.

yet undeniable message that the way to honor someone is to make them a leader. This isn't good for either men or women in the church. Men and women each have a nature, and it is best to move with the grain of that nature. The simple fact is this: churches cannot produce strong, godly men under feminine leadership. Godly men—godly husbands and fathers—can grow and thrive when they are led by men they regard as spiritual fathers. Since headship is a masculine calling, women can likewise thrive in such an environment. By contrast, men weaken under female leadership. This may be an uncomfortable fact, but it is a fact nonetheless. Both Scripture and nature attest that it is true. Isaiah 3:12 says, "My people—infants are their oppressors, and women rule over them." Being ruled by women is regarded in Scripture as a shameful sign of God's judgment.

Let me be clear about something. I'm not saying that women should never lead. We've already discussed how Adam and Eve were both created to rule in their own way. They were both created in God's image, which entails the authority to rule. Adam was a king; Eve was a queen. Nevertheless, they do not rule in the same way. Their leadership is not interchangeable. Masculine rule is direct; feminine rule is indirect. In the garden, Eve's authority was an extension of Adam's authority. Eve did not have her own authority that somehow competed with her husband's. She was his helper, which included helping him rule.

Conclusion

In summary, the church is God's human household on earth. And just as the natural family needs a man and woman to reproduce, the church needs spiritual fathers and mothers to reproduce. Just as a man and woman was needed to fulfill the Creation Mandate, both men and women are needed to fulfill the Great Commission. Men and women are both partakers of the one Spirit of grace, and both men and women have received gifts of the spirit for the building up of the church. Thus, men and women should aspire to mature into spiritual fathers and mothers who work together to bring forth spiritual children through evangelism and discipleship. Interdependence is how God designed the church to work. Men need women, women need men. These distinctions are good. No one needs androgyny. We need not minimize our distinctions but should embrace them fully and serve one another in ways conducive to those distinctions. Embracing the interdependent distinctness of our created male and female design enables the church to express its range of gifts more fully. Working together, fathers and mothers bear fruit of the gospel, a harvest of souls, who are welcomed into the household of God, where they can enjoy unity, belonging, edification, honor, and glory. Whether one is a man or woman, hand or foot, eye or ear, no one can rightly say, "I do not belong" or "I have no need of you." Everyone contributes in their own way, with love as the driving virtue.

The covenant of Jesus with his people is inextricably and eternally bound to our sexuality—and so how we confess our sexuality is inextricably and eternally bound to how we confess the gospel. This is no less true in the household of the faith as it is in the natural family. Everyone in the church is called to be faithful where God has assigned them, whether one is a man, woman, young, old, single, married, an elder, brand-new Christian, or mature believer.

CHAPTER 11

Sexual Immorality

"The next great heresy is going to be simply an attack on morality; and especially on sexual morality." [1]

G. K. Chesterton

"Flee from sexual immorality. Every other sin a person commits is outside the body, but the sexually immoral person sins against his own body."

1 Corinthians 6:18

Introduction

The road that leads from my house in Cincinnati to my parents' house in West Virginia winds through the rolling hills of Kentucky. It's a beautiful drive through rural scenery that reminds me of my childhood. My mind wanders. At various points along the way, different houses, stores, yard signs, or fences stand out from

---

1. G. K. Chesterton, "The Next Heresy," *G. K.'s Weekly*, Vol III, no. 66 (June 19, 1926), 9.

the scenery and catch my eye. There is one in particular that has taken on a deeper significance for me.

It's the site of a house fire from a long time ago. It looked like it would have been a beautiful, old house at one time, but now the grass was overgrown except in the footprint where the house once stood. Apart from some scattered debris littering the area, only one part of the house remained: the chimney. Somehow, with the rest of the house demolished, the lone chimney still reached high into the sky. I could easily imagine the house that once surrounded it, and the family that occupied it, and how they might have gathered around the fireplace and enjoyed its warmth. Perhaps a spark from this very fireplace escaped onto the floor, grew out of control, and consumed the house. Fires are like that. Fires are among the most powerful forces on earth. A little spark easily grows into an uncontrollable blaze. If it is harnessed properly, it can cook your food, keep you warm, or light up the dark. But if not, it can become an inferno, consuming everything.

Sex is like fire. Not just the physical act, but what sex means and how we understand it. As discussed throughout this book, God created two kinds of human beings, with bodies and natures that correspond to one another, and whose sexual union has the power to create new life. Human sexuality is like a fire. It's magnificence, beauty, heat, and power brings joy and delight to a home when it is chastened within the marital boundaries God designed it for. The marriage covenant is the fireplace. It keeps the fire where it belongs. The marriage covenant contains the burning heat of sexual desire, providing the necessary family support for the new life it creates. This protection keeps the fire where it belongs and prevents it from burning up everything else in sight. When sex is removed from the protection of the marriage covenant, it becomes a raging inferno that can consume and destroy everything, even a whole culture. Maybe that's what Paul had in mind when he spoke of sexual desire as a fire that burns with passion (1 Cor 7:9).

In Genesis 19, God rained down fire (perhaps a volcanic eruption) upon Sodom and Gomorrah because they "indulged in sexual immorality and pursued unnatural desire." Why? So they could "serve as an example undergoing a punishment of eternal fire" (Jude 7). Sexual immorality is a big deal to God. A high-profile pastor famously said that "God seems to whisper about sexual sin" in the Bible.[2] This is wrong and foolish. Sexual sin is no small matter to God.

The world's predictable reaction to traditional sexual ethics is a yawn and eye roll, supposing that God wants to spoil everyone's fun. This, too, is foolish. Those who think this might be shocked to know what Proverbs says about the marriage bed: "Let your fountain be blessed, and rejoice in the wife of your youth, a lovely deer, a graceful doe. Let her breasts fill you at all times with delight; be intoxicated always in her love" (Prov 5:18-19). The Bible has its steamy parts, too many to quote here. God created sex to be enjoyed, but everything has its limits. Just as God created food to taste good and be enjoyed, excess becomes gluttony. God is not anti-sex any more than God is anti-food. But he does prescribe limits and boundaries for how we may enjoy his good gifts without harm.

The Beauty of God's Design

Previously we discussed how God designed three things to go together: sex, marriage, and children. These things were obvious to most people before modern contraception changed the equation.

---

2. Founders Ministries, "Does the Bible Whisper about Sexual Sin? | Robert Gagnon," YouTube, June 23, 2021, https://www.youtube.com/watch?v=Lrb3riruWc8.

Marriage especially protects women as the ones who bear children. Her potential to create new life, and what it takes to nurture new life, is one of the most valuable treasures of the human experience. Women, and their reproductive ability, give humanity its future. Without children, and the women who bear them, humanity has no future. Therefore, as I mentioned in a previous chapter, femininity has an eschatological orientation. The feminine represents the end of things, in their completion and fulfillment. The marriage covenant binds masculine and feminine together, joining them in a one-flesh union, naked and unashamed, where they create life together and bring that life to maturity where the cycle continues.

J. Budziszewski vividly likens human sexuality to a castle containing a quiet courtyard with a secret garden. The garden has a single door, hung with a curtain. Both men and women need to protect this castle, but they do so in different ways. He says, "The castle and the garden express a primary intuition for a woman, but a secondary intuition for a man. A man builds a dwelling; a woman is a dwelling. This is true with utmost literalness of the first nine months for every human being, but it is true at many figurative levels, too. Even though a woman speaks more freely of her emotions than a man does, she lives more within herself. She is an emblem of mystery not only to men, but to herself. The very shape of her flesh is a powerful symbol, for the deepest and most secret place in her body, like the deepest and most secret place in her soul, really is open through only a single door, and really is hung with a curtain."[3]

Dallas Willard wrote, "We are sexual beings: 'male and female created he them' (Gen. 1:27). This crucial passage ties sexuality to our creation in the image of God. It is a part of our power

---

3. Budziszewski, *On the Meaning of Sex*, 115.

with which to serve him. In sexuality the intermingling of person, the knowing and being known that is characteristic of God's basic nature, is provided in a special form for embodied personality. In the full sexual union, the person is known in his or her whole body and knows the other by means of his or her whole body. The involvement is so complete that there can be no such thing as 'casual sex.' It is a contradiction of terms—something very well understood by the apostle Paul, who, accordingly, taught that fornication is a sin against one's own body (1 Cor. 6:18)."[4]

The Song of Solomon presents a beautiful picture of courtship, love, marriage, and sex. Since the woman is the gatekeeper to reproductive success, her garden should not be open to just anyone, but only to a man she deems worthy, which is demonstrated with a ring and a pledge. Before their wedding day, they do "not stir up or awaken love until it pleases" (Song 2:7). She is a "garden locked… a fountain sealed" (Song 4:12). Once she becomes his, they plant a fruitful garden sexually that brings forth new life. He says, "I came to my garden, my sister, my bride" (Song 5:2). She says, "My beloved put his hand to the latch, and my heart was thrilled within me. I arose to open to my beloved" (Song 5:4-5). The erotic imagery is unmistakable. She says, "he is altogether desirable. This is my beloved and this is my friend, O daughters of Jerusalem" (Song 5:16). "My beloved has gone down to his garden to the beds of spices, to graze in the gardens and to gather lilies" (Song 6:3). She calls out, "my beloved is mine, and I am his; he grazes among the lilies" (Song 2:14; 6:3). He is overcome with desire and delight. The fire within him burns bright and strong. Then, he says to her:

---

4. Dallas Willard, *The Spirit of the Disciplines: Understanding How God Changes Lives* (New York: HarperCollins, 1988), 171.

How beautiful are your feet in sandals,
O noble daughter!
Your rounded thighs are like jewels,
the work of a master hand.
Your navel is a rounded bowl
that never lacks mixed wine.
Your belly is a heap of wheat,
encircled with lilies.
Your two breasts are like two fawns,
twins of a gazelle.
Your neck is like an ivory tower.
Your eyes are pools in Heshbon,
by the gate of Bath-rabbim.
Your nose is like a tower of Lebanon,
which looks toward Damascus.
Your head crowns you like Carmel,
and your flowing locks are like purple;
a king is held captive in the tresses.
How beautiful and pleasant you are,
O loved one, with all your delights!
Your stature is like a palm tree,
and your breasts are like its clusters.
I say I will climb the palm tree
and lay hold of its fruit.
Oh may your breasts be like clusters of the vine,
and the scent of your breath like apples,
and your mouth like the best wine (Song 7:1-9).

This is the garden of their love, altogether delightful, as God intended. She is freely feminine and vulnerable; he is freely masculine and strong. In marriage, he has become her castle of protection. Does this sound too fairy tale-ish? Too naive and dreamy? Only if you do not believe Scripture. This is the goodness of sexual intimacy as God designed it. Feminine vulnerability is lovely, and God wants to protect it. But why? Why must it be protected? Because the fire of sexual desire can burn out of control and consume everything in its path. The bride says,

> Set me as a seal upon your heart,
> as a seal upon your arm,
> for love is strong as death,
> jealousy is fierce as the grave.
> Its flashes are flashes of fire,
> the very flame of the Lord.
> Many waters cannot quench love,
> neither can floods drown it.
> If a man offered for love
> all the wealth of his house,
> he would be utterly despised (Song 8:6-7).

Once the goodness of God's design for sexuality is recognized in all its wonder and beauty, the ugliness and horror of the sinful distortions will become clearer as well. Marriage, sex, and child-bearing belong together, and pulling them apart is disastrous. This is precisely what is happening in the modern world.

The Roots of the Problem

The problems we see in the modern world did not arise out of a vacuum but are the consequences of ideas. I made these observations in the introduction, so now I'll connect some more dots. LGBTQ+ ideology is the logical outworking of our culture's acceptance of feminism and Gnosticism. Early feminist thinkers did not hide their agenda. It was out in the open as early as 1949 when French feminist philosopher Simone de Beauvoir wrote about it. Theologian and historian Carl Trueman summarizes her agenda in this way:

1. biological sexual differences will be eliminated (androgyny),
2. heterosexual sex will be replaced by "polymorphous pansexuality,"
3. technology will be utilized to make reproduction available to both men and women,
4. the role of mother will be abolished and replaced by communal parenting,
5. technology will remove the needs for human beings to work at all.[5]

De Beauvoir wrote about these things in the mid-20th century, but it sounds like it was written yesterday. Another feminist writer, Shulamith Firestone, similarly wrote that the natural family was a form of "tyranny."[6] She also wrote that the family structure is a source of psychological, economic, and political oppression. Sadly, she died of starvation, alone in her home, at the age of 67. Her body went undiscovered for days.

These feminist thinkers weren't the only ones who thought this way. Other feminist writers spoke of the family as "oppressive."

---

5. Trueman, *The Rise and Triumph*, 262.
6. Trueman, *The Rise and Triumph*, 261.

The plainly stated goal of many of these feminists was "the destruction of the family."[7]

Fast forwarding to our day, it's plain to see that the goals of feminism have been largely achieved. Men and women are the same, and androgyny is ascendant. We have become a gnostic society, where the material body is merely a prison for the "true, inner self." We have also become a society that hates anything that is truly feminine. What we have now is bland, individualistic androgyny where everyone does what is right in his own eyes. With marriage undermined, redefined, neglected, and ignored by modern society, the raging fire of sexual passion has been set loose, burning and consuming everything in sight. The fire is out of the fireplace, raging out of control.

Sexual Immorality

In the modern world, fatherlessness is epidemic, motherhood is devalued, children are seen as a burden, not a blessing, and abortion has taken the lives of untold millions of children. Further, pornography is ever-present and becoming more common in "mainstream" entertainment. So called "gay marriage" is now seen as a legitimate union. Androgyny is the spirit of the age, where society no longer recognizes the differences between men and women. Transgender activists openly advocate for hormone therapy and even "gender affirming" surgery for children, which has become an important revenue source for many children's hospitals. Sexual abuse is rampant. I have even seen a small but growing trend of normalizing pedophilia (sex with children) as a legitimate sexual orientation. Christians and churches are not immune. Many have

---

7. Trueman, *The Rise and Triumph*, 263.

succumbed to the spirit of the age and become LGBTQ+ affirming. Churches do not discipline members for unrepentant sexual immorality. Pastors themselves have been caught up in a series of scandals of adultery or sexual abuse. God help us.

Sexual immorality dishonors God, cheapens God's gift, deadens the conscience, and damages the soul. In other words, sexual immorality destroys sex. The Greek word for "sexual immorality" is *porneia*. This word includes everything from simple lust to whatever is currently being celebrated during Pride month. *Porneia* includes pornography, fornication, adultery, rape, sexual abuse, homosexuality, incest, transgenderism, bestiality, and others. Yes, you read that right. The list includes bestiality, which is sexual activity with animals. The Bible forbids this. Why? Because people were doing it. The Bible doesn't forbid things no one is practicing. Leviticus 18:23 says, "And you shall not lie with any animal and so make yourself unclean with it, neither shall any woman give herself to an animal to lie with it: it is perversion." The excesses of LGBTQ pride month are nothing new. They happened in the ancient world as well, perhaps without the endorsement of every major cultural institution. Our culture is sex obsessed. Its normalization of all things *porneia* has created an environment that sees any restrictions to sexual pleasure as regressive. A culture that has cast aside sexual restraint and feels compelled to celebrate the latest sexual novelty is a society imploding.

Take pornography, for example. It is highly addictive. Like a drug addict, pornography lures the viewer into more novel and sometimes bizarre or perverse sexual behaviors, while deadening the conscience to its effect on the soul. Over time, one's perception of right and wrong changes, eroding his or her ability to see the sinfulness of sexual immorality as truly sinful. Without question, our society's increased exposure to graphic or even violent forms of pornography has deadened our collective conscience.

The website for Mission Frontiers reports the following:

- There are around 42 million porn websites, which totals around 370 million pages of porn.
- The porn industry's annual revenue is more than the NFL, NBA, and MLB *combined*. It is also more than the combined revenues of ABC, CBS, and NBC.
- 47% of families in the United States reported that pornography is a problem in their home.
- Pornography use increases the marital infidelity rate by more than 300%.
- The average age that a child is first exposed to porn is age 11… and 94% of children will see porn by the age of 14.
- 56% percent of American divorces involve one party having an 'obsessive interest' in pornographic websites.
- 68% of church-going men and over 50% of pastors view porn on a regular basis.
- Of young Christian adults 18 to 24 years old, 76% actively search for porn.
- 57% of pastors say porn addiction is the most damaging issue in their congregation. 69% percent say porn has adversely impacted the church.[8]

Another issue is fornication. Fornication refers to unmarried partners having sex. C. S. Lewis wrote, "The monstrosity of sexual intercourse outside marriage is that those who indulge in it are trying to isolate one kind of union (the sexual) from all the other kinds of union which were intended to go along with it and make

---

8. "15 Mind-Blowing Statistics About Pornography And The Church," http://www.missionfrontiers.org/issue/article/15-mind-blowing-statistics-about-pornography-and-the-church (Accessed July 7, 2022).

up the total union. The Christian attitude does not mean that there is anything wrong about sexual pleasure, any more than about the pleasure of eating. It means that you must not isolate that pleasure and try to get it by itself, any more than you ought to try to get the pleasures of taste without swallowing and digesting, by chewing things and spitting them out."[9] In other words, fornication is immoral because it involves a life uniting act without a life uniting intent. The word "fornication" has become less common while the sin it represents has become more common. At one time, our culture frowned upon the practice, but that's no longer the case. Now, it is considered bizarre for a couple to *not* have sex before marriage. After all, wouldn't you test drive a car before buying it?

Homosexuality has become increasingly normalized and celebrated in our culture. It is well documented but scarcely reported that promiscuity among gay men is extremely high. Since men in general have a higher sex drive than women, gay men are not as restrained sexually towards one another. Compared to heterosexual men, homosexual men are more likely to have a very high number of sexual partners, more likely to have sex with strangers, and are much more likely to have "open" relationships, where two men may commit to live and share life together while still having sex with other men. According to one survey, 28% of gay men have had sex with more than 1,000 partners. Gay men are at higher risk for health complications, such as syphilis, gonorrhea, chlamydia, hepatitis, HIV, and anal cancer. Additionally, gay men are more likely to abuse drugs and alcohol, have eating disorders, and experience depression and anxiety.[10]

---

9. Lewis, *Mere Christianity* (London, England: William Collins), 81.

10. Glick, Sara Nelson, Martina Morris, Betsy Foxman, Sevgi O. Aral, Lisa E. Manhart, King K. Holmes, and Matthew R. Golden, "A Comparison of Sexual Behavior Patterns among Men Who Have Sex with Men and Heterosexual Men and Women," *Journal of Acquired Immune Deficiency Syndromes* (1999) 60, no. 1: 83–90, https://doi.

In my pastoral experience, I've noticed an increasing number of people who cannot reconcile their Christian faith with the LGBTQ+ movement. In evangelistic conversations, people will not talk about the gospel until they know whether I affirm LGBTQ+ lifestyles or not. It's a litmus test, a "defeater belief" that is foundational to their worldview. Accepting LGBTQ+ lifestyles is so basic to their thinking that anyone who disagrees must be a hateful, bigoted dinosaur. Nevertheless, the nature of the gospel will be considered offensive to a culture that regards sexual sin as personal identity. Christians who have been influenced by endless bombardment of pro-LGBTQ propaganda have waivered in their faith, wondering why God would not simply accept LGBTQ+ lifestyles as legitimate expressions of Christian love. "Love is love," we're told. You could also say, "water is water," but that doesn't mean we should drink from the toilet.

The LGBTQ+ movement has no brakes. As our society stops creating babies in favor of creating an ever-expanding number of gender identities, there is no logical stopping point. The LGBTQ+ ideology represents a sexual impulse that is suicidal. Everyone's personal sexual identity must be absolutely respected and affirmed. Failure to affirm these identities is regarded as evidence of oppression. In a strange irony, LGBTQ+ activists have seized the moral high ground, posturing themselves as the champions of love, virtue, and moral goodness. The out-of-control nature of the LGBTQ+ movement is clear from the "plus" sign at the end because it indicates the limitless potential of sexual identities that crave recognition and celebration. The ever-growing list includes identities like non-binary, genderqueer, gender fluid, gender neutral, Two-spirit, and so on. There are also more classical terms such as polygamy, polyamory, polyandry, pedophilia, and bestiality. Where does it end? At the time of this writing, a quick Google search indicated there are 78 different gender identities and pronouns for each.

For all these reasons, Kevin DeYoung wisely wrote, "It cannot be overstated how seriously the Bible treats the sin of sexual immorality. Sexual sin is never considered *adiaphora*, a matter of indifference, an agree-to-disagree issue like food laws or holy days (Rom. 14:1-15:7). To the contrary, sexual immorality is precisely the sort of sin that characterizes those who will not enter the kingdom of heaven. There are at least eight vice lists in the New Testament (Mark 7:21-22; Rom. 1:24-31; 13:13;1 Cor. 6:9-10; Gal. 5:19-21; Col. 3:5-9; 1 Tim. 1:9-10; Rev. 21:8), and sexual immorality is included in every one of these. In fact, in seven of the eight lists there are multiple references to sexual immorality (e.g., impurity, sensuality, orgies, men who practice homosexuality), and in most of the passages some kind of sexual immorality heads the lists. You would be hard-pressed to find a sin more frequently, more uniformly, and more seriously condemned in the New Testament than sexual sin."[11]

The new sexual orthodoxy is a false teaching that must be rejected by the church. It is a deadly ideology that does harm to Christians, the church, and the cause of Christ. It is incompatible with the gospel because it makes sexuality the defining feature of a person's existence. This makes comprehending the gospel more difficult. The world tells people, "Your sexual desires and behaviors are your primary identity. That's what defines you as a human being. To be authentically human, you must order your life around

---

11. Kevin DeYoung, "A Theological Stress Test," https://kevindeyoung.org/a-theological-stress-test/ (Accessed July 7, 2022).

it. You will never be truly happy or free until you fully embrace your sexuality."

This confusion around sexuality hits adolescents particularly hard, since they are experiencing puberty, a confusing time when they are already vulnerable. Their bodies are changing, and their hormones are raging. Young men and women, who are seeking to understand their sexuality, often receive little guidance from parents and churches, so they turn to Google, YouTube, or social media for answers. These sources often set them on a painful course from which they may never recover. Those who have embraced these lifestyles and identities are image bearers of God that need to hear the good news of the gospel. We want them to know that they can have forgiveness of sin, new life in Christ, and hope of eternal life.

The Uniqueness of Sexual Sin

Sex is spiritual. It involves not only a physical act, but also an experience of transcendence. The LGBTQ+ "community" has a cult-like power over people, pulling them in and never letting them go. Some might even say that there is no human experience that can match the mystical thrill of sex. It is the strongest of the human passions, because, deep down, we long for the divine. God designed sex as a covenant renewal ceremony where man and woman become one-flesh before the God who joined them. As one novelist famously said, "the young man who rings the bell at the brothel is unconsciously looking for God."[12]

---

12. Bruce Marshall, *The World, the Flesh, and Father Smith* (Boston: Houghton Mifflin, 1945), 108.

Some Christians might raise an objection that Christians make too big of a deal about sexual sin. Some have even argued that an overemphasis on sexual purity ultimately harms people. After all, what's the harm if an engaged couple slips up sexually before they get married? Since we are under grace, not law, they argue, shouldn't Christians take a more gracious posture and leave it alone? None of us are perfect. Besides, many Christian men and women have a lot of sexual sin in their past, but they repented of it, believed the gospel, and went on to have godly marriages and to live lives of faithful service to God. May God be praised for these testimonies of grace. No sin is beyond the reach of God's grace. Another objection is to relativize the sin of sexual immorality since everyone is a sinner in need of God's grace. Why should sexual sin be any different? This problem is not new—it was previously addressed in the Westminster Larger Catechism, which asks, "Are all transgressions of the law equally heinous?" The answer is, "some sins in themselves, and by reason of several aggravations, are more heinous in the sight of God than others."[13]

Sexual immorality, however, is not like other sins. It is unique in at least three ways. First, sexual immorality is a sin against one's own body. The modern world has become more gnostic in its thinking, seeing the body as incidental to who we truly are. Gnostic thinking sees the body as a non-essential part of our personhood, more like a prison for the soul, so what we do with our bodies is relatively unimportant. No harm, no foul. If no obvious physical or psychological harm can be observed, then it's not a big deal. However, this isn't Christianity. Remember, we are embodied souls, and the physical part of us is just as much a part of who we are as the spiritual part. This is what Paul means in 1 Corinthians

13. *The Westminster Larger Catechism: With Scripture Proofs* (Oak Harbor, WA: Logos Research Systems, Inc., 1996), question 150.

6:18 when he says, "Flee from sexual immorality. Every other sin a person commits is outside the body, but the sexually immoral person sins against his own body."

Second, sexual immorality defiles sacred space. The body of a Christian is sacred space because we are indwelt by the Spirit. First Corinthians 6:17 says, "He who is joined to the Lord becomes one spirit with him." Paul goes on to say, "Do you not know that your body is a temple of the Holy Spirit within you, whom you have from God? You are not your own, for you were bought with a price. So glorify God in your body" (vv. 19-20). This text teaches that every Christian must surrender his or her sexuality to God. When Paul says, "glorify God in your body," he means we can either glorify God or dishonor God with our sexual desires and behaviors. Christ, having fulfilled the purpose of the original temple (John 2:21), sent his Holy Spirit into the world (Acts 2:4), and transformed his people into the new dwelling place of God (Rev 21:3). Now, our physical bodies are "living stones" of an eternal temple (1 Peter 2:5). A Christian embracing sexual immorality is like a church renting out its building to a prostitution ring. Paul said, "Do you not know that your bodies are members of Christ? Shall I then take the members of Christ and make them members of a prostitute? Never!" (1 Cor 6:15). Therefore, Paul says, "I wrote to you in my letter not to associate with sexually immoral people," referring to any Christian who "bears the name of brother" but embraces a lifestyle of sexual sin (1 Cor 5:9, 11).

Third, sexual immorality is associated with paganism. As discussed previously, humans are embodied souls, so sex is never a mere physical act. The OT consistently demonstrates the connection between sexual immorality and idolatry, and God forbids both (Deut 23:17; Lev 18:21). These practices indicate that sex is spiritual. It's not just something that feels good. Sex touches the soul.

The pagan spiritual underpinnings of sexual immorality should not be overlooked by modern Christians because sexuality and worship are connected. Herman Bavinck noted that men often oscillate between the extremes of oppressing women and worshiping them. He writes, "Down through the centuries and among all nations, among philosophers and among the unreflective masses, women haters have exchanged places with women worshippers. And men have hardly remained constant in their own judgment, but frequently move from the one to the other extreme. At one time or another, the woman is an angel or a devil, a queen or a vixen, a dove or a serpent, a rose or a thorn. The feminine is identified as divine, and then again as demonic. The man kneels before her in worship, only then to pin her under his foot. Frequently the conclusion is that the woman is a riddle; the man does not understand her."[14] This is an important insight that helps explain why men who murder women often develop a sick fetish that at once idolizes them yet despises them. At the other extreme are men who wish to be bound, beaten, and oppressed by women.

These are not merely perverted sexual acts. It goes deeper than that. The ideology itself is demonic. This should not be surprising, since this a consistent pattern throughout the Bible. Paganism has always sought to bend, blend, twist, invert, and destroy sexuality. In an essay about sexuality and paganism, Peter R. Jones shows how androgyny has always been a hallmark of pagan spirituality. He cites one example of a female "spirit guide" of the New Age movement who said that "sexual identity confusion in young people is a good thing, because in the New Age, people will be androgynous." The idealized future for her is a neo-pagan utopia where androgyny is the norm. Another example he mentions is Emily Culpepper, an

---

14. Bavinck, *The Christian Family*, 67.

ex-Southern Baptist turned lesbian pagan witch, who sees gays and lesbians as a form of priesthood, calling them "shamans for a future age." In yet another example, Jones cites an "evangelical lesbian feminist" who describes gays and lesbians as "God's Ambassadors." In other words, according to Jones, paganism regards androgyny as the sexual ideal.[15]

Writing in 2002, Jones correctly anticipated where things were headed. He wrote, "Do you want to capture a civilization? Change its perceptions of sexuality… The pagan agenda is the elimination of the distinction between male and female."[16] Therefore, Jones concludes, "It is evident that sexual perversion and the elimination of sexual distinctions are not incidental footnotes of pagan religious history but represent one of paganism's fundamental ideological commitments. As we have noted, the pagan priesthood is identified, across space and time, with the blurring of sexual identity via homosexual androgyny. If history is a wise teacher, we may surely conclude that paganism will always give enormous priority to destroying God-ordained monogamous heterosexuality and to promoting androgyny in its varied forms."[17]

The book of Jude has a cryptic reference to sexuality and the sin of angels. It says, "And the angels who did not stay within their own position of authority, but left their proper dwelling, he has kept in eternal chains under gloomy darkness until the judgment of the great day—just as Sodom and Gomorrah and the surrounding cities, which likewise indulged in sexual immorality

---

15. Peter R. Jones, "Sexual Perversion: The Necessary Fruit of Neo-Pagan Spirituality in the Culture at Large," in *Biblical Foundations for Manhood and Womanhood*, ed. Wayne Grudem, Foundations for the Family Series (Wheaton, IL: Crossway Books, 2002), 270–273.

16. Jones, "Sexual Perversion," in Wayne Grudem, ed., *Biblical Foundations for Manhood and Womanhood*, 263.

17. Jones, "Sexual Perversion," in Wayne Grudem, ed., *Biblical Foundations for Manhood and Womanhood*, 272–273.

and pursued unnatural desire, serve as an example by undergoing a punishment of eternal fire" (vv. 6-7). Jude is referencing the story of Genesis 6, where it seems angelic beings during the days of Noah rebelled and had sex with human women. This sin prompted the flood and the subsequent judgment of Sodom and Gomorrah for their sexual immorality. In ancient fertility cults, people had sex with prostitutes, hoping it would cause rain to fall and crops to grow. Pagan religious practices of the ancient world often included rituals that included cult prostitution, homosexuality, and child sacrifice, where infants were offered up to the pagan gods Molech or Chemosh. Satan hates children. It isn't hard to see the connection between child sacrifice and abortion. Catholic writer Peter Kreeft said, "A million mothers a year in America alone pay hired killers, who are called healers or physicians, to kill their own unborn daughters and sons. How could this happen? Only because abortion is driven by sexual motives. For abortion is backup birth control, and birth control is the demand to have sex without having babies. If the stork brought babies, there'd be no Planned Parenthood."[18]

Simply put, sexual immorality is spiritual, because human beings are spiritual. As the new dwelling place of God by the Holy Spirit, our bodies are sacred, holy, and set apart for the Lord's service. We are not our own, but we were bought with a price. Thus, sexual immorality has a unique, spiritual dimension to it because it defiles a sacred space. Satan inverts and twists reality. That's his strategy, as it was in the beginning when he attacked God's design and questioned God's word. Sexual holiness matters because our bodies belong to God, and our sexual body parts belong to God. We are called to

---

18. Peter Kreeft, "A Refutation of Moral Relativism [Transcription] by Peter Kreeft," https://peterkreeft.com/audio/05_relativism/relativism_transcription.htm (Accessed July 21, 2022).

present our bodies to God as a "living sacrifice, holy and acceptable to God, which is your spiritual worship" (Rom 12:1).

In a world that embraces sexual immorality, it is always important to keep the grace of God in view, since so many people struggle with sexual sin and regret. The grace of God calls sinners to repent and find hope in Christ. Christ conquered the grave. Jesus brings the dead to life. No sin, including sexual sin, is beyond the reach of God's grace. I highlight the seriousness of sexual sin not to heap condemnation, but to call Christians to holiness. If sin is no longer bad, then the gospel is no longer good. The matchless grace of God shines beautifully against the darkness of our wicked pasts. These are sensitive issues for many Christians who have deep regret for their past sins. Let this serve as a reminder that, in Christ, we can forget the past and, in hope, strain towards a more glorious future.

The Three Aspects of Sexuality

To understand what's happening with sexual immorality in the modern world, we need to consider three aspects of sexuality and evaluate each of them in light of Scripture. The three aspects we will examine are behavior, desire, and identity.[19] These three aspects are at the heart of the modern confusion regarding sexuality. The biggest problem in the modern world is the impulse to turn sexual desires and behaviors into new identities.

The Scriptures are sufficient to deal with all our human complexity, equipping us with what we need to glorify God with our behaviors, desires, and identity. The tactic of LGBTQ+ activists, on the other hand, is to collapse desire and behavior into the new identity category. In a world where people are desperate to discover

19. I am indebted to Jerry Armelli for introducing me to this three-fold schema.

themselves, find an identity, and authentically express who they are, this is powerful messaging. One's sexual desires and behaviors have now become fundamental categories of personhood. This isn't new, as Freud was saying this over a hundred years ago, but the idea exploded in the early 21st century. This is the genius of the modern LGBTQ movement. Sexuality is identity, period. If this is what one believes, then any notion of change or repentance becomes an existential crisis. This is antithetical to the gospel.

Behavior

We've already addressed sinful sexual behavior earlier in this chapter, so I won't devote as much space to it here. God designed physical intimacy to be enjoyed exclusively between a husband and wife. The purpose of sex is to foster relational intimacy, have children, and to prevent sexual immorality. It might sound strange to put it this way, but sexual intimacy in marriage is a duty in Scripture. Paul said, "The husband should give to his wife her conjugal rights, and likewise the wife to her husband" (1 Cor 7:3). Sexual intimacy between a husband and wife strengthens their marital bond and glorifies God. They should not deprive one another.

Since this is God's design for sexual intimacy, any sexual act outside the marriage covenant is sin. The Bible does specify and forbid some sexual sins, but there are simply too many ways people sin sexually to name them all. Any sexual activity outside of marriage belongs in the category of *porneia* and is sinful. Further, it should be noted that the marriage covenant does not sanctify *every* sexual act. Some sexual acts are inherently unnatural and degrading, even between husband and wife. Paul says "let each one of you love his wife as himself, and let the wife see that she respects her husband" (Eph 5:33). This admonition extends to the marriage bed. Marital sex is a covenant ceremony where a man and wife share their bodies with one another. It is a gift for building one another up in love. It should dignify, not degrade, the other.

Desire

Sexual desire isn't inherently sinful. It is natural, human, and God given. God created sexual desire to find exclusive expression in the marriage bed (1 Cor 7:2; Heb 13:4). The desire for one's spouse is healthy and good. The seat of desire is the heart, the control center of the whole life. When one desires something sinful, that desire is itself sin. This was a key insight from the Sermon on the Mount, where Jesus taught that sin is not merely an act of the body, but springs from deeper heart desires. In other words, sin isn't merely outer action but sin begins in the heart. A sinful act is the outworking of a sinful desire. To desire sin is sin.

Some LGBTQ+ affirming Christians have disputed this point, making the case that only homosexual *behavior* is sinful. Homosexual *desire*, however, can be holy and sanctified for Christians. This is the perspective of gay-affirming writers such as Wesley Hill. Hill describes himself as a "gay Christian" who holds traditional views on sexuality and marriage. Yet he has chosen celibacy because he believes homosexual intercourse is sinful while believing that a "gay identity" is appropriate for Christians. Hill said, "Being gay colors everything about me, even though I am celibate… Being gay is, for me, as much a sensibility as anything else: a heightened sensitivity to and passion for same-sex beauty that helps determine the kind of conversations I have, which people I'm drawn to spend time with, what novels and poems and films I enjoy, the particular visual art I appreciate, and also, I think, the kind of friendships I pursue and try to strengthen. I don't imagine I would have invested half as much effort in loving my male friends, and making sacrifices of time, energy, and even money on their behalf, if I weren't gay. My sexuality, my basic erotic orientation to the world, is inescapably intertwined with how I go about finding and keeping friends."[20]

The NT employs several Greek words to describe various types of sexual behaviors and desires.[21] We have already discussed the word *porneia,* which is the most common word for all manner of sexual sin. The word *epithumia* refers to sinful desire, commonly translated into English as "passions" (Rom 6:12), "lust" (Rom 1:24), "coveting" (Rom 7:7), and evil "desire" (Rom 13:14).[22] Another word is *aselgeia,* translated as "sensuality" in several texts, almost always with the connotation of sinful sexual desire. *Pleonexia* is commonly translated as "covet," often with a sexual connotation. Finally, the word *akatharsia* means impurity, immorality, or filthiness. Different combinations of these words often appear together in key New Testament passages about sexual sin. For example, Jesus said, "But I say to you that everyone who looks at a woman with lustful intent (*epithumeo*) has already committed adultery with her in his heart" (Matt 5:28). In Mark 7, Jesus said, "What comes out of a person is what defiles him. For from within, out of the heart of man, come evil thoughts, sexual immorality (*porneia*), theft, murder, adultery, coveting (*pleonexia*), wickedness, deceit, sensuality (*aselgeia*), envy, slander, pride, foolishness. All these evil things

---

20. Denny Burk, "Learning to Hate Our Sin without Hating Ourselves." https://www.thepublicdiscourse.com/2018/07/22066/ (Accessed July 22, 2022).

21. Johannes P. Louw and Eugene Albert Nida, *Greek-English Lexicon of the New Testament: Based on Semantic Domains* (New York: United Bible Societies, 1996).

22. See also James 1:14-15. James also uses the word *epithumia,* but he uses it in a different way. James doesn't argue that desires aren't sinful, but sinful desires lead to sinful actions which leads, ultimately, to death.

come from within, and they defile a person" (vv. 20-23). In Galatians 5, Paul says, "Now the works of the flesh are evident: sexual immorality (*porneia*), impurity (*akatharsia*), sensuality (*aselgeia*)... orgies (*komos*), and things like these. I warn you, as I warned you before, that those who do such things will not inherit the kingdom of God" (vv. 19-21). Ephesians 5:3 says, "But sexual immorality (*porneia*) and all impurity (*akatharsia*) or covetousness (*pleonexia*) must not even be named among you, as is proper among saints." Colossians 3:5-7 says, "Put to death therefore what is earthly in you: sexual immorality, impurity, passion, evil desire, and covetousness, which is idolatry. On account of these the wrath of God is coming." Jesus and Paul clearly condemned sinful sexual behaviors *and* sinful desires.

Denny Burk and Rosario Butterfield put it this way: "The Bible teaches that our desires—all of them, voluntary or involuntary—are morally implicated. Desire is teleological, and its moral character is determined by its object. If someone desires a good thing, then the desire itself is good (e.g., 1 Tim. 3:1; Matt. 13:17). If someone desires an evil thing, then the desire itself is evil, quite apart from whether or not the desire is voluntary (e.g., 1 Cor. 10:6). This holds for all human desire, including but not exclusively sexual desire." [23] In other words, *the desire to sin is sin.*

The tenth commandment explicitly forbids sinful desire. Exodus 20:17 reads, "You shall not covet your neighbor's house; you shall not covet your neighbor's wife, or his male servant, or his female servant, or his ox, or his donkey, or anything that is your neighbor's." The word "covet" means to "desire" or "take pleasure in." [24] In other words, the seventh commandment forbids the act of

---

23. Burk, "Learning to Hate Our Sin."

24. Francis Brown, Samuel Rolles Driver, and Charles Augustus Briggs, *Enhanced Brown-Driver-Briggs Hebrew and English Lexicon* (Oxford: Clarendon Press, 1977), 326.

adultery. The tenth commandment forbids the desire for adultery. It does not matter if the desire is voluntary or involuntary. It is always sin to desire sin. Jesus taught the same thing in the Sermon on the Mount when he said that a man "who looks at a woman with lustful intent has already committed adultery with her in his heart" (Matt 5:28). He wasn't being innovative. He was merely pointing out the connection that already existed between the seventh and tenth commandments.

There is another distinction that needs to be made. As mentioned previously, some sins are more sinful than others (John 19:11). All sexual lust is sinful and dishonors God. Yet, there is a subspecies of lust that adds to the offense because it is unnatural. For example, if a man and woman are engaged to be married, they may sinfully lust for one another as they anticipate consummating their marriage. This is a sinful desire for something that is natural and good, but premature. The lust is sinful because they are unmarried, not because it is unnatural. In this case, Paul says, "if they cannot exercise self-control, they should marry. For it is better to marry than to burn with passion" (1 Cor 7:9). But suppose a man lusts over another man. In this case, there is no possible context where God would sanction their union. There could never be a holy consummation of that desire because the desire itself is unnatural. Both desires are sinful, but unnatural homosexual desire entails the additional offense of sinning against nature.

But he gives more grace. Through faith in Christ, we have everything we need to overcome any sin and temptation. Peter says we have been given "all things that pertain to life and godliness," and we have even "become partakers of the divine nature, having escaped the corruption that is in the world because of sinful desire (*epithumia*)" (2 Pet 1:3-4). In other words, we are not controlled by our sinful desires. We have power over them because of the divine power at work in us.

To be clear, making the distinction between natural and unnatural sin is not intended to excuse heterosexual sin, such as fornication and adultery. But the distinction is necessary to be helpful to those who struggle with LGBTQ+ type temptations. The Scriptures warn that embracing LGBTQ+ type sins are evidence of God's judgment. Paul said, "For this reason God gave them up to dishonorable passions. For their women exchanged natural relations for those that are contrary to nature; and the men likewise gave up natural relations with women and were consumed with passion for one another, men committing shameless acts with men and receiving in themselves the due penalty for their error" (Rom 1:26-27). A few verses later, Paul adds another warning about celebrating and promoting these sins. He says, "Though they know God's righteous decree that those who practice such things deserve to die, they not only do them but give approval to those who practice them" (Rom 1:32).

In my view, the language of "same sex attraction" is misleading, especially for impressionable Christians who are not yet equipped to make finer moral distinctions. "Same sex attraction" makes a sinful desire sound less sinful, because "attraction" is a word with positive associations. Many, if not most, Christians have adopted this language in an effort to be gracious towards those who are fighting this sin, which is understandable. But it is unwise because the language of "attraction" obscures meaning. We do not say that greedy people are "attracted to money," for example. We just say they are greedy because that's more honest (Ex 20:17). Similarly, we would not say a lying man is "attracted to deceit." That obscures what's really going on, which is dishonesty. It would be wiser and more appropriate to simply speak of someone being "same sex tempted" than to say "same sex attracted."

Some have objected to this argument, citing Hebrews 4:15, which says, "For we do not have a high priest who is unable to sympathize with our weaknesses, but one who in every respect has been tempted as we are, yet without sin." Therefore, as the logic goes, if Jesus was tempted in every respect, then Jesus must have been tempted by homosexual desire. This view is incorrect.

The author of Hebrews was not indicating that Jesus was tempted by an internal desire for sin. Rather, he is referring to the incident when Jesus was tempted by Satan in the wilderness. This is an important distinction. One is an internal temptation and the other is an external temptation. James 1:13 says, "God cannot be tempted by evil." As we have already noted, the desire for sin is sin. Therefore, Jesus was not tempted by any internal sinful desire, but Jesus was tempted by an external tempter, Satan, who unsuccessfully tried to entice Jesus to sin.

The Greek word for "tempt" in Hebrew 4:15, and in the gospel accounts of Jesus' temptation, is *peirazo*. It is defined as the "attempt to cause someone to sin—'to tempt, to trap, to lead into temptation.'" [25] In other words, it refers to a temptation that is external to the one tempted, not a temptation that arises from within a person's own desires. Thus, Hebrews 4:15 does not teach that Jesus was tempted by sinful desires that arose from within him, but from an external source of temptation, Satan himself. Matthew, Mark, and Luke all use *peirazo* to describe Jesus' temptation (Matt 4:1, Mark 1:13, Luke 4:1). In Matthew's version, the word also appears as a sort of title for Satan, because he is the tempter. It reads, "And the tempter (*peirazo*) came and said to him..." (Matt 4:3). Temptation

---

25. Johannes P. Louw and Eugene Albert Nida, *Greek-English Lexicon of the New Testament: Based on Semantic Domains* (New York: United Bible Societies, 1996), 774

refers to Satan's action, not Jesus' desire. Satan tempted Jesus to sin, but Jesus never desired the sin he was tempted with. Jesus was indeed tempted in the wilderness for 40 days by Satan, but at no point in that encounter did Jesus desire anything sinful. Therefore, if Jesus experienced homosexual desire for another man, for example, he would be guilty of lust, which is itself a sin. In this case, he would be a sinner and not our savior.

Identity

We have already seen how the Scriptures treat immoral sexual desires and sexual behaviors as separate but related sin categories. Those who have sinned in such ways can repent of these sins, receive forgiveness, be adopted into God's household, and have hope of eternal life with Christ. But something relatively new has happened in recent years. Sexual sin has become an identity. One man said it well: "equating sexual desire with personal identity is a Satanic masterstroke."[26]

In the past, people got a sense of who they were by belonging to a particular family, living in a particular community, doing a particular kind of work, being connected to a particular people, and having a particular body (being male or female). In the modern world, people are alienated from these identity markers more than ever. It is common for people to feel estranged and detached. Where do people get a sense of identity, purpose, and worth now? The answer for a growing number of people is "sexual identity."

We see the concept of "sexual identity" everywhere. The language is so common that one could easily assume it's always been

---

26. I heard Jonathan Leeman say this on a Pastor's Talk podcast, but I don't remember the episode or date.

that way, but it hasn't. Homosexual sex is nothing new, of course. One could say homosexual sex was the first form of contraception—men could have sex without risking pregnancy by having sex with each other. Historians have noted how men in Alexander the Great's armies had sex with each other while they were away conquering foreign lands.[27] Being a sex toy for older men was considered part of life for many young boys in some ancient cultures. Nearly all of these men would have had wives and children, however. Even though they practiced homosexual behaviors and/or desires, they would never have considered homosexuality as an identity. That's a modern invention created by John Money, drawing inspiration from Freud. In the 1950's, John Money was a psychologist and "sexologist" for Johns Hopkins University who first asserted that one's sexual preferences should be categorized as an orientation.[28] He believed that homosexual desires were not a matter of preference but were innate and fixed. In short, sexual desires constitute a sexual identity, an entire category of personhood. Money's perspective has now gained wide acceptance, creating chaos and confusion along the way.

In Scripture there is no such thing as a "gender identity," other than male and female. Those are the only two legitimate ways to identify people by their sexuality (Gen 1:27; 1 Cor 6:9-11). These two identities include biological sex and extend to the potentialities latent within their sexuality. I'll quote J. Budziszewski again on this point: "Sanity begins with the fact that men are potentially fathers, and women potentially mothers. This is not just a fact

---

27. Philip Freeman, *Alexander the Great* (New York, NY: Simon & Schuster, 2011), 259.

28. "John Money," https://kinseyinstitute.org/about/profiles/john-money.php (Accessed July 8, 2022).

about what kind of thing they might or might not do some day, but about what kind of being they are inwardly aimed at becoming."[29]

John Money cracked open the door of gender identity and modern LGBTQ+ activists have kicked it down and burst through. Our culture is coming up with an ever-expanding list of new sexual identities that demand acceptance and affirmation. Carl Trueman wrote, "before Freud, sex was an activity, for procreation or for recreation; after Freud, sex is definitive of who we are, as individuals, as societies, and as a species."[30] The word "homosexual" is itself a relatively modern invention, coined in the late 19th century by German psychologist Karoly Maria Benkert.[31]

The King James Bible, originally published in the 17th century, uses words like "effeminate" and "abusers of themselves with mankind" to describe homosexual sex. The Sodom and Gomorrah story of Genesis 19 led to the word "sodomy" being used to describe homosexual sex. "Homosexual" was not an identity but a behavior. The notion that one's unnatural sexual desires and behaviors could be regarded as an essential part of one's personhood is a novel idea that imprisons people within a nearly inescapable ideological commitment. It convinces them that their sin is essential to their personhood. It becomes their defining feature. It is axiomatic. It's who they are. To do otherwise would be a denial of their own existence. Therefore, when someone who is tempted with homosexuality considers the question, "who am I?," they must begin with words that are most essential to their personhood, such as "lesbian," "gay," "bi-sexual," "transgender," or "queer."

---

29. Budziszewski, *On the Meaning of Sex*, 135.
30. Trueman, *The Rise and Triumph*, 221.
31. Brent Pickett, "Homosexuality," in *The Stanford Encyclopedia of Philosophy*, ed. Edward N. Zalta, Spring 2021, Metaphysics Research Lab, Stanford University, https://plato.stanford.edu/entries/homosexuality/.

A woman named Emily in my church has a twin sister who became a lesbian, got legally married to another woman, adopted a daughter with her, and has now begun "transitioning" and identifying as a male. I have prayed with Emily a number of times about her sister and her daughter. She's tried sharing the gospel but has gotten nowhere with her. Since Emily will not recognize her as a man, her sister has cut her out of her life and refuses to talk to her. But Emily continues to pray and reach out on occasion. Recently, Emily told me she sent her sister a simple text, saying "I miss you." She responded, "am I your sister or your brother?" Emily responded, "I love you no matter what," to which her sister responded, "We cannot speak again until you acknowledge me as I am." This story highlights the modern trend where LGBTQ+ activists have become the self-righteous crusaders in their cause, enacting discipline and refusing fellowship with anyone who doesn't "repent" of their regressive views.

Some Christians have bought into John Money's thinking, using it as an interpretive grid for all of Scripture. Matthew Vines, who calls himself a "gay Christian," argues that being gay is a fixed orientation, a legitimate sexual identity, and must therefore be considered "natural."[32] His sexuality is so essential to his personhood that his orientation must be read back into Scripture. The absurdity of his logic and biblical interpretation is surpassed only by its rhetorical power. It gives them an excuse to give in to their sinful desires and continue in sinful behaviors. If "gay" is a legitimate personal identity, then one must fully embrace all things pertaining to their sexual identity to be authentically human. "God made me gay, and God makes no mistakes." Rather than seeing these sexual desires or behaviors as sins to be repented of, forgiven, and

---

32. Matthew Vines, "The Gay Debate: The Bible and Homosexuality," YouTube, March 10, 2012, https://www.youtube.com/watch?v=ezQjNJUSraY.

fought against, those very desires and behaviors are what defines them as humans.

The heartbreaking reality is that treating sin as a personal identity builds a prison around that person's soul from which they feel they can never escape. This leaves them without hope. Calling them to repentance is like calling them to stop being human. This is a cruel, unforgiving worldview. Because of how politically charged the issue has become, and the aggressive, bullying tactics of LGBTQ+ activists, sexual sin has managed to become a protected class of sins with its own set of unbiblical rules. No other sin is treated this way. Any Christian who made greed a personal identity would be laughed out of the room. There have always been those within the church who want to turn the grace of God into a license for sin. Jude warns about ungodly people "who pervert the grace of our God into sensuality and deny our only Master and Lord, Jesus Christ" (Jude 4). As the pressure from the culture to affirm and celebrate LGBTQ+ lifestyles have increased, some Christians, leaders, and churches are following suit. We must not give in.

Engaging Sexual Sin with the Power of the Gospel

Many books have been written about how to deal with various sexual sins and temptations, which is beyond the scope of this chapter. For our purposes here, we will focus on two different "scripts" that can play out when someone is tempted with unnatural sexual sin.[33]

---

33. A good place to start is Joe Rigney's book, *More than a Battle: How to Experience Victory, Freedom, and Healing from Lust* (Nashville, TN: B&H Publishing Group, 2021).

The Gay Script

The first script I call the "gay script." According to the gay script, *sexuality is identity*. We see it all the time in movies, TV shows, news, social media, and so on. Here's how it goes. Suppose a young boy has a crush on another boy at school. Further, suppose they had even kissed each other during summer break and it excited him. The moment was electric, mysterious, weird, thrilling, all at once. He can't get it out of his mind. He's seen enough movies and TV shows to know that this is very significant, and it may indicate something essential about who he is as a human being. And so his mind moves quickly from the initial desire and behavior all the way to identity formation. It triggers an existential crisis. He begins to wonder, "Am I gay? Am I bisexual? Am I transgender?"

In a way, it scares him, but it also excites him. This all happened in June, where Pride month is in full swing. Everybody's talking about it, sharing their stories of how happy they are now that they're finally free to be who they truly are. He sees LGBTQ+ people treated as courageous, heroic, and worthy of admiration. The celebration of LGBTQ+ lifestyles makes him think that perhaps the unhappiness he's felt in his life could be due to his failure to recognize and embrace who he truly is. Besides, he's always felt a little awkward and unsure of himself. Maybe this is why. Like every other adolescent going through puberty, he wants to discover who he really is and what his life is going to be all about. So, he turns to Google for answers. Then to Instagram. And YouTube. He finds a 10-question "quizlet" online called "Am I gay?" and he takes it. He explores all his questions behind the safety of anonymity. Unsurprisingly, almost all the resources he finds encourage him to move towards embracing an LGBTQ+ identity. Those websites link to more websites, podcasts, books, and other resources. He tumbles down the rabbit hole, further and further. It sucks him in. Everyone he meets online is telling him to celebrate his new identity.

He starts seeing the world through new eyes, realizing that he's always been gay but just didn't know it. It is his sexual orientation. He was born this way. But living in a world that oppresses gay people, he would be unhappy because he's been suppressing his true self. But he's not alone. Others are fighting back. Drawing inspiration from the civil rights movement and the Stonewall riots, he's emboldened and becomes more determined to join the fight for equality. But first things first, he needs to learn to love his true self. The more he embraces his gay identity, and fully lives out the implications of being gay, the more hopeful he feels about who he is and who he can become. His new sexual identity becomes the defining feature of his life. Everything else in his life needs to bend towards this all-encompassing identity. Nervously, he "comes out" to his parents. He's afraid, however, because they're evangelical Christians. But his fears are unfounded. His father was quiet and somewhat ambivalent, but his mother becomes an enthusiastic supporter. She too finds a thriving online community of mothers of gay children.

She experiences more pushback than he did, especially from people she knows from church. But she's convinced that God made her son gay and accepts him just as he is. God is love, after all. When people at church aren't persuaded, one by one, she begins cutting off friendships and finding new friends who will affirm her son. Eventually, their family is surrounded by an entire community of LGBTQ+ affirming people that will celebrate this boy who has finally discovered his true self. Mother and son feel closer than ever because they have a cause to live for. Something meaningful to fill their time and thoughts. They've got a righteous cause and an enemy to defeat.

Of course, this is a made-up story based on my own pastoral experience, but the gay script is extremely common. And it's compelling. You might even notice that the gay script resembles a religious experience. "Coming out of the closet" is like a personal conversion, the "gay community" is like a church, shunning bigots is like church discipline, and gay activism is like a great commission. If he were to ever attempt renouncing his gay lifestyle, he would be cut off from his people. The LGBTQ+ community practices discipline, just the way churches do. Dissent is not tolerated. This is powerful stuff because God created people to crave meaning and purpose, and the gay script provides a counterfeit version of these things. Ultimately, however, nothing but Christ can satisfy the longings of the heart. LGBTQ+ lifestyles are unnatural and go against the grain of creation. God created us in his image, and true identity, meaning, and purpose, can only be found in him.

The Gospel Script

The alternative to the gay script is what I call the "gospel script." The gospel script gives the assurance that every human being is created in God's image as male and female and can find his or her true identity in a saving relationship with Christ. Our personal worth is demonstrated most fully and extravagantly at the cross, where Jesus died in our place, taking the punishment we deserve for our sin. Our union with Christ begins when we acknowledge our sin and need for him, repent of sin, receive forgiveness by faith, and commit to follow him with single-minded devotion. Our identity is not self-constructed from our desires or behaviors, but it is received as a gift. God made us who we are. We submit to it, trusting his infinite wisdom more than our own. Further, our sense of belonging comes from being adopted into God's household as sons and daughters of God and coheirs with Christ. Further, all believers are joined together as the bride of Christ. It is the gospel of Jesus Christ that defines us. He alone is our all-encompassing identity because he is the one who created us. True joy and satisfaction in life can only be found in total surrender to Jesus as Lord.

So going back to our previous example, suppose the same boy experiences homosexual temptation towards another boy, or even has a homosexual encounter with him. He's heard the gay script over and over his whole life, and he is drawn to it. It seems compelling in some ways, but it doesn't quite line up with what he's read in the Bible. Suppose he talks about it to his parents or to a mature and godly Christian leader. This leader leads him to the cross, helps him discern the lies of the gay script, and shows him how to fight this temptation or sin with the truth of the gospel and in the power of the Holy Spirit. Over time, this young man learns to reject the gay script because God has a better story to tell in his life.

According to the gospel script, his homosexual desires and/or homosexual behaviors are correctly identified as sin. He must reject any impulse to form an identity around this sin, as that compounds the problem and plunges him deeper into it. The Scriptures equip us with the truth we need to fight and overcome sin. Perhaps this young man only finds other boys attractive and has never been attracted to girls. Feelings of dread fill his heart. He's afraid that truly following Christ would mean being alone for the rest of his life. What he has yet to realize is that he doesn't need to be "attracted to women" in general. Unless God has called him to celibacy, he only needs to be attracted to one. The right one. Countless young men who have experienced homosexual temptation have gone on to meet a special woman that steals his heart and becomes his wife.

There have always been Christians who victoriously faced long battles with strong temptations of various kinds. Whether battles with substance abuse, pervasive bitterness, or outbursts of anger, Christians who truly believe the Bible trust that "his divine power has granted to us all things that pertain to life and godliness" (2 Pet 1:3). Homosexual temptation is no exception. This is the way of the cross.

As the Christian leader disciples this young man and continually reminds him of the grace of Jesus, he learns to walk by faith in the power of the cross, knowing that Jesus has forgiven him of every sin, and he is counted perfectly righteous in Christ. He becomes increasingly convinced that, even though his temptations are strong, the power of the Holy Spirit is stronger.[34]

You might have noticed that the gospel script could apply to any temptation, not just homosexual desires. That's because the gospel applies to every sin in the same way. Many Christians treat homosexual temptations as a protected class of temptations, as though this one issue is beyond the reach of the gospel. It isn't. I do not deny that sexual temptations can be extremely strong and difficult to overcome, but it is wrong to assume homosexual temptations are stronger than the power of the gospel. The basic framework of the gospel doesn't change for homosexual sin. We all come to Christ the same way: humble, repentant, and in need of grace. Christ will not deny us.

---

34. For stories of redemption from the homosexual lifestyle, see Becket Cook's book, *A Change of Affection A Change of Affection: A Gay Man's Incredible Story of Redemption* (Nashville, TN: Thomas Nelson, 2019), and Christopher and Angela Yuan's book, *Out of a Far Country: A Gay Son's Journey to God. A Broken Mother's Search for Hope* (Colorado Springs, CO: Waterbrook Press, 2011).

Walking in Repentance

Here are some specific ways to apply the gospel to someone who is tempted towards homosexual sin. First, reject the gay script, and trust your identity in Christ as a child of God. Every human was created in God's image, designed to be an embodied reflection of God. The Creator has made every human either male or female. By God's design, there are only two sexual identities, male or female (Gen 1:27). Every man and woman who trusts in Christ has been redeemed by the blood of Christ and forgiven of every sin.

Second, trust that God alone can satisfy your soul and fulfill your deepest desires. Sex is not the most important thing in life, God is. Sex is a gift from God, but sex is not God. We worship the giver, not the gift (Rom 1:23). To seek fulfillment in sexuality is like being adrift at sea and trying to your quench your thirst by drinking the salty ocean water. By contrast, Augustine famously wrote, "You have made us for yourself, O Lord, and our hearts are restless until they rest in You."[35] There is no sexual experience or identity that can satisfy the longings of the heart. God alone can satisfy. Psalm 16:11 says, "You make known to me the path of life; in your presence there is fullness of joy; at your right hand are pleasures forevermore."

Third, practice the gospel rhythm of repentance and faith. Repentance is not optional. One cannot follow Christ while clinging to sin or turning sin into a personal identity. Jesus didn't say, "live your truth," or, "follow your heart." He said, "deny yourself, take up your cross, and follow me" (Matt 16:24). The road of discipleship was never meant to be easy. We cannot follow Jesus while refusing to repent of sexual sin. No one can serve two masters

---

35. Augustine, *Confessions*, trans. R. S. Pine-Coffin, (New York: Penguin Books, 1961), 39.

(Matt 6:24). Either Jesus is Lord, or sexual idolatry is Lord. Therefore, Paul urges, "flee sexual immorality" (1 Cor 6:18), because "your body is a temple of the Holy Spirit" (v. 19), and "you are not your own, you were bought with a price, so glorify God in your body" (v. 20).

Fourth, find and commit to a local church that upholds the truth of scripture and does not affirm the sin of LGBTQ lifestyles. From my experience, these kinds of Christians are humble, loving, and will gladly welcome anyone who truly desires help walking in the freedom of the gospel.

Finally, repent of *specific* sins or temptations. When Paul spoke to Corinthian believers about their past sexual sins, he specifically identified the past sins Christ rescued them from. He mentioned their past idolatry, sexual immorality, adultery, and homosexual sin, saying, "such *were* some of you. But you were washed, you were sanctified, you were justified in the name of the Lord Jesus Christ and by the Spirit of our God" (1 Cor 6:11). Repentance isn't vague. Like a surgeon's scalpel, cutting in just the right place, the power of God needs to be directed at specific areas of temptation and sin. The gospel is the path of true joy and freedom because it moves us along with the grain of God's design. God's grace abounds to everyone who repents and turns toward Christ.

Where Do We Go from Here?

"If I profess with the loudest voice and clearest exposition every portion of the truth of God except precisely that little point which the world and the devil are at the moment attacking, I am not confessing Christ, however boldly I may be professing Christ. Where the battle rages, there the loyalty of the soldier is proved and to be steady on all the battle front besides, is mere flight and disgrace if he flinches at that point."

ELIZABETH CHARLES[1]

"The end of the matter; all has been heard. Fear God and keep his commandments, for this is the whole duty of man. For God will bring every deed into judgment, with every secret thing, whether good or evil."

ECCLESIASTES 12:13-14

As the sexual revolution has marched on and gained momentum, its clash with the Christian faith has become obvious. For

---

1. Elizabeth Charles, *Chronicles of the Schonberg-Cotta Family* (New York: The Columbian Publishing Co., 1891), 127.

example, a young woman in my church named Amy came to faith in college through the ministry of Young Life. Both she and her husband ended up becoming Young Life leaders and discipling high school students. Some of these high school students began questioning their sexuality and the Bible's teaching about it. This led Amy to start questioning her own views about homosexuality and the Christian faith. These doubts grew in her mind until she finally opened up to her husband about it, which is when they contacted me for help. We met several times and talked through some of her doubts, but it was too late. The fact that God doesn't accept homosexuality was a dealbreaker. She ended up abandoning the faith completely and tried to convince her husband to do the same. When he refused to follow her lead, she divorced him, even though he was willing to stay married to her. As it turned out, her allegiance to affirming LGBTQ lifestyles was higher than her allegiance to Christ. I tell this story to highlight the simple fact that the Christian faith cannot be reconciled with the LGBTQ lifestyles without becoming another religion altogether. Eventually, everyone will have to choose to either follow Christ or follow the LGBTQ movement. You can't have it both ways.

David Gushee was a prominent evangelical leader before famously adopting a pro-homosexuality position in 2016. In an editorial explaining his change, he said something that I wholeheartedly agree with: "Neutrality is not an option. Neither is polite half-acceptance. Nor is avoiding the subject. Hide as you might, the issue will come and find you."[2]

The apologetics of former generations focused on things like the existence of God, the authority of Scripture, the problem of

---

2. David P. Gushee, "On LGBT Equality, Middle Ground Is Disappearing," *Religion News Service*, August 22, 2016, https://religionnews.com/2016/08/22/on-lgbt-equality-middle-ground-is-disappearing/ (Accessed February 21, 2023).

evil, or evidence for the resurrection. But in our day, those questions have been eclipsed by questions about Christianity and sexual ethics. In the church, many Christians are confused because the world is celebrating with "Pride" what the Bible condemns as evil. What's worse, those Christians who refuse to affirm and celebrate sexual immorality are considered, at best, on the wrong side of history, and at worst, evil and bigoted. We would do well to heed the words of the prophet Isaiah:

> Woe to those who call evil good and good evil,
> who put darkness for light and light for darkness,
> who put bitter for sweet and sweet for bitter!
> Woe to those who are wise in their own eyes,
> and shrewd in their own sight! (Isaiah 5:20-21)

Sexuality has become one of the defining issues of this generation. It isn't just the LGBTQ movement. It's the more foundational questions of what a man or woman is. Faithful Christians can scarcely avoid the influence of modern sexual ideologies. It's everywhere. And Christians who maintain fidelity to the Bible's teaching on sexuality will likely pay a cost for this conviction if they have not done so already.

In light of all the things discussed in this book, it is important for Christians and churches to fortify themselves against the assaults upon the goodness and beauty of God's good design. There's more at stake than merely "what goes on in the bedroom." God's design for sexuality reflects a cosmic pattern of how God relates to his creation. As stated in the introduction, there are two truths at the heart of this book. The first is the fact that God's design for sexuality is good and beautiful, and as such, obeying God with our sexuality is an essential part of Christian holiness.

The second truth is that sexuality is a persistent area of deception, temptation, and spiritual attack. With that in view, we'll conclude this study of sexuality with some biblical applications for how Christians can prepare themselves for the future.

Final Practical Applications

There are five practical applications we can draw from Ephesians 5 that are relevant for this discussion. The first is to delight in the goodness of God's design for sexuality. We've already observed how God created sexuality to be a picture of the gospel. Paul says, "Therefore be imitators of God, as beloved children. And walk in love, as Christ loved us and gave himself up for us, a fragrant offering and sacrifice to God" (Eph 5:1-2). Paul expands on this idea later in the chapter when he compares the marriage relationship to the relationship between Christ and the church (vv. 23-25), which is truly a profound mystery (v. 32). In other words, the reason why Christians uphold the beauty of God's design is because the gospel itself is beautiful, and sexuality was created to declare the gospel.

The second thing Christians need to do is commit to sexual holiness and avoid all manner of sexual immorality. Paul says, "But sexual immorality and all impurity or covetousness must not even be named among you, as is proper among saints" (Eph 5:3). The NIV says it this way: "there must not be even a hint of sexual immorality" among Christians. As such, there should be "no filthiness nor foolish talk nor crude joking, which are out of place, but instead let there be thanksgiving" (v. 4). In other words, sexual immorality is no laughing matter. Christians should not laugh about sins Jesus died for. Paul continues with this sober warning: "For you may be sure of this, that everyone who is sexually immoral or impure, or who is covetous (that is, an idolater), has no inheritance in the kingdom of Christ and God" (v. 5). Paul's point is emphatic, "you may be sure of this." To put it bluntly, those who embrace sexual immorality will spend eternity in Hell away from Christ. Without question, this is a difficult teaching. That's why so many Christians would rather ignore it. Paul's following statement, "Let no one deceive you with empty words" (v. 6), is a warning against ignoring this hard teaching and leads to my next point.

The third point is to not be deceived. Sometimes, we're deceived because someone is trying to deceive us when our guard is down. But at other times, we allow ourselves to be deceived because the truth is hard and we'd rather not face hard truths. Nevertheless, better a painful truth than a pleasant lie. The only time we need to tell someone "Don't be deceived!" is when there's a high likelihood of being deceived. Paul knows this. He warns us to not be deceived because he knows human nature. Sometimes, however, we are deceived because we want to be deceived. Sexual immorality has become one of the most persistent areas of deception in our culture, so some Christians try to reconcile it with Christianity. It won't work, and it only provokes God's wrath and invites judgment. That's why Paul reminds us that "the wrath of God comes upon the sons of disobedience" (Eph 5:6). We should not be surprised that Satan—the deceiver and Father of lies—would be at work tempting believers to sin against God with their sexuality. Paul calls attention to this fact by saying, "therefore do not become partners with them; for at one time you were darkness, but now you are light in the Lord. Walk as children of light" (v. 7-8).

My fourth point is develop the skill of discernment. Paul says that we should "try to discern what is pleasing to the Lord" (Eph 5:10). In other words, discernment takes effort and intentionality.

Discernment is the skill of seeing or perceiving something. In this case, Paul is calling us to discern what kind of life would please God in the modern world. To do this, we need to be rooted in the Scriptures and not deceived by the world. When one discerns the good, he or she is better equipped to resist the bad.

Fifth, expose the lies of the world about sexuality. Paul says, "take no part in the unfruitful works of darkness, but instead expose them" (Eph 5:11). This is not fearmongering. It is the loving thing to do. It is important for parents, churches, and other Christian leaders to give biblical instruction to protect fellow believers from harm.

In Romans 12, Paul said, "let love be genuine. Abhor what is evil; hold fast to what is good" (v. 9). This is why I've written this book. I've written it as a resource for pastors, Christian leaders, and any other Christian who wants to be equipped to live according to God's good design. God's design is true, good, and beautiful. It should be celebrated and promoted for the wonderful gift that it is. Therefore, align your life and priorities with it. Celebrate the goodness of his design as men and women, sons and daughters, brothers and sisters, husbands and wives, and mothers and fathers. Don't be ashamed of your masculinity or femininity. It's good. Rejoice and thank God for your sexuality. Rejoice in being a man or a woman.

Men, rejoice in being a man. Rejoice in your strength. Grow into a father for other young men and women in your church. Women, rejoice in being a woman. Rejoice in your fertility. Even if you do not have biological children, there are many spiritual orphans in our midst who could benefit from the nurturing care of a spiritual mother. Parents, teach this to your kids. Start younger than you think you should because Satan already has. Guard their hearts and minds against the evil and danger of sin, but also let them see your delight in the goodness of God's design. May our churches be places where God is glorified for his wisdom in creating us male and female. May this truth ring out of our pulpits, sharpen our minds in our classes, and fill our homes with joy, all to the praise and honor of Christ.

Index

314

www.ingramcontent.com/pod-product-compliance
Lightning Source LLC
Chambersburg PA
CBHW070906120626
46546CB00001B/157